Singled
Out

Singled Out

Why Celibacy Must Be
Reinvented in Today's Church

CHRISTINE A. COLÓN
& BONNIE E. FIELD

BrazosPress

a division of Baker Publishing Group
Grand Rapids, Michigan

Published by Brazos Press
a division of Baker Publishing Group
P.O. Box 6287, Grand Rapids, MI 49516-6287
www.brazospress.com

Printed in the United States of America

Library of Congress Cataloging-in-Publication Data
Colón, Christine A., 1968–
    Singled out : why celibacy must be reinvented in today's church / Christine A. Colón
and Bonnie E. Field.
        p.   cm.
    Includes bibliographical references (p.   ) and index.
    ISBN 978-1-58743-237-8 (pbk.)
    1. Single people—Religious life. 2. Celibacy—Christianity. 3. Evangelicalism. I. Field,
Bonnie E., 1969– II. Title.
BV4596.S5C655 2009
248.4'7—dc22   2009007341

Scripture is taken from the New America Standard Bible ®, Copyright © 1960, 1963, 1968, 1971, 1972, 1973, 1975, 1977, 1995 by The Lckman Foundation. Used by permission.

Contents

Contents

Acknowledgments

We would like to thank all of the friends and family who encouraged us on our journey, read early drafts of chapters, and put up with seemingly endless discussions about celibacy.

We would also like to offer special thanks to Jane Beal, Bill Gentrup, and Joy Wooddell for reading our entire manuscript and offering their invaluable insights and suggestions. And to Laura Miguelez and Ruth Anne Reese for keeping us theologically and biblically sound.

Most of all, we would like to thank our Lord Jesus Christ who did not deliver us from the difficult times but showed us why we had to go through them.

Introduction
Our Journey

Coworker: It's easier to be killed by a terrorist than it is to find a husband over the age of 40!
Annie: That statistic is not true!
Becky: That's right. It's not true, but it feels true.

Sleepless in Seattle

"I want a man." We can't even count the number of times that sentence was uttered in the phone conversations we had with each other in our twenties. We had made it through our good, Christian college educations without the MRS degree and were now stuck, quite literally, in no man's land. Friends and family were full of consoling words: "Maybe in your new job," "Maybe in graduate school," "Maybe when you go on vacation." But as the years went by, the consolation began to transform into desperation: "Maybe you should join a gym," "Maybe you should try the internet," "Maybe you should try a new church," "Maybe you should get out of English literature and into a field with more men." We couldn't really blame our friends and family because we certainly hadn't come up with any better ideas. We were locked in a frustrating cycle, and none of our actions bore any fruit. We wanted to be married. In fact, we had done everything right to insure that when the men God had in store for us arrived, we would be ready. But they didn't arrive, and we were left wondering, "What does that mean?" "Where have we gone wrong?" As our twenties shifted into our thirties, these questions became more pointed. Our conversations were no longer punctuated with "I want a man." Instead, they were filled with "what's wrong with me?" and "why doesn't God seem to care?"

As we began to search for answers, we realized that in most of the church's discussions about singleness and celibacy, no one was really talking to us. If we had been high school students ready to sign our pledge cards, committing ourselves to wait until marriage, then, yes, we would have had a support group. As thirtysomethings, however, we soon discovered that the evangelical world, which so often revolves around the nuclear family, didn't quite know what to do with us. There were no support groups for virgins over thirty, probably because no one seemed to think we existed. But if you think the refrain of "wait" is difficult for a sixteen-year-old to hear, try being in your mid-thirties when you have already waited quite awhile for that promised mate to come along. Then you begin to realize that, despite all the positive rhetoric about your soul mate arriving when you least expect it, he or she may never arrive. The phrase "wait until marriage" begins to lose its power when you realize that the "marriage" part may never come. It wasn't that we disagreed with the sentiment, and it certainly wasn't that we were going to relinquish our moral standards and live like seemingly everyone else. But we needed more. Being celibate today means being caught between the casual sex mentality of the secular world and the family values of the evangelical Christian world. In order to withstand the pressures from both sides, we needed to arm ourselves first with a positive understanding of celibacy that moved beyond the simple command to "wait" and then with a supportive community that not only acknowledged our existence but also valued our participation.

As we continued to search for this message, we discovered that the word "celibacy" is virtually absent from all evangelical discussions of singleness. There are certainly discussions of abstinence, but by the very nature of the word, they focus on what is being relinquished or avoided. Sex is often seen as the ultimate goal, and abstinence is often promoted as a short stage to endure that will ultimately make married sex much better because of the wait. Any discussion of long-term abstinence takes on a negative tone of deprivation, so it is generally avoided. Similarly, virginity is seen as something that will eventually be relinquished, preferably to one's spouse. Both terms imply that our focus must be on guarding ourselves from sexual temptation until God grants us the blessing of marriage. But what if our thirties, forties, and fifties arrive, and we aren't married? And where does this message leave those who are no longer virgins but seek to live a God-honoring single life? Discussions of virginity in particular often leave those who were once sexually active feeling like they are damaged goods undeserving of God's forgiveness, and for those who have been sexually abused, these conversations can be painful reminders of their past trauma. Within recent years, there have been more positive discussions centering on the word chastity. These discussions have come a long way in providing a more positive image of sexuality for single Christians that moves beyond a focus on virginity. The unfortunate thing is that most of these discussions are led by Christians who practiced single chastity for only two or three years before getting married and practicing married chastity. While it is important to see chastity as a virtue that should be practiced in singleness as well as marriage, the temptation is once again to see singleness only as preparation for marriage.

Frustrated with the evangelical discussions of singleness, we turned to the early church fathers for help. Unfortunately, many of the early discussions of celibacy are predicated on the belief that sex is evil and that women are temptresses who should be avoided at all costs. Later Catholic discussions have a more positive view of sex (and women), but they generally view celibacy as a voluntary life-long decision. Such conversations do not accommodate those who would like to marry but do not know if they ever will.

Suddenly, we had a breakthrough in our phone conversations. Instead of "I want a man" or even "what's wrong with me?" we began to ask, "What would a positive evangelical discussion of celibacy look like?" "Where can we find one?" "Is it possible to have a positive understanding of celibacy that still values marriage and the role of sex within marriage?" This book is a result of our search for answers to those questions.

At first, we despaired. In the secular world everything seemed to equate celibacy with repression or childishness. As Elizabeth Abbott states in *A History of Celibacy*, "In such a sex-dominated world, celibacy is pushed into the background. Apart from the small contingent of Power Virgins, True Love Waiters, Athletes for Abstinence, and other convinced celibates, most people view celibacy as sad and lonely at best, unnatural at worst, the preserve of priests and nuns, spinsters and prisoners, and other pitiable victims."[1] In the evangelical world, we kept running into the familiar refrain of "wait," or even worse, advice from experts telling us that we weren't fully adults until we were married, that we couldn't fully participate in the church until we were married, that we couldn't develop fully as Christians until we were married, or that we were sinful for not fulfilling our God-given duties as wives and mothers.

Gradually, however, we began to piece together a more positive message: one that moved beyond the word "wait" to a more nuanced discussion of the potentially powerful role of celibacy in the Christian life. We began to recognize that we needed a conception of celibacy that bridged the gap between the message of abstinence that seemed to focus solely on waiting until marriage and the traditional message of celibacy that solely emphasized a chosen, life-long commitment. The process of discovering this message has been neither a short one nor an easy one, and we have certainly not arrived at all the answers. In fact, if our research reveals anything, it is that we need many more Christian thinkers to begin to address this topic in depth. Our book is only one step in what we hope will become a much larger discussion of the role of celibacy within the evangelical church, so that we can begin to move toward a deeper understanding of why God may call us to celibacy for a short period or for a lifetime.

While this process began as a personal quest, it soon grew to be much more, for as we began to research these issues and talk to others who were also struggling, we realized just how many older singles, male as well as female, feel excluded from the evangelical community. According to the 2006 national census, 46% of American adults are single.[2] Interestingly, the percentage of Protestant single adults (40–45%) and Catholic single adults (40–45%) comes close to mirroring the national statistics. But, according to the Barna Group, when you look specifically at evangelicals (whether Protestant or Catholic), single adults are significantly underrepresented. Fewer than 25% of evangelicals over 18 are single.[3] Why are single adults underrepresented among evangelicals?

First we should probably attempt to define what we mean by "evangelical." Barna survey respondents did not state whether or not they considered themselves evangelical. Rather, that classification was applied to those who met seven conditions that included the following:

- Saying their faith is very important in their life today
- Believing they have a personal responsibility to share their religious beliefs about Christ with non-Christians

- Believing that Satan exists
- Believing that eternal salvation is possible only through grace, not works
- Believing that Jesus Christ lived a sinless life on earth
- Asserting that the Bible is accurate in all that it teaches
- Describing God as the all-knowing, all-powerful, perfect deity who created the universe and still rules it today[4]

Based on these conditions, the term "evangelical" could be applied to some in mainline Protestant denominations as well as to some in Catholic and Orthodox churches. And on the flip side, there are probably some Christians who would describe themselves as evangelical who do not ascribe to one or more of these particular beliefs. The marginalization of singles, then, doesn't seem to be necessarily a denominational issue, but it is certainly an *evangelical* issue, particularly if we work with the definition provided by the Barna Group.

Are single adults underrepresented in evangelical churches because most evangelicals encourage singles to marry rather than cohabitate? Though that may be part of it, we believe the issue is more complicated. A 2008 poll on ChristianSinglesToday.com asked singles whether or not they had ever considered leaving the church because of the attitude toward singles. In response, thirty-eight-year-old Monica wrote, "To me, the church has always seemed aimed at families. I've sometimes had to force myself to continue attending by not thinking of myself as a single person, but as just a person in need of connection with God and community. Sitting in church by myself, or being the only single person at a women's gathering isn't easy. But I continue to do so in hopes of making connections."[5] This was the general message of most of the respondents who have stayed in the church. While the respondents didn't identify themselves as evangelical or not, our suspicions are that many evangelical churches with their strong family-centered focus could provoke this type of response, and we wonder how many single adults have left the evangelical church altogether because of similar frustrations. It is one thing for singles to leave the church because they disagree with its stance on premarital sex. It is another for singles who agree with the evangelical church's moral stance to leave because they don't feel welcome in a world that seems to cater primarily to families.

In his book, *Reaching Single Adults*, Dennis Franck, who has been working in single adult ministries for over twenty years, reminds us that "the current number of 82 million unmarried adults in the U.S. age eighteen and older represents more people than the population of most countries in the world. Imagine a country of 82 million people with no missionary. It would be out of the question! . . . This existing number of single adults represents a huge mission field that is largely untapped in most denominations."[6] The fact that very few of these singles find a home in the evangelical church is a problem that must be addressed. What would it look like if the evangelical church promoted a positive message of celibacy within the body of Christ, one that was so powerful and winsome that it provided support for Christian singles who had already decided to refrain from sex outside of marriage? *And* so powerful and winsome that it also attracted singles from the secular world who were searching for a new way to live?

Unfortunately, the majority of evangelical churches have not embraced this opportunity. Not only do many evangelical singles feel marginalized because they lack the requisite, traditional family that is so highly valued in today's evangelical church, but as soon as they leave high school or college, they are also denied a supportive community that might help them through the difficulties of remaining celibate. For many of these singles, as the struggle becomes more intense, the support system disappears. But at least many of them once had a support system that helped them to maintain their commitment to purity. What about those singles who become evangelical Christians later in life? Whom can they turn to in their desire to embrace a celibate lifestyle that is so foreign to the secular world from which they came? What about those who are divorced or widowed? What about homosexuals who struggle with same-sex attraction? All of these groups may be called to celibacy for a time or for the rest of their lives. Where is the positive message of celibacy that will help them as well?

While many have tried to refine or recast the old argument of waiting until marriage, we believe that something more must be done. We must change the questions that we ask. What would happen, for instance, if we shifted the discussion from the question of "how do we remain pure until marriage?" to the question of "what does it mean to be a single Christian even apart from the possibility of marriage?" Now, please don't misunderstand us. We are certainly not arguing for a world of celibate

Christians. The majority will be married at one time or another. But by framing the argument simply in terms of "waiting," we tend to create more problems than we can solve.

The results of the "True Love Waits" campaign, for instance, point out some problems with the rhetoric. Yes, students who sign the pledge cards are waiting, usually for about eighteen months. Is that all we are asking of them? Wait until you are more mature, or wait until you are out of high school? While the program certainly doesn't have that intention, that is what the actions of many of the students reveal, for 88% of those who made pledges not to have sex until they were married eventually participated in premarital sex.[7] When sexual fulfillment is held up as the ultimate prize, is it any surprise that some students, while holding out for as long as they feel they can, cannot wait until that moment of marriage, which is never guaranteed to anyone? And the reality of today's church is that some Christians (particularly Christian women) may never be married. While statistics indicate "that there are 4 million more males who have never been married than there are never-been-married females,"[8] many single Christian women resonate with Margaret's post on ChristianSinglesToday.com where she bemoans, "our churches and Christian circles are full of women and horribly void of single, eligible men. No matter where I go—Bible studies, church, singles groups—it is 90 percent female."[9] There may be more never-married men in the United States than women, but they don't seem to be making it to church.

What then are we to do with these "redundant" women who may never marry? Isaiah 4:1, which is found in the midst of a longer passage that prophesies the desolation of Jerusalem and recounts the large number of men who will be killed while trying to save the city, gives us one possible solution to this lack of eligible men: "For seven women will take hold of one man in that day, saying, 'We will eat our own bread and wear our own clothes, only let us be called by your name; take away our reproach!'" But we can certainly all agree that polygamy isn't the answer. Centuries later, when a similar plight of too many eligible women faced Victorian England, they created societies to encourage young women to emigrate to New Zealand or Australia where they could have their pick of men, many of whom were former convicts who had been exiled for their crimes. Today, Christian singles are encouraged to try eHarmony. But is it really the church's responsibility to insure spouses for everyone?

Or is it rather to provide a community in which the love of God will flourish in individuals no matter what their marital status may be?

In the course of this book, we would like to take you through our process of exploring the various views of celibacy that are circulating in our society as we attempt to locate a positive discussion that will counter the negative messages we receive everywhere else. We will begin with the dominant secular ideas that make celibacy difficult to maintain for anyone in American culture, but we will also explore the interesting phenomena of positive messages of celibacy that appear throughout the secular world. Might we be able to glean something from them? Then, we will turn to the evangelical world to investigate the attempts at a positive message that are dominant today. Along the way we will explore the surprisingly negative messages regarding celibacy that exist within the evangelical church and the problematic consequences they create for all Christians, single and married. After examining these current discussions, both secular and evangelical, we will begin to piece together an understanding of celibacy that draws from Scripture, church history, and contemporary Christian thought.

Before we proceed, perhaps we should say a word about some of our assumptions. First, because much of our Christian experience has been within the evangelical community, most of our critique of the church will focus on the evangelical segment of the church and its influences. That is not to say that mainline Protestant, Catholic, and Orthodox churches do not need a positive message of celibacy for their single adults as well, nor does it mean that there is not significant overlap between these various segments of the church body. But we have noticed that the issues we will be examining are markedly more pronounced in the evangelical community. And these other groups within Christendom traditionally have been more accepting of the term "celibacy" and more likely to entertain discussions about its role in the church. We consequently pull from some of these discussions in our attempt to reinvent an understanding of celibacy that can be meaningful to those within the contemporary evangelical church.

Second, although we know that an increasingly large percentage of unmarried Christians are sexually active, our assumption is that all single Christians should practice celibacy. This is not to say that we believe all single Christians should experience an undeniable "call" from God or that they should make a life-long commitment to living a single, celibate life. It does not even mean that we believe that single Christians should not date or desire marriage. It simply means that Christians should abstain from sexual relationships for as long as they are single, whether that is for a short period of time or for their entire lives. We use the term "celibacy" rather than "abstinence" because the focus of abstinence tends to be on waiting for a future marriage. The type of celibacy we propose is focused on our relationship with God rather than a future marital relationship. In addition, we use the term "celibacy" rather than "chastity" because we desire to emphasize the particular challenges that arise for single Christians, which are significantly different from the challenges that arise for those practicing marital chastity. Ultimately, the purpose of this book is not to present a biblical view of sexuality or to argue that sex should only be shared within a marriage relationship, though we do discuss this briefly in chapter three. Rather, the purpose of this book is to uncover a positive biblical understanding of singleness, specifically long-term intentionally celibate singleness, and to discuss sexuality as it pertains to the celibate single adult.

The discussion that emerges from our search is one that affects the entire church community, not just the evangelical church and not just its single members. It is a discussion focused on the body of Christ and *God's* family rather than the nuclear family. We are all called to minister to each other and the world around us. Single Christians play a valuable role within that mission, but their role cannot be fully realized unless they have the support of the rest of the church body. This support needs to begin with church leadership and be reinforced by parents who must resist pressuring their children to marry early as a means of maintaining their purity, youth leaders who must focus on more than dating and marriage preparation, and singles group leaders who must expand their horizons beyond simply seeking to find marriage partners for everyone in the singles group. But most of the burden lies with the single community, for we are the ones who need to begin seeing our singleness as a blessing rather than a curse. We need to embrace the call to singleness we have received for however long God wills and become active members within the church community. Only then will the rest of the body of Christ truly see us as valued members of the community.

Part 1

Navigating Our Path

1

Repression & Neuroses
Negative Secular Views of Celibacy

Elaine: What? Was it something I said?
Jerry: She's a virgin, she just told me.
Elaine: Well I didn't know.
Jerry: Well it's not like spotting a toupee.
Elaine: Well you think I should say something? Should I say something?
    Should I apologize? Was I being anti-virgin?
Jerry: No, no, I mean . . .
Elaine: 'Cause I'm not anti-virgin.

"The Virgin," *Seinfeld*

At a party several years ago, Christine was asked which of the characters on *Sex and the City* she was most like. Christine was at a bit of a loss since she had never actually watched an episode. Her friends pitched in to help her out, deciding that she was like Charlotte, the good girl of the bunch who was looking for love rather than simply enjoying herself with a variety of sexual partners. When Christine actually watched the show a few years later, she recalled that conversation. Her friends from graduate school who had decided that she was most like Charlotte had obviously made the connection between Christine's moral convictions about not having sex until marriage and Charlotte's commitment to finding true love, for, as Bonnie will attest, personality wise, Christine is far closer to the cynical Miranda than she is to Charlotte. The fact that her friends had drawn their conclusions based solely on Christine's and Charlotte's moral stances was intriguing, but what Christine found even more interesting was just how different those supposedly similar moral stances were. In *Sex and the City* even the supposedly prudish Charlotte, who blushes whenever Carrie, Miranda, or especially Samantha discusses her latest sexual adventures, is sexually active herself. Charlotte had her own set of lovers and one husband that she had to circulate through before finally finding her Mr. Right.

In the world of *Sex and the City*, virginity and celibacy do not exist as realistic options. In fact, in one episode Carrie has an interesting discussion with a protégée named Laurel about a book that Laurel is writing. The conversation illustrates just how far from Carrie's reality celibacy truly is:

> Laurel: Well it does deal with sex, or rather, not having sex. It's about how girls my age are saving themselves for marriage.
>
> Carrie: Saving what for marriage?
>
> Laurel: Our virginity.
>
> Carrie: Are you seriously telling me you've never had sex with a man?[1]

For Carrie, most of the other characters in *Sex and the City*, and most of the secular media, single adults have sex. It is normal and expected. While the secular media does occasionally portray virginity and celibacy positively (we will examine some of those examples in the next chapter), most of the time adult sexual abstinence is portrayed at best as odd and pathetic and at worst as a serious disorder that must be corrected. While many media savvy Christian singles are able to sift through these images and evaluate them for what they are, the fact that they have permeated society so completely can be frustrating. In fact, as we will see in chapter four, even the evangelical church has embraced many of these damaging ideas about celibacy. For Christian singles, then, these negative images can make a commitment to celibacy difficult to maintain, for they must continually fight against the damaging stereotypes that repeatedly define them as abnormal.

Sex Seen as a Biological Imperative

One of the most fundamental ideas about sex and celibacy that is expressed throughout the media today is that sex is a biological imperative. This premise is repeatedly invoked in two very different conversations about celibacy that have emerged in the late twentieth and early twenty-first centuries: the debate over the use of public funds for abstinence-only education and the scandal of Catholic priests preying upon young children. U.S. Representative Barbara Lee from California addresses the first issue. She remarks, "An abstinence-until-marriage program is not only irresponsible . . . It's really inhumane."[2] Many opponents of abstinence programs have emphasized the difficulties of asking teenagers to control their powerful sexual urges and the dangers of not teaching them about safe sex. But Lee, by condemning abstinence as "inhumane," goes further with her argument, suggesting that abstaining from sex is a cruel punishment that adults cannot inflict upon teenagers. Implicitly, then, sex is defined as a biological necessity that cannot be restrained without doing damage to the individual.

This idea about sex is echoed by Andy Rooney in one of his commentaries for *60 Minutes*. In response to the many stories of sexual abuse committed by Catholic priests, Rooney remarks, "The pledge of celibacy demanded of priests assumes that sexual desire can be suppressed by resolve. The fact is, sex isn't something a person can decide to have or promise not to have and then never have it. They might as well have ordered church bells not to ring when struck."[3] For Rooney, the problem of sexual abuse plaguing the Catholic Church stems directly from the impossibility of individuals keeping their vows of celibacy. Similar to Lee, Rooney defines celibacy as being against nature, but he takes this premise even further, suggesting that celibacy is a dangerous repression of natural impulses that is not simply cruel to the person forced to suppress his or her desires but will inevitably be channeled into criminal sexual activity.

As she concludes her discussion of celibacy in her book *A History of Celibacy*, Elizabeth Abbott remarks that "for at least three thousand years in most parts of the world, celibacy has been far from uncommon and rarely considered unnatural."[4] Why, then, does so much of the discussion of celibacy today revolve around the idea that abstaining from sex is abnormal and potentially dangerous? The most influential force in this transformation is probably Sigmund Freud whose theories of sexuality influenced not only scientific discussions but also popular culture. As Angus McLaren states in *Twentieth-Century Sexuality: A History*,

> Freud's originality lay in erecting an entire explanation of civilization based on the centrality of sex . . . His message, as spread by generations of therapists, centred on the notion that infantile sexuality existed, that the neuroses were caused by sexual repression, and that the sexual drives influenced all of human history. Most readers had only a shaky understanding of the scenario that held that the id demanded gratification, the ego judiciously regulated the promptings of the unconscious, and the super-ego internalized the restraints of society. What the public understood Freud to argue was that if the sexual drives were frustrated illness would result.[5]

By placing sexuality at the center of his explanations of human development, Freud radically transformed the way that Western society conceived of sex. Suddenly, sexual satisfaction became the sign of a normal, healthy person. Those who did not engage in sexual activity were suspect: what neuroses were they fostering by their repression of their sexual desires? Freud's ideas spread quickly, and the result was, in the words of McLaren, that "in the course of a few decades [between the first and second world wars] one had moved in Western culture from a society in which abstinence was obligatory to one in which orgasm was obligatory."[6]

Building upon Freud's ideas, researchers such as Alfred Kinsey began to argue that sexual activity was necessary not simply to escape neuroses but also to promote good health and social success. In his book *Sexual Behavior in the Human Male*, for instance, Kinsey argues that early sexual experience is important, for it helps men become "alert, energetic, vivacious, spontaneous, physically active, socially extrovert, and/or aggressive individuals in the population."[7] With all of these supposedly wonderful benefits to sexual activity, is it any wonder that abstaining from sex until marriage began to be seen not only as a quaint relic of primitive society but also as a potentially dangerous idea that would keep individuals from having fulfilling sex lives once they were married? With the development of effective and accessible contraceptives in the 1950s, the stage was set for the sexual revolution of the 1960s. While some of that enthusiasm was tempered a few decades later by the AIDS crisis, the "safe sex" campaigns and the development of new medications to help control HIV allowed this comparatively new conception of sex to continue into the twenty-first century. Now sexual gratification has a much higher priority in secular society than restraining desire does.

Popular culture provides a good primer of how these ideas continue to circulate through American society. Take, for example, the movie *40 Days and 40 Nights*, in which the main character, Matt, tries to give up sex for Lent. The response of his roommate demonstrates how thoroughly he has accepted the idea that the sexual urge is impossible to control and should not be denied: "You can't do it . . . I'm just saying no man can do it. It goes against nature. The male was biologically designed to spread his seed, Matt. You're going to piss off the seed. It goes against science. Do you want to be the man who goes against science? This isn't normal."[8] A young, attractive, single man willingly giving up sex for forty days is not only defined as abnormal but also as fascinating enough to create an entire motion picture devoted to his struggle.

In the TV drama *Everwood*, Dr. Andy Brown expresses a similar idea about the impossibility of controlling sexual desire when he talks to his son, Ephram, about sex: "You and your friends are at an age where you're deciding when or whether to have sex. I can't tell you what to do. A lot of parents try and I respect the impulse but you can't stop sex. It's too big. It's like trying to hold back the tide with a broom."[9] In the next season of the show, Dr. Brown revises his opinion, wondering, "When did we get to this point where kids just have sex and we're supposed to be okay with it?" After going through the realities of an unplanned pregnancy with Ephram's first girlfriend, he is not very eager for Ephram to begin having sex with his new girlfriend. The context in which this statement occurs, however, only reaffirms his earlier ideas about the immense power of sex, for in the midst of his frustration, he remarks, "[Ephram's] gonna do what he wants to do. There's nothing I can do about it." And his friend Nina replies, "There was never anything you could've done about it. I mean, I'm sure it was a helluva speech, but you didn't really think that you were gonna stop them from having sex, did you?"[10] Sex is still the powerful tide that can't be swept away.

Sex Outside of Marriage Seen as Normal and Expected

In response to this idea that sexual urges are so powerful that they cannot be controlled, sex outside of marriage is seen as normal and expected.

In the film version of *Bridget Jones's Diary*, Bridget struggles with what underwear to wear for a first date with her boss, thinking that the "scary, stomach-holding-in panties very popular with grannies the world over" will be the ones most likely to create the figure necessary to attain a sexual encounter but the black, lace thong will be more alluring when the encounter actually occurs.[11] For Bridget, the idea of sex on a first date is so natural that her dilemma is not whether or not to have sex but rather what she wants to be wearing when it occurs. For anyone who has watched television or films or listened to the radio in the last few decades, Bridget's dilemma comes as no surprise. Sexual activity outside of marriage is everywhere from the escapades of the doctors on *Grey's Anatomy* and Bridget Jones to sexual encounters of real women who call in to local radio stations. One Atlanta radio station, for example, used to have a segment called "First Sex Friday" in which women would call in to announce their intentions of having sex for the first time with a date and then call back on Monday to give the details.

So the question in today's secular society really isn't whether a single adult should be having sex outside of marriage but rather when is it appropriate to start having sex. American society still frowns on younger teens having sex, as was demonstrated when the "First Sex Friday" segment mentioned above came to a quick end when the horror-struck hosts realized one of their callers was a high school girl calling to tell them about losing her virginity after the prom. The media frequently emphasizes the problems that occur when young teens engage in sexual activity without being ready for its responsibilities. Whether demonstrating the immaturity of young mothers on daytime talk shows or showing the struggle of young parents trying to balance school, their relationship, and a baby in a movie of the week on Lifetime (such as their recent offering, *Mom at Sixteen*), television in particular conveys the dangers of not waiting until the time is "right." A poll conducted by NBC News and *People* magazine demonstrates that young teens (13–16) agree with these messages with 87% of them stating that they have not had sexual intercourse and 75% saying that they are too young.[12] The message changes, however, as teenagers mature, for, following from Freud's ideas that sexual repression may have serious repercussions, many representations of teenage virgins imply that they must lose their virginity at an appropriate age: they must be mature enough to handle the consequences but young enough so that they have not developed the neuroses that inevitably occur from repressing sexual desires.

Rules for Women

For women, the "appropriate" age for losing their virginity seems to be at nineteen or twenty (in the first two years of college). Young women who maintain their virginity through high school are often valorized and presented as the "good" girls, but when they go to college, they soon discover that losing their virginity is an important step in maturity that they must take before it is too late. While this tradition goes back to Donna in *Beverly Hills 90210* and Felicity in the television show of the same name, Rory from *Gilmore Girls* is a more recent example. Throughout high school, Rory is the "good" girl who is serious about studying and getting into Harvard. She has two boyfriends in the course of her high school career, but she never has sex with either of them. In fact, her virginity becomes an important plot point in an episode when she and her friend Paris are waiting for their college acceptance letters. Paris, who has just had sex for the first time, comes to Rory's house to talk over the event, assuming that Rory has already had sex. As Rory explains that she is still a virgin, her mother lurks in the hallway eavesdropping, whispering in delight, "I've got the good kid."[13] Later, when Paris receives a rejection from Harvard, she has a breakdown during a televised speech and decides that this rejection is somehow connected to her loss of virginity.

While the writers of this episode clearly demonstrate that Paris's reaction is ridiculous, they also uphold the idea that Rory's virginity makes her the "good" kid, for when she returns home she finds a mailbox full of college acceptance letters, provoking her mother to comment that she must be the "biggest virgin" in the world. Rory's intelligence and diligence are somehow wrapped up in her decision to remain a virgin. When she goes to college, however, virginity is no longer such an important commodity, and at the end of her freshman year Rory loses her virginity to her ex-boyfriend who happens to be married. In a discussion about her choice to have Rory lose her virginity, Amy Sherman-Palladino, the creator of *Gilmore Girls*, remarks, "Having sex at 19 doesn't make you a bad girl . . . It makes you a human being."[14] The phrasing of Sherman-Palladino's comment is interesting. On one level, it implies that everyone gives into temptation. On another level, it implies that sex is what ultimately makes someone a human being. Without this sexual encounter, apparently, Rory couldn't mature and develop into an adult.

Probably the most easily recognizable example of this idea is the episode of *Friends* entitled "The One That Could Have Been" where the different characters imagine how their lives might have been different. In this alternative reality, Monica is overweight and a thirty-year-old virgin; and, sure enough, this version of herself is far less mature than the regular Monica. Her immaturity is strongly emphasized in a discussion with Rachel where she reveals that she has never had sex. At first she tries to hide the fact, responding to Rachel's comment that as a single woman Monica "get[s] to have sex with whoever [she] wants" by saying, "Yeah I can! (Laughs) And don't think I don't, because I do! I mean all the time, you betcha! (Laughs)." Monica's over the top performance makes Rachel suspicious, and Monica is forced to confess that she is still a virgin. As she tries to explain her justification for remaining a virgin, Rachel's response reveals just how ridiculous we are supposed to think that decision is:

> Monica: It's not like, I haven't any opportunities. I mean, y'know, I'm just waiting for the perfect guy. I'm seeing this guy Roger, all right? He's not perfect, but umm, I think maybe I should just get it over with. Y'know, give him my flower."
>
> Rachel: Oh my God!! Do it!! Honey, you've waited long enough!![15]

For a thirty-year-old woman, Monica is incredibly immature. A conversation about sex provokes giggles and a ridiculous comparison of her virginity to a flower that might work for twelve-year-olds but sounds inane coming from the mouth of a grown woman. The writers of this episode clearly link that immaturity to her virginity.

This message is emphasized even more forcefully in a small, independent film entitled *I Love You, Don't Touch Me!* which was released in 1998. In this film Katie is a twenty-five-year-old virgin who struggles desperately to find Mr. Right. She thought she had found him at twenty-one, but when she discovered that rather than waiting for her to be ready to have sex he was sleeping with someone else, the "Ted" that she had tattooed on her behind in homage to him was transformed into "HaTed." The movie then jumps four years later to explore how this now bitter and frustrated woman finally finds true love. As a twenty-five-year-old virgin, Katie is clearly neurotic. She is plagued by an almost continual internal monologue in which she repeatedly tries to control her strong sexual desires by calling herself a slut and talking herself out of them. She also keeps trying to set up her friend Ben, who happens to be in love with her, with various girlfriends, and then becomes angry when he is attracted to one of them. And she is repeatedly told that she will never be successful as a singer because she has not had the sexual experiences necessary to really feel the music and understand the lyrics. Despite all of this, she is very smug and self-righteous as she talks to her sexually active friends about her decision not to have sex until she is in love. All of her friends, however, think that this is definitely a woman who needs to have sex to help her solve some of her problems. Ultimately, the film affirms her friends' position. While Katie's first affair is clearly with the wrong man (a self-centered composer, who, while rich and famous, is definitely not the Prince Charming that Katie thinks he is), her sexual encounters with this "bad boy" as well as the discovery of his infidelity allow her finally to see that her long-suffering friend Ben is the right man for her after all. Katie may still not be a model of mental health at the conclusion of the film, but she is finally ready to commit to the "slightly balding" Ben, who may indeed be her Prince Charming. The film may uphold the idea that love is an important component in a sexual relationship, but it also demonstrates that by not having sex at an appropriate time in her development, a woman risks becoming so neurotic and unstable that she may never find true love.[16]

Rules for Men

While women who delay having sex until after their early twenties are often portrayed as neurotic and disturbed, men are generally seen as stunted adolescents who have refused to grow up. David Letterman drew on this stereotype for his Top 10 list of the biggest disappointments in *Attack of the Clones*. One of the disappointments was "When the theater lights come back on, you're still a 40-year old virgin."[17] The 2005 film *The 40-Year-Old Virgin* masterfully demonstrates this trend of portraying older male virgins as immature nerds. Andy Stitzer, played by Steve Carell, may ultimately turn out to be a nice guy who is saner than all of his repulsive coworkers and who eventually gets the girl, but the image of him living alone in his apartment filled with action figures and using a bike as his only form of transformation is a hard one to shake. He is clearly immature and has failed to take the step into adulthood:

a step that is linked directly to sexual activity.[18] As an audience, we may be able to look back fondly (if condescendingly) on his immaturity at the beginning of the movie but only because by the end of the film he has matured as is demonstrated by his marriage, which releases him from the "immaturity" of celibacy and the adolescent lifestyle that is associated with it. The idea of a mature, well-adjusted, celibate man in his forties lies outside the realm of possibility in this comedy.

It isn't only in fiction or top ten lists that this stereotype is revealed. In a recent "Ask Amy" column in the *Chicago Tribune*, readers responded to a male virgin who wondered, "At what age does a man's virginity become a turnoff rather than a turn-on?" Out of the nine printed responses, three affirmed a man's decision to remain a virgin until marriage. The other responses provide an interesting look at how male virginity past the early twenties is perceived by the majority of American society. "Sexually Active" replied, "I would likely never marry a virgin . . . because I don't think I'd ever marry a man I hadn't slept with first." "One Woman's Opinion" remarked, "If a man hasn't lost his virginity by the time he's graduated from college, he's most likely waited too long." "A Twentysomething Woman" echoed this thought, declaring, "Past the age of about 22, his virginity is going to be considered a liability (not an asset) by most women who do not have firmly held religious beliefs." "Elizabeth" had perhaps the strongest statement of condemnation, arguing, "A sexual partner's virginity is a handicap, regardless of age or gender. Would you want to ride in a car with an inexperienced driver, or learn to drive from someone who has never driven? A sexually educated, experienced and skilled partner is a joy to find, an asset in a relationship, and I find it difficult to understand why anyone would think otherwise."[19] As these responses reveal, a virgin must lose his virginity early enough so that he has the experience to be a good lover by the time he finds "Ms. Right." Without this early sexual experience, men risk the danger of being seen as incompetent adolescents rather than skilled adults.

If we are to believe the models in the secular media, choosing a celibate life after the early twenties is an extremely risky decision: one that turns women into bitter, neurotic creatures who take out their sexual frustrations on the people around them and one that turns men into pathetic adolescents who sublimate their desires onto their fantasy worlds. For Christian singles today who are committed to a celibate lifestyle, these images are frustrating. No one wishes to be perceived as neurotic or immature, yet throughout much of the media this is how virgins, in particular, are portrayed. Because these images are so extreme, however, they may actually be dealt with more effectively than the more subtle messages that are conveyed through the media, which may ultimately be much more damaging. While celibate men may laugh at the portrayal of Andy Stitzer since they know that they have managed to become adults even without having sex and while celibate women may laugh at Katie because they recognize that they are much more well-adjusted than she is, can they resist all of the messages that say that they cannot be complete human beings without a partner?

Life Seen as Incomplete without a Partner

This idea that life is incomplete without a partner has permeated popular music for decades. Take for example the 1944 Russ Morgan song "You're Nobody Till Somebody Loves You" that has been recorded by over thirty people including Dean Martin, Frank Sinatra, Bobby Darrin, and The Supremes. And then there is the ever-popular "How Do I Live," originally recorded by LeAnn Rimes in 1997. Or there is also "Without You," known more popularly as "I Can't Live (if Living is Without You)," which has been recorded by artists as diverse as Shirley Bassey, Air Supply, Mariah Carey, and Clay Aiken. While these last two songs are about the debilitating emotional pain that comes from rejection, the message is clear that life without a partner is not a life worth living. Stephen Sondheim's song "Being Alive" from the musical *Company*, and recorded by many artists including Barbra Streisand, portrays one of the more extreme versions of this message. In much of the musical the main character, Bobby, has been enjoying his singleness and contrasting his happy-go-lucky lifestyle to the problems of his married friends. Before the end of the story, however, he has a revelation and exclaims that he is ready to be loved. Ultimately, he concludes that if he is alone, he is not alive.[20] This idea that a single life is somehow not a full and real life may not always be expressed quite as directly in other examples as it is in these songs, but it is a key theme throughout much of today's entertainment media.

In previous centuries, singleness, particularly for middle-class women, could potentially be a dangerous situation, for most had no way to support themselves until they found a man to be the head of the family. The sense that they could not live a real life until marriage was often true for spinsters who had very little control over their lives and had to adjust their dreams and desires to those of whoever in the family had the money to support them. The lucky ones could find fulfillment caring for children or other family members. The unlucky ones had to eke out an existence in poverty, becoming the pathetic object of everyone's jokes. The desperation to find a husband that is represented in eighteenth- and nineteenth-century literature is understandable. While Elizabeth Bennet's mother in Jane Austen's *Pride and Prejudice* may be ridiculous in how she goes about trying to find husbands for her five daughters, the danger that she is reacting to is real. If she can't find husbands for her daughters, they will be almost penniless, for none of them can inherit their father's estate that by law must go to the nearest male relative. Interestingly, while society has changed greatly in its treatment of women, allowing them freedom to work and support themselves without a husband, many books, films, and television shows demonstrate that the desperation to find a partner still exists. While a woman may not need a husband to support her monetarily anymore, society still says that she needs one in order to be a whole human being.

In *Bridget Jones's Diary*, which is actually a twentieth-century version of Austen's *Pride and Prejudice*, Bridget is far more obsessed with finding a partner than her nineteenth-century counterpart, Elizabeth, is. While Bridget is quite capable of supporting herself with her job in publishing and has a group of caring friends who rally around to help anytime she has a problem, she still desperately needs a man to complete her. In the film version of the novel, Bridget goes into a tailspin after hearing Mark Darcy insult her. As the opening credits roll, we see her chain-smoking and quaffing glass after glass of red wine as she sits on her couch in her pajamas singing along to Jamie O'Neal's rendition of "All by Myself" and plaintively expressing her pain over her loneliness. Bridget is terrified that she will "die fat and alone and be found three weeks later, half eaten by wild dogs." She, therefore, decides to transform herself into the perfect woman who will attract the perfect man, obsessively reading self-help books, repeatedly trying to give up smoking and drunken binges, and desperately trying to lose weight. While the film eventually reveals that Mark Darcy "likes her just the way that she is" and she doesn't need to change herself into someone else to attract a man, its romantic ending with Mark and Bridget embracing as the snow wafts down gently around them ultimately reaffirms the idea that Bridget does need Mark in order to be complete. He may like her "just the way that she is," but, as the audience recognizes, without Mark, she would be destined to be miserable and alone.[21]

Bridget may be a bit more insecure than the typical, single, career women portrayed in the media, but she is not the only one to suffer these fears. Even Miranda, the career-driven lawyer on *Sex and the City*, worries that she too may end up alone and eaten by her cat. After hearing that this kind of death was the fate of a single woman, she begins overfeeding her cat just to make sure that he doesn't turn on her. And it is not only women who often feel that their lives are incomplete without a romantic partner. In the *Friends* episode entitled "The One Where Mr. Heckles Dies" Chandler has a crisis when he realizes that he is far too similar to Mr. Heckles, his creepy upstairs neighbor who has died alone and friendless. Rachel, Phoebe, and Monica try to comfort him, but he is sure that he will be "an old, lonely man." So he decides to embrace the role. He declares, "I figure I'll be Crazy Man with a Snake, y'know. Crazy Snake Man. And I'll get more snakes, call them my babies, kids will walk past my place, they will run. 'Run away from Crazy Snake Man,' they'll shout."[22] For Chandler only two options exist: a happy partnership with someone who loves him or an eccentric existence as a weirdo who scares little children. He cannot imagine any alternative where he might be single and happy, and his fear of ending up alone like Mr. Heckles haunts him.

This idea that a romantic partner is necessary for a person to live a whole, fulfilling life becomes even more problematic as we look specifically at the conclusions of certain movies and television shows, which often begin by trying to show the independence and worth of their single characters but then end up simply returning to the idea that they must be in a romantic relationship in order for their ending to be truly happy. The film *Under the Tuscan Sun*, for instance, begins with Frances Mayes moving to Tuscany after discovering that her husband was having an affair. In the course of the film, she discovers her own sense of independence and power as she refurbishes an Italian villa and builds an unconventional family unit of people who don't seem to fit in anywhere else: immigrant construction workers, a lesbian mother who has been abandoned by her partner, and a faded actress trying to maintain her sense of youth and beauty. The film contains a wedding, but it is not Frances's. Instead, she has opened her house to a young Polish immigrant that she has befriended so that he can marry his beloved from the auspices of her household: an act that appeases the girl's conventional Italian family. At the reception Frances realizes that she now has everything she ever wanted—a family, a child, and a wedding at her house. She just didn't get these things in the way she thought she would. If the movie ended there, it would present a powerful statement of the ability to create joy and meaning outside of a conventional romance. It does not end there, however, for during the wedding, a young, handsome American writer appears, and he becomes the serious love interest that was apparently lacking in Frances's life. As the film ends, the audience knows that now she will receive the happy ending that she deserves because she has finally found a man who will be worthy of her.

While the conclusion of this film may be frustrating to those who wish that, for once, happiness was not defined by finding a romantic partner, the conclusion of the TV series *Sex and the City* may be even more infuriating. Early in the series Charlotte declares, "I believe there's that one perfect person out there to complete you." Miranda's response demonstrates the way that this idea is dealt with throughout much of the series. She replies, "And what if you don't find him? What? You're incomplete. It's so dangerous."[23] Throughout most of the show, the writers emphasize that Charlotte, Miranda, Carrie, and Samantha have the potential to be complete even without romantic partners. They are interesting, successful women in their own right. The conclusion of the show, however, subverts that idea entirely, for all of these women are neatly paired up. It might not be surprising that Charlotte finally ends up with her Mr. Right, though the audience may not have expected him to be a short, balding, Jewish man. And Miranda's baby and relationship with Steve, the baby's father, happens early enough in the series that their marriage is also expected. Also, the fact that Carrie finally ends up with Mr. Big probably pleased a majority of the audience who had waited the entire series for that relationship to work. But when you add Samantha's committed relationship to the list, it seems that no one will be allowed to remain single. All must be appropriately paired up, and the show, which shocked audiences and critics when it first premiered on HBO, ends on quite a conservative note.[24] While we may have once been asked to agree with Miranda that thinking a single person is incomplete is dangerous, we are now forced to side with Charlotte and believe that these women would have been incomplete and unhappy if the writers had not generously provided them with the men that they needed.

For many, it seems that the worst fate in the world is being single and dying without a partner. But wait, there is a worse fate than dying single and alone: dying without ever having sex. In an episode of *Everwood* two teenagers, Amy and Laynie, discuss whether or not Amy should have sex. Amy asks the more experienced Laynie what she should expect if she does have sex:

> Laynie: Uh, it's not going to be romantic. I mean, it might be and it could be, but if you build it up in your mind as this big thing that's going to change your life forever, you're just going to be disappointed. Trust me, the lower your expectations are the better.
>
> Amy: Maybe I'm not ready to do this after all.
>
> Laynie: And that's fine. Just don't wait too long and end up like Rachel Hoffer's sister.
>
> Amy: What happened to Rachel Hoffer's sister?
>
> Laynie: Twenty-nine years old and never did it. Now she's petrified that she's going to die a virgin. It's really sad.
>
> Amy: God.[25]

The message here is that sex for the first time may be "scary and uncomfortable" as one of the other characters mentions later in the episode, but it is far better to get it over with so that you do not have to worry about becoming Rachel Hoffer's sister: the virgin petrified that she will never have sex.

Is this truly what awaits Christian singles who choose to be celibate? Are they doomed to lives of immaturity and neuroses, where their only hope is to die an early death so they do not have to suffer the embarrassment of celibacy? Many Christian singles who have made it to their thirties, forties, and even beyond with their commitment to celibacy intact would attest to the fact that the outlook for individuals who don't find the perfect partner doesn't have to be so bleak. But after being exposed to these ideas repeatedly in the secular media, and (as we will see in chapter four) often meeting with similar ideas in the evangelical church, it is no wonder that many find it difficult to imagine that they may live productive, happy lives without sex and without a romantic partner with whom to share their lives. While Elaine may declare in the quotation from *Seinfeld* that is the epigraph to this chapter that she is not "anti-virgin," much of the media is. Choosing to live a life counter to the messages represented both in the examples presented in this chapter and in many more examples in film, television, books, and songs is not an easy task.

2

Power & Freedom
Positive Secular Views of Celibacy

The only thing hotter than sex is not having sex.

Sidhartha, "The Drought," *Sex and the City*

She's got the big puppy love. I mean, who wouldn't? You're handsome, and brave, and heroic, emotionally stunted, erratic, prone to turning evil and, let's face it, a eunuch.

Cordy, "Carpe Noctem," *Angel*

In a recent episode of the ABC drama *Brothers and Sisters* one of the sons jokingly blamed his mother for his relationship problems—he would never have fallen in love with a priest if he hadn't watched *The Thorn Birds* with her when he was kid.[1] The 1983 miniseries *The Thorn Birds*, based on Colleen McCullough's 1977 best-selling novel of the same name, chronicled the ill-fated romance between Meggie (Rachel Ward) and Father Ralph (Richard Chamberlain). Their story seems to have struck a chord with audiences, for even more than twenty years after the miniseries first aired, it is still repeatedly referenced. What is it about this story that captured the attention of so many people?

Certainly, the motif of forbidden love is one aspect that contributes to its popularity. As classic works like *Romeo and Juliet* reveal, truly engaging love stories generally require the tension that develops when a powerful force keeps the lovers apart. For McCullough's story, though, the fact that this tension derives from one of the lovers' devotion to God provides additional interest, for while it is easy to side with Romeo and Juliet against their warring families, how do we choose sides against God? Even in our increasingly secular society, the choice to serve God with integrity is often still respected.

It is easy to condemn the secular media for the many negative portrayals of celibacy and the assumption that individuals cannot function normally without sex, but even in the midst of all of these negative images, positive portrayals of celibacy exist. Richard Chamberlain's portrayal of the conflicted priest in *The Thorn Birds* provides us with a quintessential example of the tensions that often surround the more positive images of celibacy in the secular media. On the one hand, Chamberlain's Father Ralph is highly sexualized. His commitment to the priesthood and to celibacy not only adds to but also creates much of the sexual tension between him and Meggie. On the other hand, his vocation is portrayed seriously, and his choice to remain within it is admirable despite the pain it causes both him and Meggie. Surprisingly, some portrayals of celibacy may even go beyond this grudging respect to acknowledge that celibacy may actually be an empowering choice for certain individuals. So even as American society continually promotes the glories of sex in contrast to the repressed values of the past, it cannot completely destroy the truth that the discipline of celibacy is a valuable one.

Gaining Power through Celibacy

As we saw in the previous chapter, secular thinkers tend to portray abstinence or celibacy as unrealistic or cruel, and they fear that prolonged abstinence may have dire effects. From their responses, you would think that no one would ever consider abstinence, let alone celibacy, as an option for people in today's secular society. Interestingly, not all secular thinkers concur. In 1978, in response to the sexual revolution, educational psychologist Gabrielle Brown began writing a book on celibacy. Neither an advocate nor an opponent of celibacy, Brown simply wanted sexuality to be understood for what she says it really is, "a conscious, voluntary behavior which is learned, rather than an instinct over which one has no choice."[2] With this statement she challenges the assumption that sex is a biological imperative. But she takes this a step further and states that there are benefits to both short-term and long-term celibacy. Dr. Brown's ideas were so radical at the time that she was asked to appear on over 200 television shows, including *Donahue* and *Late Night with David Letterman*.

As Christians, we may wonder what was so radical about her ideas. After all, hadn't Christians been teaching their children to remain abstinent until marriage for almost two thousand years? Her ideas, however, were radical—not just for the secular world but for the Christian world as well. Brown not only argued that the "truths" of the sexual revolution were not necessarily true, but she also revealed a significant difference between the concepts of abstinence and celibacy—the ramifications of which are only starting to be realized today. In her book, Brown explains the difference between abstinence and celibacy by quoting a friend: "Abstinence is a response on the outside to what's going on, and celibacy is a response from the inside."[3] Celibacy, then, is much more than just not having sex. It is more intentional than abstinence, and its goal, even in the secular world, is personal growth. This distinction helps explain why some in the secular world who would probably denounce today's abstinence campaigns might still be interested in celibacy as a means of empowerment. While writers are not always consistent with their terms, often using abstinence and celibacy interchangeably, the implied meanings behind them are consistent: compelling individuals to refrain from sex by an external force is problematic, but choosing to refrain from sex for an important purpose is empowering. This distinction also has implications for the Christian world, for it might help explain why abstinence campaigns, which tend to focus on the external, might not be as successful as discussions of celibacy, which focus on the internal. Brown's book provides an interesting perspective on celibacy from the secular world that we will see echoed by many more recent writers. As Christians, we may not always seek the same type of growth as those non-Christians who practice celibacy as a means of empowerment, but perhaps there are things that we can learn from them and apply to a Christian understanding of this often-neglected discipline.

Examples for Women

The 1998 film *Elizabeth* provides an interesting starting point for the discussion of positive portrayals of celibacy since it crafts a twentieth-century interpretation of perhaps the most famous virgin in history (apart from the Virgin Mary). Queen Elizabeth's virginity has always fascinated historians, and scholars repeatedly feel the need to explain or disprove her virginity. Theories range from a physical deformity, to a psychological aversion to sex, to an obsession with a married man, to political savvy. In her biography of Elizabeth I, Anne Somerset contends that

> her virginity was to prove one of her greatest assets, for it set her apart from the common mass of humanity and could be represented as an essential part of her mystique. Moreover, by adopting as part of her personal iconography many emblems which in mediaeval literature had been associated with the Virgin Mary—the rose, the moon, the ermine, the phoenix and the pearl—Elizabeth may, perhaps unconsciously, have diverted onto herself some residue of that devotion which in Catholic times had been accorded the Queen of Heaven, and for which the Protestant faith afforded no outlet.[4]

The film follows this interpretation and even suggests that it was a conscious decision on Queen Elizabeth's part.

In the final scenes of the movie, Elizabeth (Cate Blanchett) looks upon a statue of the Virgin Mary and wonders how she was able to command the hearts of men so completely that they were willing to die for her. Walsingham (Geoffrey Rush) explains to her that men need to be able to "touch the divine here on earth" and that Protestants haven't found anything to replace the Virgin Mary. In the scenes that follow, Elizabeth transforms herself into an image of the Virgin Mary, and when she walks into court, those who previously opposed her fall on their knees in reverence. At this point she announces that she is now married—to England.[5] What the film highlights in these scenes is that by choosing virginity, Elizabeth can maintain her power over her nation, gaining not only the respect of her people but also their devotion. The 2007 sequel, *Elizabeth: The Golden Age*, may seem to question the monarch's decision to remain unmarried and celibate, portraying her to be giddy and slightly neurotic when she develops a crush on Walter

Raleigh. However, the conclusion of this film mirrors its predecessor, showing Elizabeth once again gaining power by fashioning herself after the Virgin Mary, this time appearing as the Madonna and Child. As the camera circles around the marblesque queen holding Raleigh and Bess Throckmorton's child, we hear the words of the historical Elizabeth I: "I am called the Virgin Queen. Unmarried, I have no master. Childless, I am mother to my people. God give me strength to bear this mighty freedom."[6] Ultimately, Elizabeth's celibacy is shown to be complicated but still a source of power and respect.

While Elizabeth's example may, at first glance, seem extreme, she is certainly not the only woman who has employed these tactics of using virginity or celibacy to gain authority in a society that generally does not allow women much power. Elvira Dones's recent documentary *Sworn Virgins* reveals how in one part of the world, generations of women have also used their virginity to gain power in a society that granted them very little. Albania has an ancient tradition where women are allowed to live and be treated as men if they take "an oath of lifelong virginity."[7] Dones's documentary captures the stories of several of these virgins. Apparently, the tradition began in the fifteenth century to enable a woman to provide for her family if the patriarch died. While women have historically had few rights in northern Albania, the sworn virgins were allowed the same rights as men. In fact, one sworn virgin "served as the local secretary of the Communist Party, the top office in her region. She was in charge of all the men, and though they knew the reality of her anatomy, her authority was unquestioned."[8] By swearing their lifelong commitment to virginity, then, these women were able to take charge of their lives and assume power that was not generally given to women.

While we might assume that this authority came at too high a price since these women had to relinquish their opportunities for sex and children and, in a sense, deny their femininity, Dones found "an extreme sense of beauty in [the stories of these women]. They are not bitter. They carry the stories with such dignity . . . They are so comfortable with their role."[9] These women are certainly an exception, and as Dones reveals, the number of sworn virgins is declining as women gain more rights in Albania, but the fact that for over six centuries sworn virgins have empowered themselves through their celibacy demonstrates that celibacy may be more radical than we generally imagine. But how can virginity and celibacy be seen as empowering in contemporary American society?

Queen Elizabeth and the sworn virgins might be interesting anomalies, but do their decisions to embrace celibacy have any resonance in our contemporary secular world where women don't have to foreswear their femininity in order to gain power? Contemporary fascination with their stories suggests that there is something appealing about their decisions that resonates with us today. And, perhaps surprisingly, the idea of gaining power through virginity and celibacy has permeated various elements of our culture as well.

In today's society, the common stereotype of a virgin is that she is anything but a rebel. She is the "good girl" who holds to old-fashioned values, and this is usually seen as a sign of weakness. But as we have observed with the sworn virgins of Albania, in certain cultures and at certain times, choosing virginity and celibacy can be a brave and radical act, and in some circles today, virginity and celibacy are developing more of a rebellious reputation. In her article "The New Sexual Deviant: Mapping Virgin Territory," Carson Brown demonstrates how in contemporary American society perhaps the true rebel is the virgin who refuses sexual conformity. She argues,

> In the end . . . rebellion is transformed into conformity. So it goes with sex . . . How are capitalists supposed to market their stuff if people aren't actively pursuing sex? How are they supposed to sell cars, clothes, beers, breakfast cereal, perfume, makeup, or travel on the premise that their products will get you laid if people are content to not get laid? So the market pulls out all the stops to ensure that we will remain sex-obsessed, so that we will buy things. Businesses want virgins to feel horrible about themselves, because if virgins were happy being virgins, they would be horrible consumers. As long as they are virgins desperately trying to ditch their virginity, fine. But abstinence undermines economics.[10]

From this perspective, virginity and celibacy are far more radical than sexual experimentation because celibates are able to maintain power over themselves in a way that subverts America's consumer culture. While this is a far different type of power than the one embraced by Queen Elizabeth and the sworn virgins, in today's world, which often seems ruled by marketing firms and their conceptions of "reality," it has the potential to radically transform the way we think about the issue of controlling our sexuality. No longer is this power defined as the "freedom" to engage in sex with any consenting adult inside or

42

outside of marriage, a freedom that, as Brown remarks, is increasingly defined by ad executives. Instead, it becomes the freedom to redefine sexuality apart from the pressure to have sex and the consumer culture that dictates the rules for those encounters.

Where sexual experimentation is the norm, choosing not to have sex has the potential to become a rebellious act that sets individuals apart. Celibacy has become the subject of reality television shows such as *God or the Girl* and MTV's *True Life*. And some celebrities have even used a period of celibacy to gain publicity. In 2006, for instance, several celebrity tabloids reported on Paris Hilton's decision to refrain from sex for a year. For a woman who became famous when a sex tape of her and her boyfriend began circulating on the internet, choosing a life of celibacy, even for only a year, immediately captured the attention of the press. For Hilton to do something so conservative somehow seemed radical. The same was true for *Sex and the City*'s Samantha, who is probably one of the most sexually adventurous female characters on television. Not only is she promiscuous, seeking a never-ending series of sexual experiences, but she has experimented with threesomes, lesbianism, and S&M. But what was Samantha's most deviant sexual activity? Celibacy! In "The Drought," Samantha starts seeing a yoga instructor who introduces her to the idea of celibacy as a means of preserving and increasing sexual energy. In her voiceover Carrie comments, "Amazingly, talking dirty about not having sex was the most sexually deviant activity Samantha had participated in in months."[11]

Paris Hilton and Samantha Jones may not be typical in their decisions to embrace celibacy for a short time as a radical/deviant activity, but many individuals, particularly women, are attracted to the idea of virginity and celibacy as a means of empowering themselves in a society that often does not seem to value women as more than sexual objects. The movie *40 Days and 40 Nights*, which references the power that women may derive from abstaining from sex, is an interesting example of how this idea often manifests itself in popular culture. When Matt's female coworkers discover that Matt has given up sex for Lent, they become angry. They are not angry because they want to have sex with Matt; rather, they are angry because Matt is threatening their power: "I understand what you are doing Matt. Women have been doing this since forever, so we know all about the power. You see, us having the power—that's part of the system. Now, you're taking the power . . . and

I think you can see why we can't let that happen."[12] It is no surprise to anyone that women are often portrayed as withholding sex as a way to gain power over men—to punish them or to get something from them. That is a stereotype that has often been exploited by the media. But this is not the only way that celibacy has been empowering. It is also a means to develop self-worth and independence for both men and women.

This perspective is revealed quite clearly in Wendy Keller's book, *The Cult of the Born-Again Virgin: How Single Women Can Reclaim Their Sexual Power*, where she lists ninety-one reasons why people may choose to become born-again virgins (individuals who have had sex but now choose to be celibate for either a season or a lifetime).[13] For Keller, the key question that links all of these reasons is "what if you could put yourself back in control of your own sexuality—instead of forking it over to a man, society's point of view or your girlfriends' ideas of what appropriate sexual behavior is for you?"[14] She proposes that for women in particular a time of celibacy may be essential to allow them to focus on more important issues than the physical act of sex. She declares, "We are on the crest of a new era in male-female relations. Having gone through millennia of oppression we are at last in a place where we can step out onto the platform of power and safely claim a place for ourselves too. We can finally create a masterpiece with both colors—the male and the female."[15] For Keller, celibacy may become a feminist act that allows women to discover who they are outside the sexual economy in which they have been previously trained to function.

In many ways Keller echoes ideas discussed by Wendy Shalit in *A Return to Modesty: Discovering the Lost Virtue*. As Shalit's many examples testify, the sexual revolution has actually made it very difficult for some girls to refuse sex or even to regret the loss of virginity when they are pressured into sex. Shalit remarks, "It occurred to me that in an age where our virginity is supposed to mean nothing, and where male honor is also supposed to mean nothing, we literally cannot explain what has happened to us. We can no longer talk in terms of someone, say *defiling a virgin*, so instead we punish the virgin for having any feelings at all."[16] While Shalit tends to have an over-romanticized view of the past, her attempt to make sexual modesty socially acceptable again has important ramifications, for it empowers girls and women by giving them the ability to invoke modesty as a means of saying no to unwanted sexual activity, allowing them to be true to themselves rather than simply being overcome by society's pressures. Like Keller, for Shalit, true feminism lies not in being able to "screw around" like men but rather in invoking modesty and abstinence or celibacy as a way of redefining what it means for a woman to take control of her own sexuality.

Both of these books ask their readers not only to assess the culture around them but also to question whether the transformations in sexuality and in the relationships between men and women that have occurred in the twentieth century have really made things better for women (or even for men). And they propose that the seemingly more conservative way might actually be the more empowering. This message is also beginning to make its way onto secular college campuses. In an article entitled "Students of Virginity," Randall Patterson discusses the growth of abstinence clubs in Ivy League schools. Groups such as the Anscombe Society at Princeton (founded in 2005) and True Love Revolution at Harvard (founded in 2006) have begun to stress the value of reserving sex until marriage. While many of the founders are Catholic, the groups present secular arguments for abstinence, promoting both philosophical and scientific reasons why abstaining from sex until marriage ultimately leads to a better life. Their desire is to combat the "hookup culture" of their colleges by "mak[ing] abstinence look fun, interesting." Echoing ideas that we have already heard expressed by Wendy Shalit and Carson Brown, Janie Fredell, a member of True Love Revolution, explains that abstinence is "extremely countercultural" particularly for women who are able to take full control over their bodies by refusing to give in to peer pressure.[17] These clubs and others like them on secular college campuses demonstrate that the conversations surrounding abstinence are not confined to high school abstinence campaigns promoted by evangelical churches, for secular college students are discovering how reserving sex for marriage can be a means of empowerment.

Surprisingly, in a world that seems suffused with sexual images, this idea of empowering yourself by controlling your own sexuality has also made it to a popular television show. In an episode of the ABC drama *Grey's Anatomy* entitled "The Name of the Game," Meredith, who has recently had a disastrous sexual encounter with her friend George, decides to take a vow of celibacy, replacing sex with knitting. Her friend Izzie takes the vow as well to provide Meredith with moral support. As Izzie explains this vow to a patient, she reveals that there is far more involved in this issue than simply not having sex:

45

I'm making a sweater. Actually, Meredith, that's my friend. The friend that broke George, she is knitting a sweater, she is not *really* knitting a sweater because she cannot knit. But I want her to think she is knitting a sweater because she and I took a celibacy vow. So she is replacing sex with knitting and so I am knitting pieces of Meredith's sweater so I can switch them out with hers so she can really believe she is knitting. Because if anybody needs to be celibate it's Meredith because she broke George, you know?[18]

Anyone who has watched a few episodes of *Grey's Anatomy* will recognize that Izzie is correct. Meredith has so many issues to deal with that she would benefit from a time of celibacy, for perhaps learning to control her sexuality would allow her to begin to control other areas in her life so that she doesn't continue to injure her friends and family. While her attempt at celibacy only lasts for an episode or two, the fact that the writers of the series recognize its potential value is significant.

As all of these examples demonstrate, celibacy or abstinence for women can potentially have powerful results: results that even the secular world acknowledges. For Christians, these examples may be an important reminder that celibacy is not simply holding to some abstract moral standard imposed by church tradition. Instead, it is a choice that God may use to develop us into the Christian witnesses He wants us to be. In addition, these secular examples remind us that our worth is found not in how many sexual conquests we may have in our lifetime or in whether we find our "one true love" but rather in how we are loved by Christ who values us for more than just our sexuality. We may not find our empowerment in exactly the same place as these secular thinkers, but we can agree with them that submitting ourselves to contemporary secular standards of sexuality is not a productive way to live.

Examples for Men

We might expect that positive images of celibacy in popular culture would focus primarily on women, considering that since the nineteenth century, women have often been represented as being less interested in sex than men and more concerned with not being portrayed as sex objects. This is not the case, however. Popular culture does not simply portray celibacy as a positive choice for confused women whose sex lives are out of control; it also explores the idea that celibacy may be equally empowering for men. Several male celebrities, particularly in sports, have been open about their decisions to remain virgins or embrace abstinence. A. C. Green is probably the most well-known, for anyone interested in basketball in the 80s and 90s is probably familiar with his stance on purity that resulted in him helping to found Athletes for Abstinence. He is not the only one, however. LifeAthletes.org lists over 350 professional and Olympic athletes who have pledged themselves to "living lives of virtue, abstinence, and respect for life."[19] While most celebrities are automatically associated with lifestyle choices that are anything but modest, these celebrities have chosen not only to live lives that demonstrate respect for themselves and their sexuality but also to publicize that fact, setting themselves up as role models for others. In a world in which heroism is so often tainted by steroid use, sexual indiscretions, and drug abuse, these celebrities have chosen to empower themselves by controlling their actions and setting themselves apart from the mainstream.

The athletes involved in this campaign are actually following in a long tradition of athletes embracing abstinence. Athletes in the past, however, were not quite as concerned with the moral implications of their decision. They used abstinence as a way to enhance physical and intellectual prowess, and they were occasionally joined by social reformers who also embraced celibacy as empowering for men. In *A History of Celibacy*, Elizabeth Abbott devotes an entire chapter to this idea, revealing that it has quite a long and interesting history. The fact that her examples range from Davy Crocket and Ghandi to ancient Greek Olympians, Cherokee warriors, and Indian wrestlers demonstrates just how pervasive this idea has been throughout various time periods and cultures. There are even aspects of it that continue today. The previously mentioned episode of *Sex and the City* touches on this idea when the yoga instructor explains his decision to remain celibate. He tells Samantha, "Think about really good foreplay. The sexual energy is just starting to awaken. Now imagine a three-year foreplay where all that sexual energy is coursing through your body but never gets released. It just recycles, builds, rises until your entire being is humming with that electric sexual energy."[20] Rather than celibacy being defined negatively as an unhealthy repression of sexual desire, here it becomes a way to generate power that may then be used in other ways.

Admittedly, the yoga instructor on *Sex and the City* is not an "everyman" character. His point of view is definitely in the minority. Even though Samantha is attracted to the novelty of his ideas, she certainly doesn't embrace them for long. The yoga instructor may be right, but he seems to be the only one who would be able to carry out such an "extreme" project. *Sex and the City*, then, ultimately implies that this power is only available to a few extraordinary individuals who are able to have that type of self-control. An episode of *Seinfeld*, however, demonstrates that celibacy might be even more beneficial for the common man. In an episode entitled "The Abstinence," George (a much clearer representation of "everyman") is radically transformed by a time of abstinence.

In this episode, George's latest girlfriend, Louise, gets mono and can't have sex for six weeks. George acknowledges that he has frequently gone longer than six weeks without sex and that he is a "sexual camel," but this time is different because there won't even be the *possibility* of sex. Just days into his abstinence George discovers that he is suddenly smart. Not only can he now solve a Rubik's Cube and correctly answer every question on *Jeopardy*, but he is also magically able to speak Portuguese and prefers discussing physics to sports. Jerry is the one who figures out the secret to George's newly discovered intelligence:

> Louise! That's what's doing it. You're no longer preoccupied with sex, so your mind is able to focus . . . I mean, let's say this is your brain. *(Holds lettuce head)* Okay, from what I know about you, your brain consists of two parts: the intellect, represented here *(Pulls off tiny piece of lettuce)*, and the part obsessed with sex. *(Shows large piece)* Now granted, you have extracted an astonishing amount from this little scrap. But with no-sex-Louise, this previously useless lump is now functioning for the first time in its existence.[21]

Several things are particularly interesting about this episode of *Seinfeld*. The first is that abstinence has the opposite effect on Elaine. When she gives up sex to help her boyfriend pass his medical exams, she becomes stupid. Since the ancient ideas about the power of celibacy for men revolve around the supposed power encased within semen, this disparity really isn't too surprising. The second issue, however, is more significant, for it demonstrates that the potential value of celibacy is wrapped up in the shift of an individual's mind-set. Only *intentional* abstinence has this effect on George. As long as he was unintentionally abstinent and constantly seeking sex, there were no positive effects. It is only when sex is taken off the table completely that he can free his mind up for other things.

In this episode, intentional abstinence is shown to have powerful results that can radically transform an individual for the better. In fact, once George recognizes his newfound power, he actually considers giving up sex permanently. Jerry can't understand this, but George explains, "Perhaps I can better serve the world this way . . . There was a pretty good chance I was never gonna have sex again anyway."[22] Now that his mind-set has shifted, George is able to recognize that perhaps he was placed in this world for more than just gratifying his own sexual desires. Of course, in the intensely selfish (and comic) world of *Seinfeld*, George does have sex again, and he immediately loses his short-lived genius. But by taking us through George's transformation, the writers of *Seinfeld* provide us with a fascinating portrait of celibacy. Ultimately, they affirm the power of sex over intelligence and vocation, but in the process they demonstrate that giving up sex may not be the tragedy that so many people assume it is. It may actually be the higher calling.

With this example, we can see that the idea of using a time of celibacy to gain empowerment has been taken to an even deeper level. Not only do the insight and strength gained through refraining from sex allow the celibate individual to empower himself, but they also enable him to move beyond his own concerns to think about what he might be able to accomplish more widely in the world around him. It is a move from selfishness to altruism that ultimately makes choosing celibacy not only a valid choice but also, at times, a better choice.

Giving Up Sex for a Higher Calling

As "The Abstinence" episode of *Seinfeld* suggests and other examples demonstrate even more directly, there is a tradition within popular culture in which sex is relinquished in favor of a higher calling that demands an individual's utmost attention. This tradition is often placed within a religious context as we consider individuals such as Mother Theresa who was able to accomplish amazing things through her focus on a vocation that required her celibacy. A good example of this thinking in popular culture is found in the film *Dead Man Walking*, the true story of Sister Helen Prejean, the spiritual advisor to death-row inmate Matthew Poncelet. When Poncelet (Sean Penn) asks Prejean (Susan Sarandon) if she regrets giving up men, she explains that there are many types of intimacy, not just sexual intimacy. While she has never had sex, she has had close relationships with many people. In fact, because she is not married, she is able to spend her life caring for many people rather than just a few. She admits that she is lonely sometimes but reminds him that loneliness is a part of life that everyone experiences. In this film, Prejean acknowledges the difficulties of celibacy, but by placing them in the context of the loneliness that everyone feels, she reveals that she is willing to relinquish sex for her calling to serve her world more widely. And, as the movie demonstrates, her calling is, ultimately, more important and more valuable than the pleasure of sex or even an exclusive relationship.

This type of devotion is most often connected to a specific religious vocation, but popular culture demonstrates that relinquishing sex for a higher calling does not have to be limited to religious vocations. One area of popular culture where this idea is seen repeatedly is in the world of superheroes where sex is often the sacrifice they must make for their special powers. Although not all superheroes are celibate, there is definitely a tradition of celibacy amongst those who fight evil. Of course there are several reasons for this, not the least of which is sexual tension. The Superman story isn't as interesting without the love triangle between Superman, Lois Lane, and Clark Kent. In fact, when the writers of the various Superman incarnations feel compelled to show the Man of Steel in a sexual relationship, there is invariably a plot device (e.g., dream, memory erasure, etc.) to reverse the situation and restore the tension. But the more significant reasons for the celibacy of many superheroes are tied to the famous line from the film version of *Spider-Man*: "With great power comes great responsibility."[23] Although superheroes fall in love, they realize they have a responsibility both to the ones they love and to the world at large.

If Superman, for instance, pursues a relationship with Lois Lane, he puts her in danger, and the same is true for several other superheroes and their objects of affection. How many times has Lex Luther kidnapped Lois Lane in order to trap Superman? And how many times has the rest of the world faced annihilation while Superman attempted to save Lois? The sacrifices that accompany this responsibility are most clearly seen in *Superman II*, when Lois realizes Superman's true identity. Blinded by his love for Lois, Superman relinquishes his superpowers in order to be with her. But once he becomes mortal, he is subject to defeat. The only way he can save the world is to become Superman again and erase Lois's memory so that she has no recollection of his true identity. In this film, Superman realizes the truth of Humphrey Bogart's famous line in *Casablanca*: "The problems of three little people don't amount to a hill of beans in this crazy world."[24]

The TV series *Smallville* emphasizes these difficulties in Clark Kent's younger years as he struggles between his love for Lana and his responsibilities as a superhero. In the episode "Arrival," for example, Clark Kent is faced with a life-changing decision: does he keep his promise and return to Jor-El at the Fortress of Solitude before the sun sets, or does he break his promise and stay with Lana, even though he knows there will be dire consequences? Initially, he chooses Lana, relishing the idea of becoming mortal and consummating their relationship. His choice, however, results in his death, and although Jor-El revives Clark and restores his powers, he warns Clark that a price must be paid—someone he loves will die.[25] Ultimately, his father is the one to pay that price. While the next few episodes are unclear as to whether or not Clark returns to a celibate life after his resurrection, the writers eventually reveal that he certainly does. The price for sex has proven to be too high.

Why do superpowers require celibacy? Clark initially explains that he doesn't know whether or not he will be able to control his powers during a moment of arousal, and he doesn't want to hurt Lana. But he later confesses that the real reason is that he can't keep his true identity from Lana if he is intimate with her. He doesn't want their relationship to be based on a lie. Clark's love for Lana is the driving force behind all of his decisions, but, interestingly, every time he allows it to control his actions, it has disastrous results. This dynamic sets up an odd tension in the show. Jor-El tells Clark that his human emotional attachments are his weakness. He should distance himself emotionally from humans and accept his destiny. But Clark realizes that his emotions are what make him human. Isn't it good to care for others? What is the point of having superpowers if you don't use them to help others? Clark doesn't seem to realize that the point is, whether Jor-El and the writers of *Smallville* realize it or not, that loving one person above all others distracts him from his special calling to love and protect all humanity. The problem isn't the emotion. The problem is the exclusivity.

This point is made even clearer in *Buffy, the Vampire Slayer* and the spin-off series *Angel*. The characters in these two shows are far from celibate, and it would be difficult to argue that they make a case for celibacy, but they do teach that there are some things that are more important than romantic love, even more important than *true* love. In the early seasons of *Buffy, the Vampire Slayer*, Buffy Summers is a high school student who must learn that she has a special calling and that this calling requires certain sacrifices. Like the Clark Kent of *Smallville*, she just wants to be a normal teenager, and normal teenagers go on dates. When her Watcher, Giles, cautions her that "maintaining a normal social life as a Slayer is problematic at best," she replies, "This is the 90s. The 1990s, in point of fact, and I can do both. Clark Kent has a job. I just wanna go on a date."[26] But whenever she does go on a date, the boy ends up in mortal danger.

With Buffy, the point isn't simply that her calling makes her incompatible with normal teenage boys who can't know about or understand her vocation. When she falls in love with Angel, a vampire with a soul who helps her fight the evil forces in Sunnydale, she finally connects with someone who knows about her abilities and her special calling. In fact, in many ways he understands her calling better than she does. Even though they have what could be considered a shared calling, their dating life couldn't be more complicated. At the end of the second season Buffy loses her virginity to Angel, but thanks to a gypsy curse, the "moment of true happiness" results in Angel losing his soul and becoming his evil counterpart, Angelus. In the episodes that follow, Angelus threatens, tortures, and/or kills everyone Buffy cares for. The reign of terror doesn't end until Buffy kills him and once again saves the world. When Angel returns, soul intact, the following season, Buffy and Angel must learn to have a platonic relationship. They know that if they go too far, Angel will lose his soul again and Angelus will return, and the temptations are so great that Angel eventually leaves town. In season four Buffy makes a guest appearance on the show *Angel*. In the episode "I Will Remember You" Angel gains what he has sought for over 200 years, his mortality. He and Buffy can finally be together, but after one day of bliss, he realizes that, as a mortal, he is powerless against the forces of evil. Like Superman in *Superman II*, he decides to sacrifice his own happiness so he can spend his life helping others.[27] Again, sex (and even true love) is revealed to be less important than his calling.

The usual message found in movies and television shows can be summed up in the famous line from the song "Nature Boy," a line that is repeated throughout the movie *Moulin Rouge*: "The greatest thing you'll ever learn is just to love and be loved in return."[28] While there is truth in that message, especially if you are talking about God's love, it is usually interpreted to mean that anything can be justified in the name of romantic love. While the examples we have looked at do indicate that giving up a romantic relationship is the ultimate sacrifice, they also show that it can, and sometimes should, be sacrificed for the greater good. A similar message can be found in U2's song "Miracle Drug," in which Bono sings about being willing to give up romantic love in exchange for a cure for life-threatening disease.[29] While romantic love and sex are so often presented as the ultimate goals for everyone in our society, these examples demonstrate that they are occasionally called into question even in the realm of popular culture.

Interestingly, the message that "with great power comes great responsibility" sounds remarkably like Jesus's words in Luke 12:48: "From everyone who has been given much, much will be required." If we look at this verse in context, we will see that it concludes the parable of the servants waiting for their master to return from the wedding feast. The master could return anytime, or he may be some time in coming. What are the servants doing while they wait? Are they preparing for the master's return, or do they think they have plenty of time and indulge their own desires? If we look back at the rest of the chapter, we will see that this parable immediately follows the warning against storing up treasures on earth and the reassurance that God will take care of all of our needs.

In Scripture we are clearly asked to focus on what needs to be accomplished before the master returns, and while that certainly does not mean that we should avoid marriage and the responsibilities that come with it, it should perhaps compel us to pause and think whether our entire focus in life should be finding that perfect mate. As we will see in chapter four, some Christians do think that finding a spouse is our primary goal here on earth, for they believe that it is this relationship that will develop us into mature Christians, but perhaps Christians could learn something from these aspects of secular culture, which remind us that there is more to ourselves as individuals and as Christians than our sexual desires. Through celibacy we may learn to focus our attention on our true vocation of living out the will of God on earth.

3

Chastity & Holiness
Positive Christian Views of Celibacy

Who knew that virtue turns women on?!
    Simon, "Virgin," *7th Heaven*

Why shouldn't you be slutty? You have absolutely no mother-taught
morals standing in the way of you and your sluttiness.
    Lane Kim, "So . . . Good Talk," *Gilmore Girls*

In the hit TV series *Gilmore Girls*, Rory Gilmore's best friend, Lane
Kim, is the product of a conservative Seventh Day Adventist upbringing.
Although she has rejected most of the teachings of her strict mother,
she is horrified to discover that one rule has stuck: no sex before marriage. This also comes as a surprise to her boyfriend, Zach. When Zach
tries to seduce her, Lane exclaims, "I have to wait until I get married."
A bit shocked, Zach responds, "I didn't know that," and Lane replies,
"Neither did I." Although they both admit that they aren't sure if they
are okay with this decision, they do, in fact, wait until they are married.
When Lane looks back on all of the rules taught and enforced by her
mother, she wonders,

How did this happen? I started listening to rock music when I was seven years old. I snuck makeup on at school. I managed to join a band without anyone knowing. I had a boyfriend who my mother thought was a Christian guitarist. And I ate spicy condiments like they were going out of style. I drank soda, ate hamburgers, wore jewelry, I danced . . . And then I moved out and I lived with two guys. I mean, nothing else stuck. Nothing. So why this? Why couldn't the gluten-free thing stick? I could've lived with that.[1]

Like Lane, we both grew up in conservative families, and we both got the message loud and clear: no sex before marriage. We have occasionally joked that between the messages received from our families, our churches, and our Christian schools, it seemed as though there was a footnote in our Bibles next to the unpardonable sin that said, "See sex." Our overdeveloped senses of guilt convinced us that if we ever had premarital sex we would not only get pregnant and contract every venereal disease known to humanity, but we would also become cautionary tales for teenage Christians across the world. For us, the scare tactics worked. And, to some extent, we are grateful. But we also realize that we are in the minority, and many Christians have to deal with either guilt over past sexual sin or pain over past sexual abuse.

The issue of premarital sex is not an easy one for the church to address. In *Growing Strong Daughters*, Lisa Graham McMinn gives us a good example of one of the problems inherent in the discussion. She recounts an experience when she and her daughter heard a song on the radio about a high school girl who gets pregnant and commits suicide. When the song was over, McMinn's daughter expressed how she would probably do the same thing if she got pregnant because having sex before marriage would be such a horrible sin. While McMinn was pleased to know that her daughter recognized the importance of reserving sex for marriage, she was also dismayed that she had "picked up a belief in the extraordinary awfulness and shame of sexual sin."[2] Is sex before marriage the unpardonable sin? Of course not. And in our attempts to show the value of abstinence and celibacy, we need to be careful not to promote such a potentially damaging message not only for those who have fallen into sexual sin but also for those who suffer the repercussions of sexual abuse. But we both know many Christians who go too far the other way. They may believe that premarital sex is wrong, but they unquestioningly assume that their children will have sex before they are married. The reasoning usually goes something like this: "Sure, we hope they wait until they are married, but we didn't, so how can we expect anything different from them? We just hope they are safe." How, then, do we teach God's truth when it comes to sexual matters without conveying the idea that sexual sins are unforgivable or that individuals who are no longer virgins are "damaged goods"? How do we learn to value virginity but also keep it in perspective? Many of the messages emanating from the evangelical church are aimed at helping teenagers and young adults negotiate these difficulties. Even though they don't necessarily provide a developed understanding of celibacy, many at least provide a positive view of abstinence for young Christians.

Abstinence Programs and Support Networks for Young Singles

The most visible attempt to convey this important message about the value of purity is seen through the abstinence programs that gained prominence in the late-twentieth century. The philosophies behind these programs often stem from the traditional values of the Christian church. Despite wavering cultural attitudes toward premarital sex, the official message communicated by most evangelical churches as well as most Catholic churches presupposes that Christians use scripture as a moral guide and that scripture is very clear about sex outside of marriage. Beginning with Genesis, they emphasize that God ordained sexual activity between one man and one woman within a marriage relationship. Citing Genesis 2:24, they focus on God's declaration that a man and wife are to be "one flesh" and often emphasize that this statement is reaffirmed by Christ in Mark 10:8. Paul also invokes this idea of "one flesh" in 1 Corinthians 6:15–20 to counsel against fornication, reminding the Corinthians that by engaging in sexual activity (*porneia*) with prostitutes they are yoking the temple of the Holy Spirit with uncleanness. Here, it becomes very clear that the idea of a husband and wife becoming one flesh in marriage is tied directly to sexual activity, and Paul's discussion of sexuality in 1 Corinthians 6:12–7:9 is often referenced in arguments for the need for Christians to keep themselves from all types of sexual immorality.

Biblical scholars may debate the actual meaning of the word *porneia* (which has been translated variously as fornication, adultery, homosexuality, and incest), and some may wonder if premarital sexual activity is covered by the term. But those Christians involved in the abstinence campaigns generally concur that *porneia* does include premarital sex, and is, therefore, harshly condemned not only in 1 Corinthians 6 and 7 but also in 1 Thessalonians 4, where Paul asks the Thessalonians to be wary of lust and to keep from acting upon it as the Gentiles do. They would agree, then, with Lewis Smedes who remarks in his book *Sex for Christians: The Limits and Liberties of Sexual Living*, "Fornication [*porneia*] is sin; intercourse by unmarried people is fornication [*porneia*]; therefore, intercourse by unmarried people is sin."[3] Based upon these scriptures, then, the commitment to abstinence before marriage is expected for those who strive to live their lives in accordance with the word of God.

Need for Abstinence Programs

While many of the abstinence campaigns go further than this to explore why God might have put these limitations on sexual activity and to discuss why abstaining from premarital sex is a good idea even for those who may not be Christians, the connection between many of the ideals behind the abstinence campaigns and these traditional Christian values is clear. What is perhaps not so clear is why there arose a need for these abstinence programs to support what had always been traditional church doctrine. While the shift in values that occurred in the twentieth century is a key element in the development of these programs, there is also a deeper issue that illustrates why the evangelical church in particular needed help from these abstinence programs to support its moral stance.

Within the early Catholic Church, the repudiation of sexual activity before marriage was supported by a strong tradition of celibacy where both men and women could choose to relinquish their desires for marriage and children to serve God. With the Reformation, however, came a shift in emphasis for the Protestants from celibacy to marital chastity. For many Protestants, celibacy was no longer seen as a spiritual discipline; rather, it became an extremely rare state that few could achieve. Many saw the Catholic Church's support of celibacy as an important sign of its tendency to come between the people and God—in this case controlling their sexuality and implicitly declaring that celibates were more holy than the laity. In addition, many began to focus on the abuses of celibacy as an example of the corruption of the church since many monks and priests were known to break their vows of chastity. Protestants repeatedly invoked the Catholic Church's support of celibacy as an example of the power and corruption of the Catholic Church that needed to be reformed. For many Protestants, celibacy was no longer a viable option, so the focus shifted from conceiving of celibacy as a spiritual discipline supported by church doctrine and tradition to simply emphasizing the need to remain pure until marriage and chaste within marriage. This rejection of celibacy and emphasis on marital chastity set the stage for problems as the culture began to change.

While society continued to uphold the idea of the sinfulness of premarital sex, the Protestant Church really did not need to emphasize a strong theological argument for abstinence. Augustine acknowledged that the women of his time were kept virgins by external laws enforced by parents and society,[4] and for four centuries after Martin Luther, unmarried Protestants without an affirming message of celibacy in the church still had a social morality that upheld an ethic of chastity. Although premarital sex was certainly not uncommon, it was not encouraged. For the upper classes and the emerging middle classes in particular, virginity before marriage was essential (at least for women) to insure that property was passed on to a legitimate heir. And once we reach the nineteenth century, these concerns about legitimacy become linked with the attitudes about sex that we now term "Victorian." The excessive concern that the Victorians had with propriety led them to repress sexuality in ways that now seem problematic and damaging, but these attitudes did contribute to a society that strongly emphasized that sex was to be reserved solely for marriage.

In the twentieth century, however, cultural attitudes toward sex changed significantly. At first, many of the changes in sexual attitudes stemmed directly from a reaction against the sexual repression that many associated with their Victorian parents. They may have also been a response to the horrors of the First World War. In the Roaring Twenties, the young experimented with everything from fashion to sex as they attempted to break away from the confining mores of the previous generation and reclaim their lives after the devastation of war. With the Second World War, however, this rebellion was curbed as attention was directed first to the war effort and then to creating model families for soldiers when they returned from serving overseas. In the 1950s, the family values that are so often invoked today became prominent as people tried to create a sense of stability that had been lost during the war. At the same time, though, as we explored in chapter one, the rise of Freudian thought combined with new research into sexual issues by Kinsey as well as Masters and Johnson set the stage for the sexual revolution of the 1960s, which reacted strongly against the supposedly model families of the 1950s. And with birth control being safe and easily accessible for the first time in history, waiting for sex until marriage became passé.

In response to declining social morality, the Protestant Church, beginning in the second half of the twentieth century, had to promote its own moral teaching for the unmarried. No longer could the church rely upon social values to insure that their single members remain abstinent until marriage. The question for the evangelical church, then, was how to reaffirm biblical morality in a world that no longer accepted either scripture or its moral principles. The church now had to combat a social ethos that generally defined abstinence as unnatural and potentially harmful, and it no longer had the tradition of celibacy to utilize. And with the rise of scandals in the Catholic Church regarding priests who were anything but celibate, the Catholic Church also had to combat a tainted image of celibacy.

Popularity of Abstinence Campaigns

The most easily recognizable result of this shift is the growth of abstinence programs designed to help teenagers withstand pressures both from their peers and from a secular media that often portrays sex for teenagers as natural and expected. Abstinence campaigns such as True Love Waits, Worth Waiting For, The Silver Ring Thing, and Wait for Your Mate have moved beyond individual churches to become active nationwide, with all stemming from the desire of evangelical and Catholic churches to promote morality for their teenagers.

The intention of these programs is admirable, and they have certainly had some positive results. A 2001 study by the National Institute of Child Health and Human Development revealed that teens who take virginity pledges do not have sex as early as those teens who do not make virginity pledges.[5] Three years later the National Longitudinal

Study of Adolescent Health conducted another study which revealed that teens who take virginity pledges "are less likely to experience teen pregnancy," "to be sexually active while in high school and as young adults," "to give birth as teens or young adults," "to give birth out of wedlock," and "to engage in risky unprotected sex."[6] While there are some problematic aspects to these results that we will discuss later, the fact that more and more teens are becoming aware that they do have a choice to say no to sex before marriage is positive. Through these abstinence programs, Christians are making sure that the values of Christianity are being affirmed even within a secular society that does not generally embrace them.

In fact, these ideas have become so prominent that they have even entered into popular culture. One TV show in particular that has wrestled with some of these questions is *7th Heaven*. Like many shows that deal with moral issues, the family drama about a Protestant minister and his family has received criticism from some for being too conservative and pedantic and from others for not being conservative enough. The characters rarely mention Christ and have a weak understanding of scripture, but the show does take a surprisingly strong stand on the issue of premarital sex. In the seventh season, Simon Camden, a high school junior who will become the only one of the seven children to have premarital sex, and his girlfriend, Cecelia, come to the conclusion that they are ready to have sex. They believe their parents will be supportive as long as a good argument is made in support of the decision. The argument that they love each other and they get good grades does not convince either's parents, and Simon and Cecelia decide that maybe they aren't ready after all and continue to struggle with their temptations.[7]

Two seasons later, when the issue comes up again, the writers continue to emphasize the value of reserving sex until marriage. Simon returns home from college with a new girlfriend, Georgia, and a bad attitude. After several poor decisions by all involved, Simon talks to his dad about the fact that he is having sex with Georgia even though he doesn't really like her. Simon then asks his father to tell him what most television fathers would say at this point: "Say that what was right for you might not be right for me. Say that what I did was okay." But Reverend Camden can't give his son what he wants. Instead he says, "Simon, I don't like what you have been doing, and it's really difficult to believe after growing up in this family you could so easily abandon what you have been taught and what I think you believe." He goes on to tell Simon that he is not like other guys and cannot practice casual sex because he has "more than a casual relationship with Christ."[8] While the show never provides concrete biblical reasons for why premarital sex is wrong, it does, in fact, clearly demonstrate that for some Christian families sex is still something to be reserved solely for marriage and that this choice is not simply one of tradition but rather it is wrapped up in one's relationship with Christ.

This message has also transcended the high school audience and begun to affect singles in their early twenties, for there are pockets of twentysomethings who see the message of abstinence until marriage as a radically powerful way to live. In his article "The Young and the Sexless," Jeff Sharlet introduces his readers to a group of twentysomething Christian singles in New York City. They see abstinence as countercultural: a way to fight the materialism and consumerism of our age by rejecting the idea that anything (e.g., sex) can be bought and sold. Taking their cue from the authors of *Every Young Man's Battle*, they arm themselves with abstinence so they can be part of God's army. Although they openly talk about sex and are far from prudes, they abstain from all sexual contact and hold each other accountable for their actions. And in a gesture that sounds reminiscent of the infamous contest on *Seinfeld*, they even wear "masturbands" which they have to remove if they are no longer "master of their domain."[9] This group has taken the Christian message of sexual purity and embraced it in a radical way, creating a lifestyle that transcends the world of high school virginity pledges and makes the message real for them.

Many of these Christian singles are affirmed by a number of urban churches and some large suburban churches that have committed themselves to supporting their many single members. As we will see in the next chapter, this type of church seems to be in the minority, but for those who attend one, it can become an empowering community that enables singles not only to resist the temptations of the world but also to assume an important place in the body of Christ as they begin to minister to others. Redeemer Presbyterian Church in New York City is just one example of a church in which singles, who comprise 80% of the congregation, are encouraged to come together as a community, find their unique spiritual gifts, and begin to reach out to others. In his article "A New Kind of Urban Church," Tim Keller, the pastor of Redeemer Presbyterian, discusses his strategy for creating "a dynamic counterculture" in the cities in order to influence society. Interestingly, one aspect of that counterculture (and, indeed, the first point he mentions in the article) speaks directly to the lives of singles. He remarks, "Regarding sex, the alternate city avoids secular society's idolization of sex and traditional society's fear of it. It is a community that so loves and cares for its members that chastity makes sense. It teaches its members to conform their bodily beings to the shape of the gospel—abstinence outside of marriage and fidelity within."[10] For Keller, a right understanding of sexual purity is not only a means of supporting the single members of the church but also a way to be a countercultural witness to the secular world.

Through their Citilights ministry in particular, Redeemer Presbyterian helps Christians in their twenties and thirties not only find a meaningful place within the church community but also reach out to the unchurched. They are encouraged to meet others for meals after church services, attend praise nights, and hang out at coffee houses. Loneliness is often the greatest problem that singles have to deal with, and many Christian singles who attend churches where they are far outnumbered by the families that surround them will attest to the need to feel valued in their Christian community. Churches like Redeemer Presbyterian, then, provide an important support system for many Christian singles from which they may, then, demonstrate the radical message of celibacy to unbelievers.

Self-Help Books and Dating Services

While most twentysomethings are most likely not part of a group wearing "masturbands" to demonstrate their commitment to abstinence and may not even have a church that is strongly supportive of Christian singles, they are probably familiar with a whole host of dating guides that are designed to help them negotiate the difficult world of Christian dating. Perhaps one of the most well known is Joshua Harris's *I Kissed Dating Goodbye*, where he asks his readers to avoid "defective dating" that trivializes intimacy and doesn't truly prepare individuals for marriage. He counsels singles, saying,

> God gives us singleness—a season of our lives unmatched in its boundless opportunities for growth, learning, and service—and we view it

as a chance to get bogged down in finding and keeping boyfriends and girlfriends. But we don't find the real beauty of singleness in pursuing romance with as many different people as we want. We find the real beauty in using our freedom to serve God with abandon.[11]

He develops his ideas further in *Boy Meets Girl: Say Hello to Courtship* where he ultimately sets up "courtship" in contrast to "dating" (though he has problems with both terms). While "dating" carries with it all of the connotations associated with secular relationships such as "playing the field," having casual sex, and kissing many toads before you find that prince, "courtship" compels Christian singles to recognize that the ultimate goal of these relationships is not simply fun, excitement, and experimentation but rather a committed relationship in a marriage devoted to God. Harris's ideas have had some problematic results, which we will explore in later chapters, but by creating a model of relationship building that directly counters the model constructed by contemporary secular society, Harris does provide support for Christian singles who refuse to be conformed to the world.

For those who find Harris's ideas a bit too serious and intimidating, there are also books like *The Unguide to Dating: A He Said/She Said on Relationships* by Camerin Courtney and Todd Hertz who agree with the foundational moral principles that Harris sets out but also acknowledge that there is a place for fun, casual relationships even for Christians. Addressing issues such as "The Dating Drought," "Changing Gender Roles," "Internet Dating," and "Sexual Temptation," Courtney and Hertz deal with the realities of the dating world for many older Christian singles with humor and attempt to help them negotiate the craziness of a world in which "the traditional route to the altar has become as outdated as an Atari game system."[12] While *I Kissed Dating Goodbye* and *The Unguide to Dating* have two very different messages about the dating world, both provide support for those Christian singles who long to live lives of purity in the midst of a secular environment in which that commitment is seen as hopelessly conservative.

Those who need a little more help with the realities of the Christian dating world may also turn to eHarmony, a very practical way for Christian singles to find others who share their values. Neil Clark Warren, the founder of eHarmony, emphasizes the importance of compatibility, and his questionnaire helps singles think about who they are as well as what they desire in a partner. In his book *Date . . . or Soul Mate?* Warren reveals that his goal is to eliminate divorce, creating strong marriages that will withstand the test of time. In order to accomplish this, he attempts to help single men and women address the issues in their lives that have kept them single so that they may find the perfect mate. The ideas that Warren expresses in his book and that serve as a foundation for eHarmony are valuable, for he not only emphasizes the importance of shared values as a strong foundation for a marriage but he also helps singles look at their lives, explore how their values are manifested, and work to change the elements of their lives that aren't working. The many television commercials for eHarmony showing rapturously happy couples are certainly evidence that, for some, his advice seems to have worked.

His comments, however, also demonstrate a dangerous train of thought that may be found throughout many of these Christian dating guides as well as in the rhetoric of the abstinence campaigns: the idea that singleness is simply a stage to pass through on the way to marriage and that if you just have enough faith or just correct a few problems in your life, the right person will automatically arrive. Warren never condemns singleness. In fact, he remarks, "In all my seminars throughout North America, I keep stressing one fundamental truth: You can be deeply content without being married."[13] He does, however, fall into the trap of implying that if you fix yourself first, then you will find the perfect mate. He almost goes so far as to guarantee this: "I promise that when you have read through this book—and implemented the strategies I recommend—you will be significantly more attractive to the person you most want to marry."[14] And then later he remarks, "If you follow the principles for marrying the right person, you will be successful at the most important part of human living."[15] For Warren, as well as for many others, singleness is characterized primarily as a time of waiting that should be used productively to prepare for the inevitable future marriage.

Whether it is seen in the titles of so many of the abstinence campaigns that simply ask teenagers to "wait" until the right person comes along or it is implied in the supportive dating advice that asks its readers simply to hold on through a few more bad dates until Mr. or Miss Right comes along, the assumption is that waiting and preserving your purity in the midst of that wait will one day be rewarded with the perfect partner and amazing sex. Many of us know couples who can attest to the success of eHarmony. And others who will swear that once you stop looking, God will bring along the perfect person. Jeramy Clark, author of *I Gave Dating a Chance: A Biblical Perspective to Balance the Extremes*, uses his personal experience as proof that his advice will work for everyone, remarking, "I hope you understand that [my wife] Jerusha and I weren't handed some exclusive deal for only the few."[16] Others may not state it quite as directly, but the assumption is that all singles are in a "season" that will soon be transcended when they find someone to marry. We all may know that God doesn't give us all the same gift in the same way, but in desperation we may also cling to these stories and hope we will be able to tell our own version of the story some day. But is that the best way to think about singleness?

In an episode of *Sex and the City*, Carrie states in one of her voice-overs, "The primitive Greeks clung desperately to myths to explain the random hopelessness of their miserable lives. Do modern day singles need modern day myths just to help us get through our random and sometimes miserable relationships?" Miranda goes on to describe the urban relationship myth: "Unbelievable fairy tales concocted by women to make their love lives seem less hopeless." And Samantha interjects, "Except it makes you feel even more hopeless because this fabulous magical relationship is never happening to you."[17] As singles in our late thirties, we can relate to that sentiment. When Jeramy Clark (as well as many others) seeks to give singles hope by talking about how he didn't get married until his mid twenties, we have a tendency to roll our eyes and think, "What does *he* know about waiting?" And the sting is even deeper for those of us who are Christians because so much of the advice we receive is predicated on the assumption that if we are good Christians and we are right with God, God will bless us with a mate. Carolyn McCully writes in her article "Sex and the Single Woman" that this kind of thinking "creates a works-based mentality to receiving gifts, which can lead to feelings of condemnation. The Lord doesn't require that we attain a particular state before he grants a gift."[18] But with so many Christian writers on singleness emphasizing that God *will* provide a mate if we are only patient enough, holy enough, or well-adjusted enough, it becomes difficult to remember this truth.

Thankfully, there are others within the church who acknowledge this difficulty and help singles to focus on God not as a means of improving our marriage potential but rather as a means of developing into the individuals that God wants us to be even if that means remaining single. Books such as Camerin Courtney's *Table for One: The Savvy Girl's Guide to Single-ness*, Connally Gilliam's *Revelations of a Single Woman: Loving the Life I Didn't Expect*, Jason Illian's *Undressed: The Naked Truth about Love, Sex, and Dating*, Jennifer Marshall's *Now and Not Yet: Making Sense of Single Life in the Twenty-First Century*, Wendy Widder's *Living Whole Without a Better Half*, and Holly Virden and Michelle McKinney Hammond's *If Singleness Is a Gift, What's the Return Policy?* offer support for singles. Sometimes it is helpful just knowing that you are not alone, that you are not the only one who feels hopeless at times, and that you are not the only one who questions whether or not God has someone special for you. While all of these books acknowledge the difficulties of negotiating a world in which singleness is often seen as "an incurable disease, doom-ing [us] to a life of loneliness and despondency,"[19] they also remind their single readers that our focus as Christians needs to be our walk with God and not our walk down the aisle.

Grappling with Theological Truths regarding Singleness

Books like those listed above and Web sites such as ChristianSinglesToday.com, can provide encouragement for singles during difficult times. But sometimes we need more than an anecdotal support system. While an-ecdotes may be comforting, they do not necessarily deal with the deeper theological issues that often fuel our frustrations: What does it mean to have faith in God? If we don't have a spouse, does it mean we don't have enough faith? If marriage is ordained by God, why would he withhold this good gift from some of his children? Ultimately, these are the types of questions we struggle with, and anecdotes about our lives do not really answer these questions. Many of the books reach the conclusion that we need to trust God, and that is certainly true. But perhaps we need to rethink what we are trusting God for. Does our hope in God lie simply in finding a mate? Or are we challenged to hope in God even if he chooses to have us remain single?

Bible Studies and Devotionals

Moving beyond self-help books and anecdotal support systems, there are a few Bible studies and devotionals written specifically for singles.

These books generally use scripture as their basis and provide discussion or application questions to help singles apply the principles to their daily lives. Unfortunately, most of these books are written for singles in their twenties and end up focusing on marriage. One of the better studies is Andrew Farmer's *The Rich Single Life*. As part of Sovereign Grace Ministries' Pursuit of Godliness Series, its goal is to focus on sound doctrine and personal application of spiritual truth. Accordingly, the book starts by having a very clear focus on the gospel. It places a strong emphasis on scripture and stresses the importance of seeking our identity in God, understanding God's grace and what he has done for us, and practicing discipline in our lives. While these are topics important for all Christians, regardless of our age or marital status, they are discussed specifically with the single adult in mind. Unfortunately, the second half of the study focuses on more typically "single" issues as it moves from discussions of the gospel to discussions of gender roles, courting, and marriage. Even though Farmer emphasizes the importance of seeking your identity in God and serving him with undivided focus, one can't help but notice the main message of the chapter on marriage: "The rich single life embraces a biblical vision for marriage with sober but faith-filled anticipation."[20] Farmer acknowledges that marriage should not be our goal, but marriage is still assumed as something that will come and should be anticipated. Even in a book that discusses Paul's theology of singleness, emphasizes the providence of God, argues that if we are single we have the gift of singleness, and encourages us to view everything with an eternal perspective, there is still no real understanding of long-term celibacy. Marriage plays such a central role in our evangelical culture that even many positive discussions of singleness eventually end up focusing on marriage.

Thankfully, there are also several books that help singles wrestle with the difficult questions of celibacy in ways that move beyond the myth that the perfect mate will definitely arrive one day. In *They Were Single Too: Biblical Role Models*, David Hoffeditz, an associate pastor and assistant professor of Bible and Greek who happens to be single, takes his readers through an examination of eight biblical role models, each of whom represent a different type of single Christian. In addition to discussing Paul, who had the gift of celibacy, Hoffeditz also devotes chapters to other singles throughout Scripture—including Anna, who spent most of her life as a widow; Ruth, who was a younger widow that eventually remarried; Martha, who was a busy single woman; Jeremiah, who was commanded not to marry; Joseph, who resisted temptation as a single man and eventually married; Nehemiah, who was possibly a eunuch; and John the Baptist, who devoted his life to preparing the way for the Messiah. Hoffeditz concludes that "these individuals understood the true meaning of life. It concerns not a spouse, an education, or a lucrative job. Rather, a life worth living remains faithful to His calling, follows the Lord despite the costs, and presses forward to the prize."[21] One of the most refreshing things about this study is that there isn't any advice regarding dating or marriage. Instead, the focus is on undivided devotion to God.

Another refreshing aspect of this study is that Hoffeditz does not shy away from addressing one of the greatest challenges that singles have to face: loneliness. While many books aimed at singles mention that loneliness is something that we may struggle with, few move beyond acknowledging that it is a problem and encouraging singles to forge relationships with more people. Hoffeditz turns to scripture to remind us that God often works most powerfully through times of solitude. In the midst of his discussion of Jeremiah, for instance, Hoffeditz acknowledges some of the difficult questions that often remain unanswered for singles: "If Jesus truly loved me, could He not at least provide one or two close friends as I bear this 'gift' of singleness?"[22] As he points out, Jeremiah asked similar questions, and Jeremiah had every reason to be lonely. God commanded Jeremiah to forsake marriage and even social events such as weddings and funerals, and God also called him to a despised profession—that of a prophet. Not only did Jeremiah struggle with loneliness and depression, but he also suffered persecution. Like many of us, he even questioned God's nature, accusing him of being a "deceptive stream" (15:18): someone who promises hope but provides none. Hoffeditz observes that Jeremiah, like David in Psalm 13, comes to realize that "our trust is not rooted in false hope or fanciful dreams. Our confidence in the Lord's love for us and His all-powerful hand resides in who He is and what He has done in our lives. Despite bouts of loneliness and the knowledge that he would always be single (16:1–9), Jeremiah confidently declares that the Lord is 'my strength, and my fortress, and my refuge in the day of affliction' (16:19 KJV)."[23] By using the example of Jeremiah and turning his readers' attention to the faithfulness of God even in the midst of loneliness, Hoffeditz provides support for singles as we negotiate the difficulties of our reality. Rather than simply asking his single readers to hold out until God brings a mate, he encourages us to recognize that God is faithful even if that mate never comes.

For singles who are frustrated by simplistic suggestions that we should simply pray harder or have more faith that our mate will arrive, Hoffeditz's study provides hope that someone not only understands more of the complexities of our lives but also sees how God is faithful in the midst of them. Marva Dawn's book *I'm Lonely Lord—How Long? Meditations on the Psalms*, which looks at how many of the Psalms express God's eternal faithfulness to us even in the midst of extreme loneliness, may also help singles develop a more mature conception of God's faithfulness. She begins with Psalm 13, echoing David's cry, "How long, O LORD? Will you forget me forever?" (v. 1) and acknowledging the depths of despair into which people may fall for various reasons, including loneliness. As she guides her readers through the Psalms, she also helps them to negotiate the process that David moves through in Psalm 13: a poem that begins in lamentation but ends with David trusting in God's unfailing love. Rather than trying to dismiss the pain of loneliness, arguing that we simply need to become better people to withstand this pain or providing advice on how to find the perfect Christian spouse so that we are no longer lonely, Dawn reminds us that God is with us throughout all of these trials. Dawn also reminds us that God may work through our pain and uses her own life as an example, remarking, "Out of my loneliness came ministry. That had been the story of my life all along. God kept turning around things that caused me pain and continued to use them as vehicles for witness and service." [24] For both Dawn and Hoffeditz, the answer to loneliness lies not in finding a mate but rather in letting God work through the pain to accomplish the work that he wishes to do in and with our lives. With these books, then, both authors address the deeper difficulties of singleness and provide hope for singles who are no longer convinced that if we simply have enough faith, God will automatically provide a partner.

Theology

With their devotionals Hoffeditz and Dawn begin to move beyond simply providing anecdotes and advice to exploring theology as they ask their readers to grapple with the realities of the God that we serve. This type of deeper analysis is essential for older singles in particular as we begin to wonder how to reconcile our singleness with the truth of who God is. *Sex and the Supremacy of Christ,* edited by John Piper and Justin Taylor, also encourages us to start thinking through these theological issues. Throughout the book, the authors work to create a theology of sex based upon scripture. Their advice, then, flows from this theology rather than simply from personal experience. The volume devotes two chapters to singleness: the first, with sections authored by Mark Dever, Michael Lawrence, Matt Schmucker, and Scott Croft, addresses single men and the second, authored by Carolyn McCulley, addresses single women. The chapter focusing on single men is not quite as successful as the chapter focusing on single women at escaping some of the dangerous messages that permeate so many of these discussions. Many single Christian men may cringe when reading Mark Dever's exclamation that "if you are not called to celibacy, get married!"[25] For many single men as well as single women, the issue is not lacking a desire to be married but rather not meeting anyone with whom that desire may be fulfilled. As Dever continues, he reveals that the issue may be a bit more complex, admitting, "Of course, the desire to be married is no guarantee that it will happen. And for that, I have no great answer."[26] The chapter, however, is based on the assumption that if a man wishes to be married, he eventually will be.

Despite Dever's assumption, the chapter's discussion of sexuality does raise important issues about the purpose of sex and goes beyond "a list of do's and don'ts."[27] In his part of the chapter, Michael Lawrence reminds his readers that "sex is not the arbitrary reward you get for getting married . . . Rather, sex has a God-given theological meaning and purpose that transcends 'my' experience and opinions about it."[28] The rest of the chapter, then, sets out this theology based upon the idea that "sex outside of marriage makes a mockery of the covenant God instituted and to which he is witness."[29] By creating an argument for chastity based upon a strong theology of sex that moves beyond a "just say no" mentality to demonstrate the purpose of sex not just within marriage but also within God's overall plan for humanity's relationship with him, the authors provide answers to many singles' questions about the value of celibacy.

The chapter by McCully provides an even more powerful discussion of singleness and sexuality. Reminding her readers that "we need to clearly see our singleness through the lens of Scripture and not our desires," McCully leads us through a discussion of scripture that reveals that singleness needs to be accepted as God's will and used for "the common good of others." [30] While McCully does not deny the possibility of marriage, she counsels her readers saying, "We're not on hold. Waiting in faith is our high form of worship. And though we may not be married, we are eternally embraced in the arms of everlasting love." [31] In both of these chapters, but particularly in McCully's chapter, sex is seen within the context of God's commands in scripture, and singles are challenged to focus on God's Word rather than their own desires or frustrations.

This message is an important one, but it is one that is often lost amidst all of the other discussions that focus solely on the need to wait in faith for a spouse. Few acknowledge the reality that some of us may remain single for our entire lives. In fact, Lori Smith, in her book *The Single Truth*, provides a rare perspective when she acknowledges that she may not get married. For Smith, as well as McCully, hope does not lie in a potential marriage but in the knowledge that God is in control. For some, acknowledging God's control is synonymous with blaming God for denying us what we believe to be his blessings. It is easy to feel that way when you think God is giving everyone else the desires of *your* heart. But as these authors remind us, our focus should not be on this life but on the eternal. While many of the dating books and even the books designed to commiserate with fellow singles concentrate on the daily realities of being single in a Christian world that is seemingly designed for the married, Smith's book and the essays in *Sex and the Supremacy of Christ* remind us that God's truths do not presuppose a world of married individuals. They speak directly to singles who must also learn how to glorify the Lord in whatever state we are placed.

Sexuality

The question of how singles serve the Lord in the midst of singleness is often wrapped up in issues surrounding our sexuality. While many Christians assert that singles cannot refrain from sex and, therefore, cannot be effective Christian witnesses, others have begun to explore the possibility that celibate Christians may embrace sexuality in a way that honors God. This desire to articulate a theology of sex that affirms Christian singles in their holy service to God informs Lauren Winner's book *Real Sex: The Naked Truth about Chastity*, and for Christian singles who desire to think through the issues of singleness and celibacy in more depth, Winner provides a good discussion. In her introduction, Winner expresses her frustration with many of the Christian books on sex and singleness: a frustration that many of her readers will probably resonate with. She complains that they are "out of touch with reality," "designed for people who get married right out of college," "theologically vacuous," and "dishonest because they make chastity sound easy."[32] Rather than relying on the familiar refrain of "just wait until marriage," Winner explores chastity as a spiritual discipline that applies both to those who are single and to those who are married, and her discussion provides insight into issues that are rarely addressed by contemporary thinkers.

One of the strengths of Winner's argument is that she places her discussion of singles' sexuality in the midst of a long tradition of spiritual discipline, allowing her to refute many of the misconceptions about sex that permeate other works. After exploring various lies that the secular world and the Christian world tell about sex, Winner concludes:

> We Christians don't want to—cannot—accept the culture's story about sex: that sex is only for fun, that sex has no consequences, that what I do with my body is none of your business, that the goodness of sex is evaluated by the mind-blowingness of the orgasm. But nor ought we err on the side of Gnosticism that tells us that sexual desire is bad, that bodily longings are to be stamped out of existence. Neither of these is the Christian approach, for the Christian approach is neither hedonism nor obliteration; it is discipline.[33]

As she continues her argument, Winner explains what it means for chastity to be a Christian discipline: "doing sex in a way that befits the Body of Christ, and that keeps you grounded, and bounded, in the community. As we've seen, that means sex only within marriage—which means, in turn, abstinence if you're not married, and fidelity if you are."[34] By defining chastity as a spiritual discipline and placing it firmly within the context of Christian community, Winner moves far beyond the discussions of personal frustrations with singleness and instead posits a world where chastity not only helps develop individual Christians in their walks with God but also helps to build up the church, reminding the married members that our supreme loyalty is given to God and not to our spouses or families. Unlike many contemporary Christian writers who deal with singleness, Winner recognizes an important place for singleness in the church and sees value in singles learning to develop the discipline of chastity.

The discipline of chastity is also an important component of Doug Rosenau and Michael Todd Wilson's book *Soul Virgins: Redefining Single Sexuality* where they, like Winner, attempt to define sexuality appropriately for Christian singles. They too see a huge gap between secular conceptions of sex typified by "the backdrop of MTV, reality dating shows, and so many other pop-culture influences" and Christian conceptions of sexuality, which, even if they are appropriate, are often not expressed as strongly as they should be.[35] Their goal is to create "a whole new paradigm—a whole new way of thinking."[36] An early step in this process is to shift the focus from finding a mate to concentrating on God. They remark, "Here's a radical thought: what would happen if you took the desperate energy you spend looking for a mate and instead redirected it into a *desperate seeking after God*?"[37] For singles steeped in discussions of what they must do to find a spouse, Rosenau and Wilson provide an important reminder of where our focus really needs to be.

They also provide probably the most in-depth discussion of sexuality for singles, not only presenting guidelines for singles that are based firmly on scripture but also acknowledging the complexities of sexuality that make lists of dos and don'ts untenable. Rather than simply addressing sexuality as being limited to intercourse, they acknowledge that sexuality encompasses far more. Perhaps the strongest element in their book is the discussion of the "sexual ache" that Christian singles often feel. Rather than asking singles to deny it or repress it, they counsel singles to redirect it and reframe it: "*Redirecting* takes sexual energy and uses it to motivate other activities and accomplishments. *Reframing* sees into the deeper meaning of sexual desire, allowing such perspective to inspire greater wholeness."[38] Rather than denying these desires, the authors ask singles to let the desire lead us into positive community within the church where we may be spurred "toward compassion, depth of character, and adventures in true intimacy."[39] By acknowledging these longings and helping singles know how to channel them into positive work for God's kingdom, the authors help singles address the realities of our situation and demonstrate why singleness is an asset to the church at large. For older singles in particular, this discussion, which addresses the complexities of sexuality and helps individuals see a higher purpose in chastity, is a breath of fresh air in the midst of the majority of books on singleness.

Persistent Messages of Waiting

Books like *Soul Virgins* and *Real Sex* demonstrate that positive discussions about singleness are occurring within the evangelical church. Both present strong theological arguments for the value of abstinence and allow singles to see themselves as an integral part of the church. They ultimately challenge the church to view sex in a proper context. Unfortunately, they too occasionally fall into the trap of seeing marriage as the eventual goal for everyone. Admittedly, their discussions are far more nuanced than presentations such as one that occurred at an abstinence rally sponsored by Silver Ring Thing in which one of the leaders began by leading the auditorium full of teenagers in a chant of "Sex is great!" After this went on for several minutes, the leader added, "within marriage," and encouraged the teenagers to postpone sexual activity until they had a ring on their finger. Then, the video screen showed a close up of his gold wedding band, and the Hallelujah Chorus began to play. Lauren Winner, Doug Rosenau, and Michael Todd Wilson would all agree that this view of abstinence with its simplistic glorification of sex within marriage is problematic, particularly for singles who are no longer in junior high, but throughout their books they cannot entirely escape the idea that marriage is the ultimate goal. The fact that these authors, who present such strong, scripturally based arguments for single chastity still invariably see singleness as a stage before marriage demonstrates just how difficult it is to create a positive discussion of celibacy apart from the idea of waiting for marriage.

For Winner this problem is revealed as she discusses the need to place sex within the context of the church community. She quotes from an essay by Wendell Berry in which he "urges married couples to integrate their sexual lives into the larger, holistic project of creating a household,"[40] and in her discussion of this essay, she uses an interesting metaphor to explain Berry's ideas of community: "Perhaps the more appropriate metaphor is the wedding cake. At the very top are a bride and groom, and they are supported by a layer of household, a layer of family, and a final layer of community and society."[41] While this metaphor may be useful to describe the support a married couple needs, it is woefully inadequate if we use it as a vision of Christian community. Later, Winner will discuss the need for singles to be integrated fully into the church community, but this metaphor tellingly reveals why that is often so difficult. With the bride and groom at the top, singles are relegated to a bottom layer of "community and society." They may play a supporting role but clearly must find a spouse if they ever hope to receive support themselves.

In *Soul Virgins* the problem is even more overt. One of the foundational points in Rosenau and Wilson's argument is expressed in a chart, which they title "The Relationship Continuum Bridge." The bridge, which moves from "connecting" to "coupling" and finally to "covenanting" is designed to help singles see what types of behavior are appropriate for the different stages of a relationship. The fact that it is a bridge, however, and that the final goal is marriage implies that singles who don't marry are stuck on the wrong side with a huge gulf of "erotic sexual behaviors" between them and those who are married. That marriage is the final goal is also emphasized at the end of the "radical thought" that we quoted earlier, which asks singles to focus on God rather than searching for a mate. While the authors begin by asking singles to shift their focus from marriage to God, they conclude, "What a foundation you would build for intimate coupling with a potential future mate!"[42] From this conclusion it is too easy to assume that becoming a stronger Christian has one main goal: to provide a strong foundation for a future marriage. While the authors never state this directly (and probably don't even believe it), much of their rhetoric unintentionally implies it.

Their discussion also implies that singles must learn to survive on their own without the support of the married members of their churches. In an extended metaphor that occurs in their final chapter, the authors compare marriage and singleness to two different dinner parties. One is an intimate affair between Brad and his wife. They sit alone at a private table in a private room and have eyes only for each other. The other is a buffet where Molly samples the food and talks to the various single people who also fill the banquet hall. While the authors argue that both parties are enjoyable even if they are different, the point that stands out to us is that the people in the two parties are never allowed to meet. They are carefully segregated from each other. True, this is only a metaphor, but on the previous page the authors highlight the separation that will inevitably occur between singles and their married friends: "Deeper connecting relationships other than with one's spouse become difficult to maintain. This is the reason many singles who marry begin spending less and less time with their single friends. It's not that they no longer care to be around them; it's just their priorities have changed—and rightly so."[43] At the conclusion of *Soul Virgins*, then, Rosenau and Wilson posit a world in which singles are excluded from the lives of their married friends. Rather than viewing the church as a community in which everyone works together to support everyone else, Rosenau and Wilson construct the church as pockets of nuclear families supporting themselves while singles look on wistfully, longing for the day when they too will find a spouse to whom they may devote their entire attention.

Even the very positive images of celibacy in the church that Winner, Rosenau, and Wilson uphold generally leave something to be desired, for, directly or indirectly, they often imply that singles must eventually be married in order to participate fully in the community of the church and even in the blessings of God. Even though some of these writers may not really believe that is true, the fact that it permeates their illustrations and rhetoric shows how accepted this idea is in the church. For older singles, this message becomes progressively more difficult to handle, for it implies that something must be wrong with them if they are excluded from the one thing that will seemingly make them a full member of the body of Christ. And these are the messages that they receive from many of the *positive* images of celibacy within the church. The picture only gets more dismal as we move into an exploration of the overtly negative messages that the church today often directs toward Christian singles. As we will see even more explicitly in the next chapter, Christian singles need a much more powerful message of the value of long-term celibacy within today's church to withstand all of these disheartening messages.

4

Sin & Selfishness
Negative Christian Views of Celibacy

Everywhere I looked people were standing in twos. It was like Noah's west-side, rent-controlled ark.

Carrie Bradshaw, "Bay of Married Pigs," *Sex and the City*

Martha O'Dell: [Given your Christian beliefs], would you have a problem doing a sketch about premarital sex?
Harriet: I don't have a problem *having* premarital sex. It might be the only sex I'll ever have.

"The Long Lead Story," *Studio 60 on the Sunset Strip*

Recently, Bonnie had the courage to broach the subject of celibacy in the church with her neighborhood Bible study. The previous week someone had brought up speaking in tongues, so Bonnie thought the members of the predominantly Baptist group might be willing to explore another controversial topic. As Bonnie prepared the lesson, she wondered how a group that, in addition to her, consisted of four couples and one divorced man who was engaged, would respond to the topic. Bonnie started the discussion by pointing out various scripture passages that focused on the value of celibacy. While the consensus of the group seemed to be that, yes, there is a positive representation of celibacy in scripture, the discussion quickly turned from scripture to whether or not this message is seen in the evangelical church and whether or not singles are supported in their local churches. As Bonnie began to express some of her frustrations with how she, as a single woman, is often treated in the church, she was surprised at the responses she received. No one seemed to acknowledge it as a problem. The responses ranged from "We've got singles at our church" to "If people make derogatory comments about singles, you shouldn't care. It doesn't matter what other people think of you. You just need to consider what God thinks of you." Bonnie was shocked that the treatment that had been so obvious to her was not only completely unseen by the other members of the group but also quickly dismissed.

Singleness and Demographics

For many of us who are single, the problem of the way we are often treated in the church is so obvious that we don't even question it or debate it. We just sit around and swap horror stories. It is surprising, then, to find that many married couples don't see the same issues that we see, or, even more surprising, are the people who seem to think that celibacy and singleness are upheld in evangelical churches even more than marriage and family. In her book *Getting Serious about Getting Married: Rethinking the Gift of Singleness*, Debbie Maken remarks, "Condoning singleness from the pulpit is in large part responsible for causing singles to resign themselves to their unfortunate and less-than-ideal fate. With the benefits of marriage systematically downplayed and the supposed freedoms and hyper-sanctification of the single lifestyle glorified, protracted singleness becomes a self-fulfilling prophecy."[1] For the moment leaving aside her denigration of singleness as an "unfortunate and less-than-ideal fate," let's consider her premise that pastors are "glorifying" singleness. Perhaps some are, but they have certainly not been part of our church experiences. For more than thirty years, both of us have attended suburban churches that cover a range of denominations (Anglican, Assemblies of God, Baptist, Christian and Missionary Alliance, Church of the Nazarene, Evangelical Free, Presbyterian, and non-denominational), and we have rarely heard a sermon glorifying singleness. True, there might have been a few comments about singleness in a sermon or two, but in that case, the pastors usually presented singleness simply as a "season of life" to be endured before marriage. There might even have been an entire sermon or two about singleness as part of a longer series on marriage, but when you balance these one or two sermons with the hundreds we have heard on marriage, there is no doubt that the scales tip in favor of marriage.

Now, granted, we are seeing the issue primarily from our perspective, which certainly does not encompass all evangelical churches in the United States. Particularly in urban areas, there are churches that minister primarily to singles, and perhaps these are the churches that Maken has observed. The majority of singles, however, do not seem to be encountering these affirming messages of their singleness. In fact, many Christian singles don't even seem to be making it to church at all. If you look around the congregations in many suburban, evangelical churches, you will find a large number of families; a few widows, divorced women, and single mothers; even fewer widowers, divorced men, and single fathers; perhaps a handful of women over twenty-five who have never been married; and perhaps one or two single men over twenty-five who have never been married.

Church demographics certainly do not support the idea that single men and women are being affirmed in the church, particularly when we consider the large number of single individuals within American society. According to the Barna Group's 2006 and 2007 statistics, not only do singles make up approximately 50% of American adults, but they also make up approximately 50% of adults who say they have made a personal commitment to Jesus Christ.[2] However, singles are less likely to attend church than those who are married (38% to 50% respectively).[3] These numbers may not seem that significant, but when we look specifically at the statistics for the evangelical church, we see some alarming results. Only an approximate 25% of evangelicals over eighteen are single.[4] When you consider that 60% of single adults are under thirty, that leaves us with a mere 10% of evangelicals over thirty that are single.[5] While the Barna statistics show that single adults are less likely to attend church than married adults, they do not show *why* this is the case. A poll of over 1000 singles on ChristianSinglesToday. com provides some insights. Singles were asked, "Have you ever been tempted to stop going to church due in some part to your singleness?" Of the single adults who took the Christianity Today Web site poll, 59% replied in the affirmative.[6]

These statistics support the experience of many of the singles we know, for they have expressed frustration about feeling invisible in the church, feeling like a problem that needs to be fixed, or even sometimes feeling like the enemy amidst a world of couples and families. For many singles, the evangelical church (despite a tradition of abstinence) has become a place that no longer recognizes the role of celibacy and therefore neglects to nurture or support singles appropriately. A survey of the evidence that exists within local churches as well as in Christian media will demonstrate that singles are not imagining the problem; rather, we are seeing the realities that married couples are able to ignore.

Singleness and the Local Church

Considering the demographics of many suburban evangelical churches, it is not surprising that some single men and women have difficulty even entering the doors of their local church. With congregations filled with couples and families, the few singles who arrive for a Sunday morning service may find themselves feeling out of place. Christine, for instance, once attended a very small neighborhood church in Sacramento. The church was so small that any visitors were quite obvious to the rest of the attendees. On the first Sunday that she visited the church, several women came up to her to introduce themselves. After the initial round of names, the next question was whether or not she had any children. As soon as she revealed that not only did she not have any children but also she wasn't married, the conversation ended and the women quickly moved away to talk to someone else. Christine continued to attend the church, but always felt as if she didn't quite fit in. This lack of connection to the church body was emphasized a few months later when her parents came for a visit, for that Sunday she noticed people clustering around her parents, asking them whether they would be joining the church and whether they would like to be involved in various ministries. It suddenly became very clear that the members of the church knew how to relate to and interact with other married couples. They could have interesting conversations, and they could invite new couples into their community. They had no idea what to do with a single woman with no children. The truth is that most of us tend to gravitate toward the people who are like us. It is easier to converse with those with whom we share things in common. Unfortunately, in many churches the things that hold the community together center around marital status and children rather than our mutual love of Christ. And singles can end up feeling like outcasts.

If you question whether this focus on marriage and children is truly the emphasis of many suburban churches, just look at church bulletins. Many are full of Sunday school classes for engaged couples, married couples, married couples with preschoolers, married couples with teenagers, empty nesters, etc. And they have various activities for these families: father–daughter campouts, mother–daughter teas, father–son baseball games. For singles trying to connect to our local churches, the fact that we are automatically excluded from so many of the events listed can be extremely frustrating. Even events that aren't necessarily designed for families can be difficult for singles. How many single men or women have the courage to show up at a potluck or church picnic, knowing that we may have no one to talk to through the whole event? If no one will converse with us at the Sunday morning service for longer than an exchange of names, how will we ever survive an entire afternoon or evening of feeling like an outcast?

As any single who has ever looked for a church will confirm, the church bulletin is often the first clue whether the church will ultimately accept singles or not. A few years ago, both of us had to relocate for work, with Christine moving from California to the Chicago suburbs and Bonnie moving from Arizona to the Atlanta suburbs. As we searched for churches to attend in our new locations, both of us encountered churches that had just started a month-long series on marriage. Christine remembers staring at the bulletin, seeing the list of various topics on marriage that were going to be discussed in the Sunday morning services, the Sunday evening services, and the Wednesday night services, and wondering if all the single people in that church simply went on vacation for the month. While constructing a godly marriage is certainly an important topic of study, what does it say to the singles in the church when it becomes the sole focus of the church for an entire month? Needless to say, both of us continued our searches for a church community in which we would feel nurtured.

If Christian singles manage to survive walking in the door of the church and reading the church bulletin, there is always the Sunday morning message to remind us that we just don't quite belong. Think of all of the examples pastors use to convey their points. How many of them have to do with marriage and/or children? How many times have we heard that marriage is the perfect metaphor for the church's relationship with Christ? Now, we are certainly not arguing against the use of these illustrations. They are often appropriate. But do they have to be the only kinds of illustrations that are given? As pastors prepare their messages, they obviously think about what illustrations will be most appropriate for their audiences: what will they relate to? As singles, we often wonder if pastors even acknowledge that we are part of their congregations as well. Yes, marriage is used in scripture as a metaphor for Christ and his church, but aren't there other metaphors as well? Why does it have to be THE metaphor that is repeated over and over again in sermon after sermon? While married couples may never recognize the number of these illustrations because they fit so perfectly with their experiences, singles definitely do, particularly when they are placed in the previous contexts of the church demographics and the activities presented in the bulletins. In her article, "Single on Sunday Morning," Camerin Courtney expresses the plight that many singles feel when confronted with these issues: "I hate to admit it, but one of the loneliest times of my week is Sunday morning. Sitting alone in a pew amidst a sea of happy couples and families, I listen to sermons about how to be a more God-honoring spouse and parent and to announcements about church-wide family picnics I won't attend because, as a single, I'd feel too out of place."[7]

But, you may ask, what about singles groups? Certainly the large number of singles groups at various churches indicates that the evangelical church isn't blind to the plight of Christian singles. True, many churches do try to connect with the singles in their congregations by providing a place for us to support each other, but are these singles groups truly the way to integrate singles into the church? Unfortunately, they often seem to create a singles ghetto that simply reinforces the isolation that singles feel from the rest of the church. In her article "Bringing in the Single Sheep," Wendy Widder clearly delineates the problems that often occur when churches divide their attendees into groups according to stages of life:

Most churches structure adult classes around an "age-and-stage-of-life" format. Young marrieds meet with young marrieds, parents of teens fellowship with other parents of teens, and so on, each according to their "own kind." This kind of arrangement has advantages, but it also has costly disadvantages. When we segregate into age groups, we struggle to learn from those who have done life ahead of us and to teach those who are coming after us. At best, we dance around Paul's instruction for the older members to instruct and encourage the younger (Titus 2) and at worst, we disobey it. Also, when we spend most of our time with people like us, we begin thinking everyone is like us—or should be. We develop myopic views of life and ministry.[8]

Ultimately, this division is productive neither for singles nor for couples, for it simply reinforces the distance that already exists in most church congregations.

In addition, these types of divisions can often alienate those who fall between the cracks. When Bonnie was searching for a church, for instance, she discovered one that had two singles groups: "College and Career" and "Single Again." For someone in her thirties who had actually taught college and didn't feel comfortable in that age group, she wondered what had happened to the "Single Still" group. And even if these divisions aren't clearly marked out in the bulletin, they are often implicit within the groups themselves. Bonnie's friend Danielle shared one of her recent experiences with us:

A few years ago I mustered up the courage to go to the brand-new singles' worship night at a local mega-church. I was my typical early self and went inside and sat down at one of the dozen or so empty round tables that were set up. I watched over the next 15 minutes as people continued to trickle and then pour into the room, and not one of them approached me. People came over and asked to borrow chairs so they could cram extra people around their own table. Finally, someone approached me—a nice lady who looked old enough to be my grandmother. Her first question after she sat next to me . . . "So how long have you been single?" "Always," I replied with a smile. "Oh!" she said, and quickly began searching the room, not knowing how to talk to me anymore. I tried asking her a few questions but her short answers and eyes that were looking everywhere but at me left us soon sitting in an uncomfortable silence. After a few more minutes, three gals about my age all came to the table and asked if they could join us (the only table with any space left). We quickly introduced ourselves and their first question to me was "How many kids do you have?" When I replied that I had none, the light in their eyes shut off and they spent the rest of the evening talking amongst themselves. I became the amazing invisible woman . . . that rarely seen freak of nature who has arrived at her 30s and has never been married and never had children.

Ironically, even in singles groups where supposedly everyone has singleness in common, the type of singleness is extremely important. The statistics seem to support these experiences. The Barna Group found that even though 50% of born again Christians over 18 are single, only 19% have never been married.[9] It certainly seems that once you are over a certain age and have never been married or had children, you don't fit in anymore.

This alienation of never-been-marrieds over thirty may illustrate another problem with these singles groups: the focus on getting all the singles married as quickly as possible. Most Christian singles over thirty have probably heard the following from friends, family, or even church leaders: if you can't find a husband or wife at your church, find another church. And many singles groups seem to embody the truth of this idea as the members search desperately for a mate. Is finding a spouse truly the main thing singles should be looking for in a church? This type of thinking often leads to the "meat market" mentality of many singles groups: a phenomenon common enough to find its way into pop culture. In an episode of *7th Heaven* entitled "Sunday," Lucy expresses her frustration with this exact problem, stating, "Church is not a pick-up joint. This is a place of worship. And it's Sunday. Sunday is not the new Saturday night."[10] Even the leaders of singles groups aren't necessarily immune from treating the church group as a Christian dating service. For instance, one evening Bonnie's sister invited her to go to Starbucks with a group of friends from her singles group. That evening one of the leaders announced, albeit half jokingly, that his goal for the next year was to create more quitters. By "quitters" he meant those who quit the singles group because they get married. Is the success of a singles group to be measured by how quickly it puts itself out of business?

All of this pressure to marry off the singles seems to have interesting repercussions, for many Christian singles have noticed strange trends in our churches. On the one hand, many Christian singles are experiencing a dating drought that has spanned several years. In her article "Why Aren't Christians Dating?" Camerin Courtney comments on this issue:

I was chatting with my friend Margaret about how seldom she and I and nearly all our single Christian sisters seem to get asked out. If it was just one or a couple of us experiencing a dry spell, I could understand. But when so many of the vibrant, put-together, intelligent, God-fearing, reasonably attractive single women I know spend nearly all of their Friday and Saturday nights for practically years on end hanging out with each other—not always by choice—I've got to think maybe this is a trend. In fact, a recent poll on the Singles Channel revealed that 54 percent of you (both males and females) haven't been on a date in more than two years.[11]

With all of the focus on marriage, why are so many Christian singles not even dating? What is it about the culture of the evangelical church that is making dating difficult? Is there perhaps too much pressure to "find the right one" so that normal social interaction is stunted?

On the other hand, many Christian singles have found themselves in church singles groups that have embraced the "meat market" mentality so fully that traditional Christian values have seemingly disappeared. Sexual activity before marriage is common, as is a couple living together without the bonds of marriage. Research from the Barna Group shows that 25% of born-again Christians have cohabitated,[12] and research from the Center for Disease control shows that approximately 45% of unmarried men raised in Fundamentalist Protestant homes are sexually active.[13] For a friend of ours, the recognition that this was going on in her church singles group came as quite a shock:

> One night, I arrived early at the small group to borrow the leader's computer to look for a book online. As he was taking me through the web search, a rather "inappropriate" book cover popped up, turning me a BRIGHT red. My embarrassment soon turned to horror when the leader said, "Now, now . . . I think it's safe to say that given our ages everyone here has 'experience' in that area." I quickly assured him that was NOT the case and that I was still waiting for marriage, and after the shock wore off he said, "Oh, well . . . that's great . . . for you . . . and I'm sure if I get married again I'll be faithful, but until then . . ." Yes, this was the LEADER of the small group, and that was my last night in that small group.

For singles who wish to maintain traditional Christian values, this type of singles group is certainly not providing the support that we need, and it certainly lends credence to the idea that singles must be married off as quickly as possible because after a certain age we can no longer say no to sexual activity.

Neither of these extremes is healthy, yet both are far more common than we would like to admit. And both illustrate that something is terribly wrong with the way singles groups are often handled in evangelical churches. For singles, then, the local church often provides a host of minefields that we must work hard to avoid, and even beyond simply avoiding these issues, singles must also work hard to keep from becoming bitter and cynical as we come up against these issues time and time again. As the previous example demonstrates, the church is not immune from the values of the secular world. In fact, they may have come to influence the evangelical church more than we realize.

Singleness and the Secularization of the Church

In January 2006 a show entitled *The Book of Daniel* premiered on television. In this show Aidan Quinn played Daniel Webster, an Episcopal priest with an addiction to prescription drugs and with a very dysfunctional family: a daughter who is arrested for possessing and selling drugs; a straight, teenage son who is sexually active; a homosexual son who hasn't come out of the closet to everyone yet; a wife with a drinking problem; and a father who, despite being married and a bishop in the Episcopal Church, is having an affair with another bishop. As to be expected, many conservative Christians were offended at the portrayal of the clergy, and the show only ran for a few episodes before disappearing from the channel's lineup.

This show was not written or produced by Christians, and it certainly did not reflect the values of most evangelical Christians. It does, however, provide an interesting perspective on the secularization of Christianity in our culture. The fact that Aidan Quinn could argue in an interview with the Associated Press that *The Book of Daniel* was "a pretty down-the-middle wholesome show" indicates that the definition of "down the middle" has certainly shifted.[14] In this show, addiction, premarital sex, homosexuality, and adultery are portrayed not as sins but as issues that every normal family experiences, and if these activities don't seem to be hurting anyone else, no judgments are made against them. While many of the show's critics found the storylines extreme, others saw the show as an accurate representation of their ideals. In fact, a friend who is Episcopalian loved the show because she could relate to it. For her it represented "the story of my people."

The Book of Daniel may have only run for a few episodes, but the values it embodied, particularly with regard to sexuality, are becoming more acceptable, especially in mainline denominations. In his book *In the Ruins of the Church: Sustaining Faith in an Age of Diminished Christianity*, R. R. Reno explores the debate over homosexuality in the Episcopal Church but then shifts to discussing the underlying problem of attitudes regarding sexual freedom. He remarks,

> Plenty of divorced men and women want reassurances that it is OK to enter into the world of "date, then fornicate." Plenty of parents want the priest to tell them that having their son's girlfriend sleep in his bed during a visit over Thanksgiving break is OK. Plenty of unmarried thirtysomethings want to go to church as couples, eager to normalize their lives and test the deeper waters of adult responsibility, and do so without judgment . . . Sex is like the public library: we want our children to feel free to explore their interests. In this way we can reassure ourselves that our commitment to sexual freedom . . . is just a sensible revision of traditional Christian moral strictness.[15]

As Reno observes, for many Christians, the idea of reserving sexual activity for marriage has unfortunately become hopelessly outdated: a relic of a moral code that must be revised to keep up with the times. And while many conservative, evangelical Christians might like to see this as a problem that exists only in mainline denominations, the truth is that these ideas have also found their way into many suburban evangelical churches.

We have already seen how these ideas may affect some singles groups where the assumption is that if you are single and in your twenties and thirties, you must be sexually active. The question is why is this occurring even in churches that are doctrinally more conservative than many mainline denominations. Are evangelical churches implicitly accepting a "sensible revision of traditional moral strictness"? For many churches, the answer would be "yes." With the rise of the "seeker-friendly" mega church, the desire to draw in new attendees has often outweighed the need to speak the truth about moral standards. Speaking about sexual activity outside of marriage as sin is not exactly the best way to draw a large audience, and in many churches Sunday morning services focus much more on God's love and desire for his followers to prosper than on the standards he has set up for his followers in Scripture. Now, granted, many "seeker-friendly" churches design their Sunday morning services explicitly to draw in visitors, hoping that once they get more involved in the church, they will receive a deeper education in the truths of Christianity. The question is whether or not this is actually happening, particularly for singles who attend the church. Often, the singles ministry is also designed to attract visitors, providing them with an easy way to integrate themselves into the church. The focus is often on fellowship and activities rather than teaching from scripture. Sexually active singles, then, may never encounter anyone who questions their choices in light of scripture even if, doctrinally, the church stands behind the traditional value of sexual activity only within marriage. In practice, many evangelical churches end up being no different from the supposedly more liberal denominations in their treatment of extramarital sex.

Singleness and Its Implications

But what about those Christian leaders who are standing up for traditional morality and resisting the secularization of Christianity? What support do they have to offer to Christian singles? Interestingly, they often end up reacting to the same assumption that forms a foundation for the more liberal desire to revise traditional morality: the idea that sex is the one temptation no one can avoid forever. In *Sex and the Single Christian: Candid Conversations*, Tim LaHaye calls celibacy "an idealistic and unnatural standard,"[16] and he implies that only those with "lower sex drives" will be called to celibacy.[17] The supposition is that individuals can't say no to sex; they can only say wait. And the hope is that Christian singles will get married before eventually giving in to the temptation. Marriage, then, becomes the focus of most discussions, and singles who are not married in an appropriate timeframe (usually before we are thirty) are generally ignored, pitied, or condemned.

As we have already seen in our glance at church bulletins, the focus of many churches is marriage and the family. On the Web site embrace marriage.org Ron Pinkston, Senior Pastor of the East Bay Fellowship Foursquare Church in Danville, California, provides a testimonial that clearly demonstrates the philosophy of many churches: "One of the most important foundations of a strong and healthy church is the marriages of that church."[18] With the intense focus that the evangelical church provides on families, what is the place of the single Christian? Interestingly, James Dobson's Focus on the Family has fairly recently recognized that in its attention to the family, it was ignoring singles, so in 1998 it began a ministry called Boundless that was designed to target singles. Their editor, Ted Slater, delineates the goals of this ministry: "helping single adults make the most of their years of transition . . . and more importantly helping singles prepare to have rich, successful, happy marriages."[19] Yes, Focus on the Family is beginning to acknowledge the single members of the family of God—but only if we see ourselves as in "transition" and only if our main concerns are our future roles as spouses and parents. For older singles, who are perhaps struggling with issues of loneliness, frustration, and bitterness and are even perhaps feeling abandoned by God as we realize that this time of "transition" may actually be permanent, this discussion is woefully inadequate. By relying on the assumption that all Christian singles will be married and married early, Focus on the Family ignores older singles and our unique challenges.

Focus on the Family's inability to deal effectively with older singles is also illustrated by an interaction that Bonnie had with the organization. As someone who had purchased a transcript from a recent broadcast, Bonnie was sent a link to an online survey. Focus on the Family said it wanted to know more about her so that it could better serve its constituents. Bonnie was told that the survey would take twenty to thirty minutes to complete, depending on her answers. Since she saw this as an opportunity to share the perspective of the ever increasing demographic of singles in the church, she decided to participate. The first question asked about her marital status: "single, never married." The second question asked the number of children she had: "none." She was then thanked for completing the survey and told that Focus on the Family didn't have any further questions for her. While we can all acknowledge that singles without children are not Focus on the Family's core audience, Bonnie's experience with the survey indicates that we do not even figure into the discussion. Certainly, whoever designed the survey had no intention of offending any single individual without children who attempted to respond to it, but he or she obviously did not think that singles would respond or that our responses might be instructive. With this attention to the family, singles become invisible.

When we are acknowledged, the emphasis is usually on trying to get us married as quickly as possible. As mentioned previously, one of the great fears is that Christian singles will give in to sexual temptation rather than learn to resist it. In January 2004 Dr. Al Mohler, president of Southern Baptist Theological Seminary, spoke at Joshua Harris's New Attitude Conference for Singles. One of his themes was that Christian singles need to marry early:

> In the year 1900, the average boy reached sexual maturity at about age 15 and married, generally, by 20. The average girl reached sexual maturity at about 14 and married somewhere between 18 and 20 or somewhere thereabouts. The average age for a first marriage of a white male in America, according to the 2000 census is 27.5, and updated data indicates that it's now over 28. The average first marriage of a white female, just looking at this statistical data, is about 26.4. Now, what have we done here? We've created this incredible span of time where sexual passion is ignited but there is no holy means for it to be fulfilled . . . If you're 17, 18, 19, 20, in your early 20s—what are you waiting for?[20]

While Mohler is correct that individuals are getting married later in life, we wonder whether getting them married off as soon as possible simply to avoid temptation is really the best advice. In the past, people did get married earlier, but life expectancies were much shorter and individuals were encouraged to mature earlier. Is a typical American eighteen-year-old really ready for the responsibilities of marriage? Once again the assumption seems to be that celibacy is an unrealistic expectation, so rather than providing a positive foundation for it, Christian leaders like Mohler push for teenagers to get married right out of high school.

For those who might argue that teenagers are not mature enough and do not have a clear enough sense of their personal identity to be strong marriage partners, Mohler and others have responded that marriage is what creates personal identity and maturity. According to Mohler, "The more you, as an adult, define yourself as an 'I,' the longer you do so resiliently, the harder it's going to be to become a 'we.'"[21] With this statement, Mohler echoes Danielle Crittenden who, in her book *What*

Our Mothers Didn't Tell Us, remarks, "The truth is, once you have ceased being single, you suddenly discover that all that energy you spent propelling yourself toward an independent existence was only going to be useful if you were planning to spend the rest of your life as a nun or a philosopher on a mountain top . . . In preparation for a life spent with someone else, it was not going to be helpful."[22] For both Mohler and Crittenden personal identity is found primarily within a marriage. Their rhetoric implies that anything outside of that is at best useless and at worst dangerous to a person's future marriage.

In addition, in many of these discussions those who delay marriage end up being characterized as stunted and immature. In an early episode of *Sex and the City* a married woman bluntly expresses her opinion of the difference between single and married women: "It's all about what you want out of life. Some people like me choose to grow up, face reality and get married. And others choose to what? Live an empty life of stunted adolescence."[23] This type of thinking is not far from the thoughts of many writers who talk to Christian singles. Crittenden, for instance, warns women that "by spending years and years living entirely for yourself, thinking only about yourself, and having responsibility to no one but yourself, you end up inadvertently extending the introverted existence of a teenager deep into middle age."[24] And Mohler warns Christian singles that "the Scripture makes it clear that [the crucible of our saint-making] will be done largely through our marriages."[25] Gary Thomas in *Sacred Marriage* takes this discussion even further, arguing, "If you want to be free to serve Jesus, there's no question—stay single. Marriage takes a lot of time. But if you want to become more like Jesus, I can't imagine a better thing to do than get married."[26] From the tone of these discussions, it is clear that the speakers are targeting younger singles and warning them to avoid the mistakes that are currently crippling older singles. But what about those older singles? Is it true that we are immature, stunted, limited in our ability to be like Christ? Our observations of many mature Christians who also happen to be older singles suggest otherwise, but from all of these comments about older singles, you would think that all of us are pathetic losers who deserve to be single.

These scare tactics that emphasize what lies in wait for those who do not marry young are often directed specifically toward women while attacking single men in the process. Crittenden presents a nightmare scenario of a woman just past thirty who waits longingly to find the man of her dreams only to be presented with "immature, elusive Peter Pans who won't commit themselves to a second cup of coffee, let alone a second date; neurotic bachelors with strange habits; sexual predators who hit on every woman they meet; newly divorced men taking pleasure wherever they can; embittered, scorned men who still feel vengeful toward their last girlfriend; . . . men who are simply too weak, or odd, to have attracted any other woman's interest."[27] The assumption is that in her pursuit of a career this woman has let all the good men pass her by only to be left with the rejects. Debbie Maken takes the nightmare scenario even further, condemning the woman who marries in her late thirties: "Without doubt, the story of the woman who narrowly manages to marry before the age of forty is more a grim reminder of a society gone awry than of the good providence of God. This woman will not enjoy the full benefits of marriage. Aside from reduced or no fertility and all that goes with it, she has had to live without sex for the past twenty-plus years (we hope she did anyway)."[28] For young singles, these horror stories should be enough to drive them to the altar with anyone just to avoid such pathetic futures. But what do these discussions and stories do to older singles?

Rather than being applauded for doing what everyone seems to think is impossible—remaining celibate throughout their thirties and forties (and even beyond)—these singles are derided and blamed for remaining single. The assumption seems to be that all of us have chosen to be in this position and must now suffer for our choices. Many authors and speakers such as Dobson and Mohler blame feminism for the plight of older singles, saying that women have become so aggressive and focused on their careers that men no longer know how to approach them. Interestingly, we have yet to meet a Christian single woman who has rejected marriage with a strong, Christian man in order to pursue a career. There may be some, but the reality for most Christian single women over thirty is that there were no choices. The godly, Christian man whom everyone said was waiting hasn't shown up yet, and rather than wasting our lives in the vain pursuit of any man who crosses our radar, we have decided to serve God where he has placed us. Rather than seeing this as a positive decision, many Christians have begun to talk about the sin of delayed marriage. Singles are told that "the Bible is clear: *It is God's will for people to marry*"[29] and that "the Bible starts out with

God commanding two single people to leave, cleave, and become one
. . . [Nothing] in the Old Testament or the New Testament [rescinds]
that command."[30] The implication is clear: anyone who remains single
in his or her thirties, forties, or beyond is obviously disobeying God.

Singleness and Christian Advice

If the implications of remaining single are truly that serious, you would
think that there would be plenty of useful advice for older singles on
how to escape the sin of our singleness. Interestingly, there is not. Most
of the advice that is out there is either geared toward a young audience
or it is so overly simplistic that it is insulting rather than useful. Take,
for example, Jeramy Clark's *I Gave Dating a Chance*, which is directed
toward high school and college age students. In this discussion, Clark
speaks quite a bit about the need for patience, and he references his own
experience of waiting a long time to be married. While waiting until
your mid-twenties to be married may seem long to some (as it did to
Clark), people in their thirties or forties have far more experience with
this type of patience, and Clark's naïve pep talk about waiting really
isn't very helpful. Neither are statements such as "I believe God has a
prince or princess for almost everyone. After all, you're a son or daughter
of the King, so it's only fitting that you marry someone of nobility and
character."[31] Relying on the fairy-tale motif may work with some high
school girls, but older singles and savvy younger ones may resent the
complexities of our lives being reduced to this simplicity. Besides, this
scenario places God in the role of the fairy godfather waiting to bestow
the perfect mate upon his deserving child. Is that really how we should
be thinking of God? What if the perfect mate hasn't shown up yet? Is
it because God doesn't care, or is it because we aren't worthy? Either
way, this type of thinking creates a distorted view of God, his love for
us, and his ultimate purpose for us here on earth.

Even books aimed at older audiences often sidestep important issues
in their attempts to advise singles. In Henry Cloud and John Townsend's
Boundaries in Dating: Making Dating Work, the assumption is that once
you fix whatever is wrong with you, you will find the perfect partner.
Their first suggestion in the chapter entitled "Dating Won't Cure a Lonely
Heart" is to "put a boundary around your wish for a relationship. *Cure*

that fear first, and *then* find a relationship."[32] In the next three pages, they proceed to explain that process which consists of improving your relationship with God, developing your relationships with other Christians, getting involved in various activities, and "pursuing wholeness." Setting aside the fact that they condense some very serious issues into just a few pages, there is nothing wrong with any of these ideas except for the fact that many older singles have already worked through these issues and are still single. What are we to do? Cloud and Townsend provide little additional help except to warn us to "be afraid of wasting time . . . In reality, you can't wait forever, because you don't have forever. There is such a thing as 'too late.' "[33] So, singles are expected to release our fears of not having a relationship while at the same time worrying that we have waited too long and will be single for the rest of our lives. Are we the only ones to see a contradiction here? The rest of the book, which provides basic dating advice, does not give any other answers for those Christian singles who aren't currently dating. The only reason we are left with for our singleness is that somehow we are not good enough for someone else to want us or for God to reward us with a spouse.

In "The Problem with Platitudes" Camerin Courtney reflects upon the advice about singleness that she has received from others: "They mean well, bless their hearts. All those kind, well-meaning souls who offer us answers to questions we never asked. You know what I'm talking about. You've heard these answers, too: 'Just trust God to meet all your needs.' 'Stop looking and the right one will show up.' 'No matter how it appears, God is still sovereign.' 'Your maker is your husband.' 'Focus on being the right one instead of looking for the right one.' 'There is so much more to life than marriage.' " While her list of comments comes from various people she has met rather than from Christian self-help books, most of the published material really isn't any better. And as she mentions later, "Their words don't come close to acknowledging the depth of our pain or wrestling and therefore sometimes feel insulting."[34] For singles who may feel alienated from our local churches, condemned by Christian leaders, and frustrated by our own emotions, we need a message that will address the complex realities of our situations, but too often, we are at best ignored or patronized and at worst ridiculed or made to feel inferior or sinful.

And what is perhaps even more disturbing is the fact that these issues are no longer simply affecting older singles. College-age students are already struggling with them. In an editorial for *The Record* (the Wheaton College newspaper), Leila Noelliste, a student at the college, expresses her frustrations with the way singleness is treated in the evangelical church:

> Many single women are conditioned to believe that their lives are insignificant because they lack a man's romantic affection. . . . Single women are encouraged to put themselves out there "in faith." So, they make preemptive attempts to connect with men on a romantic level, rendering themselves vulnerable to those who might dismiss them on the basis of immutable properties like personality and appearance. Women also hear that singleness is a punishment for those who have not attained a certain level of spirituality. Single women often live with a sense of inferiority, wondering what defective aspect of their lives has made them privy to the horrors of partnerlessness. Most damaging is the notion that singleness is something unpleasant to be endured, like swallowing a bad-tasting pill or walking through a foul-smelling tunnel. The stories singles hear are of women who cry out continuously to God for a man and are delivered. The biblical phrase "weeping may endure for a night but joy cometh in the morning" is often used in reference to the intense sadness brought on by singleness and the subsequent joy and relief of finding a partner.[35]

Young Christian women like Leila have already been taught what it means to be single in today's evangelical church, and the picture that Leila paints is not a pretty one. Instead of individuals focusing on their relationships with God, looking for exciting ways that he can use them, and striving everyday to be more like him, they are desperately looking for marriage partners so that they may avoid the pity and condemnation that await them should they fail to find a partner. Are these truly the messages we want them to receive?

Part 2

Encountering Dangerous Messages along the Way

5

Lust & Avoidance
Dangerous Messages about Sexual Temptation

Pete: And your solution is, what, put her in surgery? This woman is not
  gonna die if she doesn't have sex.
Addison: Oh, please. If it was you going without, you'd be begging to
  go under the knife.

"In Which Addison Finds the Magic," *Private Practice*

Halal: You must wear this. You must put the veil over your hair.
Harriet: Why must I cover my hair?
Halal: With the deepest of respect, the sight of a lady's hair may distract
  the men from their devotions.
Harriet: You can't make men chaste by keeping women out of sight.

Fortunes of War

A few years ago Bonnie developed the habit of stopping by Starbucks on
the way to work. She had an hour commute, and there was a Starbucks
with a drive-thru about fifteen minutes into her trip. Several months, a
few pounds, and far too many dollars later, she decided she needed to
stop. Then it started—the lust for a mocha. It was not just a *desire* for

a mocha; it was *lust*. She did not think, "Oh, a mocha would taste good right now." She thought, "I *have* to have a mocha." She could think of nothing else as she passed the Starbucks. She could almost feel the car turning into the parking lot on its own accord. If she managed to drive by without stopping, she began thinking about an alternative route she could take to work that would take her right by another Starbucks. Okay, it was on a road with a lot of traffic, and it would add ten minutes to her commute, but that didn't matter. Bonnie suddenly had insight into the power of addiction and non-sexual lust.

But how was Bonnie to deal with this lust? Should she *never* go to Starbucks again? Should she decide that it was a sin for her to drink coffee? Some might suggest these extremes, recognizing that lust is dangerous and that it is sin to be completely and uncontrollably consumed by anything besides God. The truth is that we need to bring all of our desires to God and let him direct our response to them. The difficulty lies in how to manage this process in a way that not only honors God's prohibitions against lust but also doesn't imprison us in a legalistic world where we end up depriving ourselves of the good blessings that God desires us to experience in the world around us.

Lust is a reality, whether it is for a Starbucks mocha or for an unattainable man or woman, and singles as well as marrieds must learn to deal with their desires in ways that honor God. Unfortunately, the messages about sex and temptation that Christian singles are receiving both from the secular world and the Christian world don't necessarily help them deal with lust effectively. The secular messages tend to encourage lust as something that is normal and must be indulged, and the Christian messages tend to oversimplify both the problem and the solution. By looking more closely at these messages, however, perhaps we can begin to formulate a more complex vision of this struggle and, as a result, derive important lessons on how to negotiate these complexities.

Dangerous Message 1: Sexual temptation cannot be resisted, so Christians must avoid it altogether

As the evangelical church, we often pride ourselves on how our views differ from those in the world. We find comfort in our reverence for the nuclear family and our desire to teach our kids abstinence. But do our values really differ that much from those embraced by the world? Unfortunately, the church has been influenced by the world's view of sexuality. We share a belief that sex is the ultimate human experience. While we may not say this directly, it is the foundation of many of the discussions surrounding sex and abstinence. There is never any real discussion of celibacy. Marriage is always assumed, not necessarily as a covenant before God but rather as the only way sexual activity will be permissible. Within this context there is the often implied and occasionally stated message that sex is the one temptation that cannot be resisted long-term. Although groups promoting abstinence would never tell teenagers that they cannot resist sexual temptation, the message is inevitably implied within the message of "wait until marriage." Like Freud and Kinsey, the church generally believes that sex is a biological imperative. It is impossible to comprehend a lifetime without sex.

If the world's message is true and we are *not* able to resist sexual temptation, how are we to avoid giving in to immorality and lust? The standard advice is, run! Follow Paul's advice in 1 Corinthians 6:18 and Joseph's example in Genesis 39, and flee immorality. This is certainly good advice. Scripture is clear that we are to flee immorality, which is generally taken to mean sexual intercourse with anyone besides your husband or wife. In today's society, however, when teenagers are openly engaging in sexual activities that were thought risqué for married couples a few decades ago, this definition doesn't go far enough. Far too many Christian singles think they are free to engage in any sexual behavior they want, with or without their clothes on, as long as they don't actually have intercourse. They have heard the message that they shouldn't have sex before marriage, but they don't have any real understanding of chastity, let alone an understanding of celibacy.

Acknowledging the seriousness of this issue, more and more Christians are beginning to address the importance of chastity and the dangers of giving in to lust. Unfortunately, despite attempts to avoid legalism as we encourage singles to practice chastity, we often end up focusing simply on regulating individual behaviors. Joshua Harris, for instance, spends a lot of time focusing on the importance of avoiding all "lust triggers." Most of the lust triggers he discusses, however, are not things that encourage you "to go outside God's guidelines to find satisfaction,"[1] which is part of his definition of lust. They are, instead, things that trigger sexual desire. Granted, triggers to sexual desire are much easier to identify because they are usually external while our reaction to them is what would cause us to "go outside God's guidelines." To give Harris credit, he only discusses his own personal boundaries and relates how he and his friends choose to avoid the lust triggers in their lives. He is careful to tell his readers that he is not prescribing a list of dos and don'ts but only giving some practical suggestions. In fact, he is very careful to warn his readers against legalism, emphasizing the futility of trying to control lust with merely a set of rules. However, in our human desire to search for a quick fix to our problems, it is often easier to take someone else's personal guidelines and treat them as the solution rather than examine our own sinful hearts. And far too often this turns into legalism as we intentionally or unintentionally impose those restrictions on others.

According to some of the more popular dating guides, not just those written by Harris, what should men do in order to avoid lust? Don't go to the video store; don't go to the gym; don't go to the beach; don't watch commercials; when you go outside during the summer, stare at the sidewalk so you don't have to see a woman in shorts; etc. And then there are the ever-popular words of advice to young women: Don't hug, don't flirt, and be careful what you wear (this can include everything from don't wear short skirts to make sure your bra strap doesn't show to don't wear anything that accentuates your curves). While some of these guidelines may be good for some people who struggle with particular temptations and while we all need to practice modesty, it is perhaps a bit unrealistic in our society to expect everyone to avoid everything that might cause them to lust. It's like telling someone who might become addicted to coffee and who happens to live in Seattle never to drive by a Starbucks or look at a cup of coffee. In a world where we are surrounded by potential lust triggers, we need to be careful that we don't avoid taking responsibility for our lustful thoughts, simply blaming members of the opposite sex for causing us to stumble and hopelessly trying to avoid them.

Recently, a group of young college men were encouraging their female friends to stop wearing their purses diagonally across their bodies because this accentuated their breasts, thus causing the young men to lust. These young men obviously never stopped to wonder *why* their female friends carried their purses like this. They didn't consider that a college student might need her arms for other things, like carrying books. Or perhaps the young women were told that this is the most secure way to carry a purse, making you a less likely target for purse snatching. These young men just knew that a woman's figure caused them to lust, even if it was appropriately covered. (Would they also want women to avoid wearing seat belts for the same reason?) Rather than taking responsibility for their thoughts, they made the women responsible for the lust trigger.

One of the many problems with this approach to lust is that it is very male-oriented. Many male authors don't acknowledge that women even deal with sexual lust. Or if women do, it is only desire for romance or a relationship, not sex. Most women would tell you that couldn't be further from the truth! We might not lust in exactly the same way, but a lot of men would probably be very surprised by how a woman can talk about a man's physical qualities. Let's face it. None of us has experienced lust as a man *and* as a woman, so no one *really* knows how alike or different we are. But it does seem that in some ways a woman's lust triggers can be even more difficult to regulate than a man's. Sure, we have known women who are turned on by a man in tight jeans and no shirt, but we have also known women who are turned on by things as varied as Roman noses, strong yet graceful hands, wire-rimmed glasses, and long sleeve white shirts. But you don't see any dating guides telling men to cover up their noses or not wear glasses because they might cause a woman to lust.

Ramifications and Response

While the advice to avoid temptation is a good one, it can be taken too far. As we have discussed before, most books written for singles are written for teenagers, and teenagers generally do need clearly defined boundaries. But what ramifications do these principles have when applied to adults? Camerin Courtney and Todd Hertz address the difficulties of dating as an older single in their book *The Unguide to Dating*. In their introduction Courtney writes about the things she does and doesn't have in common with the teenagers to whom most of the dating books are written. What other issues must older singles deal with? Courtney remarks,

> But as a thirty-four-year-old dater, I also have a solo apartment, a changing body, marriage on my mind, a biological clock that keeps tick-tick-ticking, family and church pressures to pair off, friends who are getting

married and friends who are getting divorced, shifting demographics, and, consequently, an overall changing climate in which to date. Unfortunately, no one's addressing these things. Dating advice within the church seems to peter out at around age eighteen.[2]

Some would argue that the same guidelines apply whether you are eighteen or eighty. But do they? Adults certainly are not immune to lust and its effects, and there are definitely activities that should be avoided. Certainly, we should not view or read pornographic materials, and we should not put ourselves in compromising situations. But when we believe that the only way we can resist sexual temptation is to avoid any interaction with the opposite sex, or any acknowledgement that God created our bodies differently, we have gone too far.

A good friend of ours, a single Christian woman who dresses modestly and does not flaunt her sexuality, used to work for a company where the owners and most of her coworkers attended the same conservative church. She was under the impression that being single would be an advantage in the workplace because she could leave on a business trip at a moment's notice. But she was told quite plainly that the opposite was true. Because she was a single woman, the men of the company had to bring their wives along on business trips as chaperones. If their wives did not come, she would have to stay in a separate hotel (not a separate hotel *room*, a separate hotel). And of course she would have to go to dinner by herself because the men of the company could not go to a restaurant with an unchaperoned single woman. If they had to drive across town for a meeting, they had to take separate cars. Once, when her car broke down, a coworker called his wife to give her a ride home because he couldn't be alone with her in a car. So much for chivalry!

This may seem like an extreme case, but it is a natural result of the belief that we are unable to control our sexual desires. We are all familiar with the effects that lust and immorality have had on a number of high-profile Christian leaders, and we may have even heard that Billy Graham was able to remain above reproach because he made sure that he was never alone with a woman who was not his wife. But this certainly doesn't mean that Billy Graham would have committed adultery if he had given a stranded woman a ride to the nearest telephone. It could have provided some tabloid journalist the opportunity to write lies about him, but most of us are not followed by paparazzi. Behavior like this may also be appropriate if there are past incidents of impropriety or suspicion, but as a general rule, it can cause serious problems. Not only does it isolate single adults even more than they already are, but it causes suspicion and distrust between the sexes. It also propagates the belief that men are mere animals who cannot be trusted, encourages wives to be suspicious of their husbands, and paints single women as evil temptresses. In their book *Captivating: Unveiling the Mystery of a Woman's Soul*, John and Stasi Eldredge emphasize the dangers of this type of thinking for Christians: "Far too long we have lived in a culture of fear in the Church, fearing that any relationship between men and women will end in an affair. Sadly, we have forsaken so many opportunities to call one another forth with the grace of our genders."[3] Unfortunately, their characterization of the evangelical church resonates with far too many singles.

The fact is we will never be able to eliminate or avoid everything that could awaken sexual desire. Even if we did seclude ourselves and never let ourselves be exposed to any lust triggers, we still have our thoughts, our fantasies, and the physiological reactions of our bodies. Jerome, the fourth-century ascetic and translator of the Latin Vulgate Bible, provides a good example of this difficulty, for he recounts a time when he struggled with lustful thoughts even though he was fasting in the desert and his flesh was "as good as dead."[4] If even this extreme mortification of the body can't completely stifle sexual desire, perhaps we need to rethink the rather simplistic advice that we should just avoid temptation.

The good news is that we *can* resist sexual temptation. When confronted with the argument that without marriage sexual self-control is impossible, evangelical Christian leader and life-long celibate John Stott replied, "We Christians must insist that self-control is possible. We have to learn to control our temper, our tongue, our greed, our jealousy, our pride: why should it be thought impossible to control our libido? To say that we cannot is to deny our dignity as human beings and to descend to the level of animals, which are creatures of uncontrolled instinct."[5] Similarly, Doug Roseneau and Michael Todd Wilson write, "Sexuality is much broader and more all-inclusive [than intercourse]. Sexuality is really more of a soul thing. Our bodies give us visual input and hormonal arousal, but we interpret and build on these sexual cues using our minds, hearts, and wills. Unlike those in the animal kingdom, humans *make choices* to create erotic arousal. We can pursue sexual feelings or not."[6]

105

As we mature as Christians, our focus needs to move away from simply eliminating those things that might trigger temptation (something that is impossible to do successfully) to surrendering to God and learning how to respond appropriately to the temptations that may come.

Let's go back to the ever-popular story of Joseph avoiding the sexual advances of Potiphar's wife. Genesis 39 tells us that the first time she made a sexual advance he told her "no" and explained why. As the advances continued, he tried to avoid her. Finally, when he felt trapped, he ran. This passage is often used to justify avoidance of all potentially tempting situations, but notice that Joseph did not sequester himself away from society for fear that he might see a woman. He fled when he was relentlessly pursued. The difficulty, though, is figuring out when a simple "no" and explanation will suffice, when we need to avoid contact, and when we need to drop everything and flee.

Christian thinkers have approached this difficulty from various perspectives in their attempts to move beyond legalism to a process that emphasizes our submission to God's will. In *Soul Virgins*, for instance, Roseneau and Wilson strive to avoid legalism and resist answering the clichéd "how far is too far" question because they realize that this doesn't get to the root of the problem. Instead, they encourage singles to practice chastity, which they call "soul virginity," by celebrating and protecting God's design for sexuality. For Roseneau and Wilson, soul virginity requires singles to think about their sexuality in terms of their relationship with God, acknowledging their creation as sexual beings that long to be in community with others but recognizing that sexual intercourse must be reserved for marriage. Within this framework they provide a simple, easy to remember guideline for those who want clearly defined boundaries: don't touch anything that would be covered by a bikini.[7] They don't say that everything else is fair game, but they recognize that God-honoring single adults need to draw those lines for themselves.

When it comes to drawing these boundaries, Marva Dawn adds to the discussion by positing a helpful question. Throughout the Old Testament, most notably in the book of Hosea, Israel is compared to an unfaithful bride. Dawn uses this metaphor to show how important it is for us to practice our sexuality appropriately. She states, "The sexual lives of God's people, therefore, are always judged by this question: Are we symbolizing God's fidelity or imitating Israel's faithlessness?"[8] When we think of fidelity, we usually think of fidelity within a marriage, but those of us who are not married also need to practice fidelity. Many Christian dating and relationship books emphasize the importance of being faithful to one's future spouse. But what if you never marry? As scripture continually points out, our ultimate fidelity belongs to God. When we view others lustfully, as mere objects to satisfy our desires, we end up placing our sexual desires before God. Just as Israel was tempted to serve the pagan gods of other nations, we are all too often tempted to serve the gods of our world, particularly the god of sex. Rather than asking ourselves how far is too far, perhaps we should ask ourselves if we are merely following (or trying to circumvent) a set of rules, or if we are demonstrating our humble response to God's faithfulness in how we live our lives.

As we think about how we demonstrate faithfulness to God, it might also help to consider how we define lust and what those definitions say about the steps needed to resist it. When Pope John Paul II talks about lust, for instance, he focuses on the condition of our hearts. He states that lust reduces "the riches of the deep attractiveness of masculinity and femininity to mere satisfaction of the sexual need of the body."[9] Richard Foster expresses a similar view of lust when he defines it as "an untamed, inordinate sexual passion to possess."[10] When we try merely to avoid anything that might trigger sexual desire, we neglect the root of the problem. According to these definitions, lust is a lot more than sexual desire. It is the objectification of another person. It is seeing someone else only through our own desires, and these desires can be emotional as well as physical. Seeing someone only in terms of our desire for intimacy or security can be just as objectifying as seeing them in terms of our desire for sex. Rather than fearing the opposite sex, or even our sexual desires, perhaps we should focus on viewing others as individuals created in the image of God. John 12 gives us a wonderful example of this. In this passage we are given an account of Mary anointing Jesus with expensive perfume and wiping his feet with her hair. Jesus did not condemn Mary for performing what could be seen as a potentially erotic act. Rather, he saw it for what it was—an act of devotion that foreshadowed his death.

Often when Christians discuss sexual temptation, they turn to Paul's advice to the Thessalonians that they should test all things, hold on to that which is good, and avoid evil. In response to this passage, Joshua Harris, for instance, asks, "Are you testing? Are you avoiding every kind of evil? Are you holding on to the good? Remember, media is after your heart. It's not trying to reason with you—it seeks to disguise its message so that you'll welcome it and let your guard down."[11] Harris jumps very quickly from "testing" to avoiding, already assuming the evil influences rampant in the world around him. But, as we have already explored, this type of avoidance is nearly impossible, for even while fasting alone in the desert, temptations may arise. And this type of avoidance leads too easily to a legalistic faith that focuses far more on avoiding the externals than on transforming the internal state of the heart.

The poet John Milton, however, provides us with a very different response to Thessalonians, emphasizing the "testing" part of the passage. In "Areopagitica," he writes, "Read any books whatsoever come to thy hands, for thou art sufficient both to judge aright, and to examine each matter ... To the pure, all things are pure; not only meats and drinks, but all kind of knowledge either good or evil; the knowledge cannot defile, nor consequently the books, if the will and conscience be not defiled."[12] This may be comparing apples and oranges. Harris is talking about sexual lust, and Milton is talking about ideas put forth in books, but both use as their starting point 1 Thessalonians 5:21–22 which is actually talking about false teachings. But interestingly, Milton does later apply the same reasoning to all types of temptation. Whether it is temptation of the mind or temptation of the flesh, Milton encourages a mature faith, a faith that is tested and holds true: "He that can apprehend and consider vice with all her baits and seeming pleasures, and yet abstain, and yet distinguish, and yet prefer that which is truly better, he is the true wayfaring Christian. I cannot praise a fugitive and cloistered virtue, unexercised and unbreathed, that never sallies out and sees her adversary, but slinks out of the race."[13] This is certainly not an excuse to seek out temptation or to put yourself in compromising situations, for we must not forget that we are challenged to hold on to what is good. But by focusing almost solely on the message of avoidance, are we missing the opportunity to develop our Christian faith and take up the challenge that Milton (and perhaps Paul) places before us? Whenever we find ourselves falling into lust, we should ask ourselves why. Is it simply because we are controlled by our biology and our physiological impulses? Or is it because we believe the lie that all of creation is here to satisfy our desires?

Dangerous Message 2: Sexual temptation cannot be resisted, so Christians should marry early

We really shouldn't be surprised that many Christians today accept the teaching that sexual temptation cannot be resisted. The idea of the irresistibility of sexual temptation has been espoused by Protestants since Martin Luther. Allan Carlson, President of The Howard Center for Family, Religion, and Society, provides one recent example, and he actually turns to Luther for inspiration. He believes that Martin Luther's ideas regarding marriage, family, and sexuality are not only "remarkably contemporary" but also provide a "powerful and relevant message for Christians—and others—in the twenty-first century." Although he states that he does not agree with Luther's claim that it is virtually impossible for adults to remain celibate, he bases much of his argument on precisely this point:

> Except among those rare persons—"not more than one in a thousand," Luther said at one point—who received true celibacy as a gift from God, marriage and procreation were divinely ordained. "For it is not a matter of free choice or decision but a *natural and necessary* thing, that whatever is a man must have a woman and whatever is a woman must have a man." [emphasis added] The intentionally celibate adult had no warrant from God. Indeed, Luther added: "They cannot boast that what they do is pleasing in God's sight, as can the woman in childbirth, even if her child is born out of wedlock." [*The Estate of Marriage*][14]

In his zealousness to praise marriage and procreation, Luther not only devalues celibacy, but he goes so far as to imply that God prefers fornication to celibacy because fornication might result in new life. As alarming as this is, it is perhaps even more disturbing that Carlson believes this message is "powerful and relevant" for twenty-first century Christians. Even if we understand Luther's comment as hyperbole, it remains clear that he did not see celibacy as a realistic option, and he believed that chastity could only be found in marriage.

In support of the view that marriage is necessary in order to keep one chaste, Carlson quotes from *An Exhortation to the Knights of the Teutonic Order That They Lay Aside False Chastity and Assume the True Chastity of Wedlock* (1523) in which Luther addresses the problem of the supposedly celibate knights who would take advantage of unsuspecting women. This was certainly a legitimate concern for which Luther had every right to express righteous indignation. Unfortunately, his argument gives way to generalization and the assumption that all unmarried men are dangerous predators when he writes, " 'Single men cannot be trusted very far; even married men have all they can do to keep from falling [into adultery], although among them there is more justification for hope and confidence. With single men one can have neither hope nor confidence, but only constant fear.' "[15] In Luther's opinion, single women don't fare much better. In his letter "To Several Nuns" (1524), Luther writes,

> Though womenfolk are ashamed to admit to this, nevertheless Scripture and experience show that among many thousands there is not a one to whom God has given to remain in pure chastity. A woman has no control over herself. God has made her body to be with man, to bear children and to raise them as the words of Genesis 1 clearly state, as is evident by the members of the body ordered by God Himself.[16]

Luther may be writing from the perspective of a man steeped in sixteenth-century German culture, but his message still resonates throughout many discussions of sexuality in the late twentieth and early twenty-first century evangelical church, remaining a predominant view toward sexual temptation and one that informs many of our beliefs and decisions regarding sexual issues.

The idea that sexual temptation cannot be resisted is at the core of the recent "Get Married" campaign that is often discussed on the Boundless webzine, Focus on the Family's Web site devoted to singles. In her many articles and her 2008 book, *Get Married*, Candice Watters, the founding editor of Boundless, argues that if we are single our main focus should be getting married. Quoting Pastor John MacArthur on 1 Corinthians 7, she argues that marriage is an imperative for everyone who lacks self-control: "The Greek tense for 'let them marry,' says John MacArthur, is a command, a strong imperative 'since a person can't live a happy life and serve the Lord effectively if dominated by unfulfilled sexual passion.' "[17] Then, taking this even further, she implies that almost everyone falls into this category. Quoting one of her mentors, Watters adds,

> "Marriage is such an important part of honoring God as sexual beings," said Mary Morken. "I don't know how people can make it morally with-

out getting married. I've met very few who have." Research supports her experience. With the rate of premarital sex among Christians mirroring that of unbelievers—77 percent of men raised in "Fundamental Protestant homes" admit to premarital sex—it's clear that Paul's admonition to marry is as relevant as ever.[18]

Rather than examining why so many Christians give in to sexual temptation and discussing the need to encourage each other to practice self-control, Watters assumes that the only solution is to get married. While she does give advice on how to avoid temptation while dating, this is seen only as a temporary solution. But will all of our struggles with temptation miraculously end if we marry? The number of Christian marriages damaged by pornography and infidelity suggests otherwise.

Watters is not the only one who reasons that since resistance and total avoidance are both futile, the only option singles have is to get married, preferably while they are still young, so that they will have an outlet for their sexual desires. In chapter four we saw that Al Mohler views high school as a time when "sexual passion is ignited but there is no holy means for it to be fulfilled." His solution is to get married as soon as possible.[19] Similarly, Joshua Harris sees marriage as a solution for those who struggle with masturbation. In fact, he is quite direct about it: "Here's my advice: Get married." Fortunately, he does qualify this advice by adding that he is not advocating this for fifteen-year-olds, that it should not be our driving motivation for marriage, and that he does not want anyone to make a hasty or rash decision.[20] But he still emphasizes early marriage as a means of dealing with sexual desire.

As support for this idea of the necessity of early marriage among Christians, Debbie Maken argues that the Bible actually prescribes the appropriate time for marriage. She concludes:

> The phrase "wife of your youth" or "bridegroom of your youth" is often used in connection with marriage (Proverbs 5:18; Malachi 2:14–15; Joel 1:8). But what does "youth" mean? It refers to a time when two people (a man and a woman) ought to be prepared to marry and be given in marriage. Biologically this refers to a time when the two are relatively young and can make the most of their sexuality and their childbearing years. The term means spring of one's life, as opposed to the summer, fall, or winter. The term "youth" denotes a time when all the rights and privileges associated with marriage can be enjoyed.[21]

With this discussion, Maken conveniently ignores the complexities of a polygamous culture in which older men would often marry younger wives who could give them more children once their older wives had passed their child-bearing years. She also ignores the fact that lifespans were much shorter then. Instead, Maken interprets these passages as a biblical command that transcends time and culture—a command based on the false assumption that sex is automatically more enjoyable when one is young.

Many of these messages to marry young are prompted by what Mohler, Watters, and others see as an alarming trend of twentysomething single men being more interested in "playing the field" than getting married. The proponents of early marriage often see marriage as *the* tool for teaching maturity and responsibility. While they acknowledge that a rare few may have the "gift" of celibacy, they believe that the key sign of such a gift is the absence of sexual desire. So, their advice is, if you have sexual desires, get married, and the sooner the better.

In contrast, John Stott is one church leader who encourages singles to wait until they are older to marry. In an interview with Albert Hsu, Stott responds to the question of whether or not he has any final advice for singles with a resounding, "Yes! Don't be in too great a hurry to get married. We human beings do not reach maturity until we are about twenty-five. To marry before this runs the risk of finding yourself at twenty-five married to somebody who was a very different person at the age of twenty."[22] What Stott, a celibate man, is able to recognize is that it is possible to control desire so that young Christians don't have to be rushed into marriage.

Studies have shown that marriages have a better success rate if the couple is older when they marry. In "The State of Our Unions: The Social Health of Marriage in America" (2002), for instance, Barbara Dafoe Whitehead and David Popenoe use U.S. Census material to explore different trends in marriage, and they conclude, "A large body of evidence indicates that marriages of very young people, that is, teenagers, are much less stable and successful on average than are first marriages of persons in their twenties and older." Then, moving beyond an analysis of teenage marriages and looking at the stability of marriages in general, they conclude, "Indeed, age at marriage is one of the strongest and most consistent predictors of marital stability ever found by social science research."[23] Certainly, rushing into marriage at eighteen or nineteen simply because you desire to have sex is not the best way to begin a lifelong commitment.

Ramifications and Response

Our intention is not to advocate a particular age for marriage. Certainly there are some who are ready for marriage in their early twenties, but advising everyone to marry early creates problems for young Christians who find themselves married before they are mature enough to deal with the realities of that commitment. We mentioned earlier that most of these discussions advocating early marriage are aimed at young men who reject marriage in favor of either going out and playing the field or staying in and playing video games. Marriage may teach some men responsibility, but this is not always the case. Many married men lack responsibility and prefer to spend their time "playing" with their friends. One is reminded of the joke that men marry assuming their wives will never change, but they always do. And women marry assuming their husbands *will* change, but they *never* do. Of course it is easy for both men and women to find this joke offensive. But isn't this the type of scenario that is created when immature singles are encouraged to marry, hoping this commitment will create maturity? Rather, shouldn't young singles be encouraged to mature in their relationship with Christ and become productive God-honoring members of society? Then their focus can be on serving God, whether or not that includes marriage.

Not only does the advice to marry early create potential problems for young Christians, but it also ignores or condemns those who don't marry early, often assuming that all older singles are sexually promiscuous. Frankly, there really isn't a lot of advice for us even though there are more and more of us all the time. Although Joshua Harris does acknowledge we exist, he does so dismissively: "I understand that there are many people who want to marry but haven't been able to. I'm sorry if you find this counsel [to marry] frustrating."[24] Maken is much more direct and addresses what she sees as the dire consequences of long-term singleness, especially for women:

> It produces women who have had to live in a sort of limbo and the possibilities that may go with it—failed relationships, a heartbreak or two, repentant bouts of fornication, cohabitation, unwanted pregnancy, abortion, a doubly-increased chance of being raped without having the

protection of a father or husband, strained relationships in substitute families made up by roommates, an overall feeling of isolation and loneliness, resentment toward God and men for their single state, and so on. There is the fear that if they marry too late, they may not be able to have children or will have increased their chances of breast cancer if they become pregnant for the first time past the age of thirty. (In actuality, the odds of pregnancy decline in the late twenties.) If they do become pregnant at a later age, the baby's chances of Down's syndrome increase, as well as other complications down the road.[25]

The picture that Maken draws is not a pretty one. It is designed to compel women in particular to find a husband as quickly as possible so that they may avoid this horrific future. While not all present the future for singles in such bleak terms as Maken does, all those who focus on the necessity of early marriage do create a sense of desperation in many singles.

Those who advise singles to marry early are generally the same ones who suggest going to extreme measures to avoid any situations that could potentially cause lustful thoughts. This makes sense. On the positive side, they value marriage and want to discourage any behavior that may endanger it. But their advice may prove to be counter-productive, especially for those who graduated from the high school or college youth group when Reagan was president. In fact, their advice may be at the root of what has come to be called the "dating drought." While there are certainly those who date their way through all of the church singles groups in their town, it is not unusual for Christian singles over 25, even those who would like to marry eventually, to go years without a date. As we mentioned in chapter four, Camerin Courtney addressed this issue in her singles column. Not only did she receive 250 e-mails from singles across the country, but an informal poll of 671 respondents revealed that 54% had not been on a date in more than two years.[26] Does that mean that at least half of the single adults in the church just aren't date worthy, or is there something else going on here?

Many blame this phenomenon on single men. The few single men who are in the church have been accused of being everything from lazy to afraid of commitment and responsibility to downright disobedient. While this may describe some single men, it certainly does not describe all of them. Not only is there no acknowledgement that these men might have a good reason for not marrying, but they are blamed for depriving all of the godly single women out there from fulfilling their God-created role of wife and mother. Debbie Maken recounts a friend's attitude toward unmarried men:

> Single at the age of thirty-four, my friend Anna desperately wanted to be married. Her boss asked if she'd be interested in dating "a very godly forty-five-year-old" lawyer. Her response? "If this man is so godly, why isn't he married by now?" She explained that she wasn't about to "reward a slothful forty-five-year-old man with someone eleven years his junior," but that she could recommend some woman who was well over forty, had lost the beauty of her youth, and would have trouble conceiving. She explained that this was the kind of candidate for this man since his inaction in finding a wife had caused this outcome for some other woman.[27]

Maken's friend's response may seem extreme, but the basic sentiment is expressed by highly respected Christian leaders and writers, including Elisabeth Elliot:

> Everywhere my husband and I go we meet lovely Christian women, beautifully dressed, deeply spiritual, thoroughly feminine—and *single*. They long for marriage and children. But what is it with the men? Are they blind to feminine pulchritude, deaf to God's call, numb to natural desire? . . . Where are the holy men of God willing to shoulder the full responsibility of manhood, to take the risks and make the sacrifices of courting and winning a wife, marrying her and fathering children in obedience to the command to be fruitful? While the Church has been blessed by men willing to remain single *for the sake of the Kingdom* (and I do not regard lightly such men who are seriously called), isn't it obvious that God calls most men to marriage? By not marrying, those whom He calls are disobeying Him, and thus are denying the women He meant for them to marry the privileges of being wife and mother.[28]

Elliot expresses a frustration felt by many single women in the church. In some cases, this is certainly a legitimate problem. There are far too many Christian men who want to marry and who date godly women but fear making a commitment that lasts for more than a few months. However, while it might be easy for single women to blame the single men in the church for not fulfilling their supposed duty by marrying early, is this a fair characterization of all older Christian men?

Todd Hertz recounts one of his experiences that demonstrates how difficult the Christian dating world may be for men:

I received a bizarre response from a Christian woman I asked out shortly after I graduated college. She was puzzled by the invitation and replied, "I'm sorry, I don't get asked out. I don't know what that means. I think we could go to a movie or something, but I don't understand what a date *means.*"

Perhaps the key confusion in the Christian dating world is that no one really knows what "dating" is. What's a date? What kind of commitment does dating involve? Should we even be dating? Should we be courting instead? Should we just let our parents prearrange the whole thing and exchange some goats between families?[29]

For Hertz and many single men and women like him, then, the problem isn't selfishness or laziness but rather the conflict between the intense desire to be married and the difficulty of negotiating the world of Christian dating.

If you look at the messages singles receive regarding relationships between men and women, is it any wonder that we have so much trouble connecting, even as friends? When Christian singles are repeatedly warned to avoid all temptation from the opposite sex, how are they supposed to get to know each other, let alone develop a relationship deep enough to lead to marriage? In *I Kissed Dating Goodbye*, for instance, Joshua Harris does acknowledge that friendships are possible between single men and women, but he puts some very strict guidelines on them. He argues that "the key to friendship is a common goal or object on which both companions focus. It can be an athletic pursuit, a hobby, faith, or music, but it's something *outside* of them."[30] While he acknowledges that emotional intimacy is good, he states that it should occur only after a commitment is made. Harris is careful to tell men not to avoid relationships with women, but when you consider that he generally views friendship as the first stage of courtship and that the purpose of courtship is marriage, there really isn't much room for true friendship that isn't in some way based on the goal of marriage. When Harris wrote his dating books, he was trying to address a very real problem—the problem of intensely emotional and physical relationships between young people who had no intention of marrying anytime in the near future. But this huge gap between platonic friendship and friendship leading to courtship might be what helps to cause so much of the confusion in Christian dating, especially among older singles, for it almost compels individuals to define their relationship and goals even before they have a chance to get to know each other.

Matt Schmucker, writing to a slightly older audience, takes these ideas even further and thereby demonstrates how problematic they are for older singles. He states that a single man should not do anything with a single woman that a married man should not do with a woman that is not his wife. If he were referring only to physical sexual behavior or intimate emotional connection, we would be a little more open to his point, but his examples include sharing a meal, meeting for a cup of coffee, and having extended conversations about each other's lives.[31] When you come right down to it, this married man basically seems to be saying that men and women shouldn't have any meaningful interactions with each other until they are officially courting or married.

Given that so many people find erotic overtones to sharing coffee and conversation, are we surprised that so many singles are faced not only with the confusions of whether to date or not but also with loneliness and a lack of Christian community? By creating a sense of desperation in singles whom they claim must marry early to avoid the horrors of enforced celibacy and then creating an intense fear that interacting with members of the opposite sex will inevitably lead to sexual sin, many of those advising singles are actually creating more problems than they are solving.

Dangerous Message 3: If you are celibate, you are not sexual

Let's go back for a moment to the advice on how to deal with lust, which often revolves around avoiding anything that causes sexual desire. We have already seen the problems that arise from that perspective when it comes to developing a mature faith. In addition, this perspective creates an oddly mixed message about the sexuality of single adults. When all sexual desire outside of marriage is seen as lust, singles are viewed as either immoral or asexual. The assumptions tend to be that either Christian singles are filled with uncontrollable desires and must marry as soon as possible, or they have been given the "gift of celibacy" and no longer have any desires at all. Joshua Harris, for instance, writes, "Unless God has removed your desire for sex and has given you a clear vision to serve Him as a single person, then assume that you're supposed to get married and either make yourself ready or begin pursuing it."[32] Likewise, in *What's a Girl to Do? While Waiting for Mr. Right* Janet Folger gives her interpretation of 1 Corinthians 7: "It seems to me Paul is saying that if you really want to be married, then you *should* be married. It's not only okay; it's what you should do."[33] For Harris and Folger, the realties of the Christian single life are quite simple: if you have sexual desires and/or the wish to be married, you should marry as soon as possible; if you are not meant to be married, God will take away those desires. But is it really that simple?

Harris and Folger are not alone in this view. In fact, they are in good company. In his *Large Catechism* on "The Sixth Commandment: Thou Shalt Not Commit Adultery," Martin Luther writes that marriage is commanded by God and the only ones who are exempt from this commandment are those who are "especially excepted" by God "so that they are not fit for the married estate, or whom He has released by a high, supernatural gift that they can maintain chastity without this estate." Unless you fall into one of these two categories, "it is not possible to remain chaste without marriage."[34] This understanding of sexual desire is directly connected with the idea of the "gift of celibacy" or the "gift of singleness." Throughout history, many have assumed that this is how God works, and many who have taken vows of celibacy acknowledge God's "special graces" when it comes to their sexual desires.

While God does work this way for some people, it is dangerous to believe that God works this way for everyone. In 2000, several years before the Boundless "Get Married" campaign, one reader wrote in to ask "Professor Theophilus" how you know whether or not you have been called to singleness. The question was deferred to a single youth minister who expressed the difficulty of recognizing "the call":

Apart from a direct word from God, I am not convinced that anyone can know they are called to permanent (lifelong) singleness. Those in the Catholic faith have the clarity of a mandated vow of celibacy to accompany their call to full-time ministry. Protestants do not have such a clear choice. Of all the Protestant singles in full-time ministry who I have read or know about personally, all have a desire and hope for marriage, but for one reason or another it has simply never worked out (yet). But they have also come to the realization that their desire for marriage is one more thing that gets to be laid on the altar of living a surrendered life. They have also discovered exceptional grace to live life with much joy in undivided devotion (1 Corinthians 7:32–35).[35]

This minister's perspective echoes the messages we have heard from many Christian singles who find that discussions of the "gift of singleness" tend to trivialize the complexities of their reality. Rather than receiving "special graces" from God at one point in their life that remove all sexual desire, they receive God's grace on a daily basis as they struggle and cope with the difficulties of being a human being in a fallen world.

Ramifications and Response

The belief that God removes all sexual desire from those called to singleness can lead to two negative ramifications. The first ramification is the belief that God bases his callings on our desires. Imagine for a moment a married Christian assuming that God wants him or her to be single because he or she no longer wants to be married. This is, of course, preposterous, but as we have seen, this is often the assumption regarding singleness. If you have a desire to get married, God must want you to be married; otherwise, he would take away that desire. But the example of Scripture shows that God doesn't necessarily base his call or his gifts on our desires. Moses certainly did not have a desire to lead the Israelites out of Egypt. But God had different plans, plans that showed God's strength in the midst of Moses's weakness. While the apostle Paul certainly had a desire to remain single because he saw how his single state enabled him to better serve the cause of Christ, that does not mean that God was controlled by Paul's desires. Paul also had a desire for God to remove his "thorn in the flesh," whatever that might have been. Paul prayed for God to remove it, but he did not. God's answer was, " 'My grace is sufficient for you, for power is perfected in weakness.' " And what was Paul's response? "Most gladly, therefore, I will rather boast about my weaknesses, so that the power of Christ may dwell in me."[36] The message here is that God's grace is sufficient in times of struggle, not that God's grace removes the struggle. Why do we have such a hard time believing that God's grace is sufficient for those of us who are single? Is not God's grace sufficient when it comes to dealing with loneliness and temptation? Cannot God help us to have a proper understanding of our sexuality and our desires?

The second ramification is the belief that we are not sexual beings unless we have sex. ChristianSinglesToday.com conducts regular polls regarding issues affecting singles. One such poll had to do with how singles handle issues of sexuality. One woman responded to the poll by writing,

> I've heard that as singles we should "embrace our sexuality," but I've never quite been able to figure out how or why. It almost seems as though we don't *need* it for anything since we're not supposed to be sexually active . . . As a divorced person, I've found myself almost *hating* the sexual part of myself because of going from sexual freedom within the boundaries of marriage to suddenly having to do without under all circumstances . . . I'm still not sure why God doesn't just shut off the sexual part of singles.[37]

This idea that sexuality is just sexual intercourse is a common misperception that often leaves singles wondering how they can be sexual without having sex.

Roseneau and Wilson do a good job countering this misperception, explaining that sexuality encompasses all types of relational intimacy: "Sexuality describes *who we are* more than what we do. You are at your very core a sexual being, whether or not you ever engage in sexual behaviors."[38] Ultimately, they argue that we need a deeper understanding of sexuality, for they believe that sexuality and sexual desires were created by God to move us toward an "intimate connection" with him and "with other members of the body of Christ."[39] As the responses to the survey on singles' sexuality reveal, however, this perspective is often ignored, leaving Christian singles feeling that they must either deny their sexuality or desperately pursue marriage since they have obviously been denied the supposed "gift of celibacy" that will miraculously remove their sexual desires. But is singles' sexuality truly an either/or proposition? Many Christian singles today feel as if we are caught in the middle. We refuse to deny our sexuality and instead wish to discover how to embody it effectively in order to glorify God, and we also refuse to be utterly consumed by the desire to find a spouse, choosing instead to trust it to God's will and timing. For the Christian singles who are living in the "no man's land" between these two extremes, the complexities can be difficult to negotiate, and the reality is that we are receiving little advice on how to survive.

Coping with These Dangerous Messages

We are all sexual beings, and to some extent, most of us have sexual desires. Unfortunately, we too often accept the secular world's message that these desires cannot be controlled. In the evangelical community, this often leads to disturbing messages about lust and temptation. Christian singles are told to avoid everything that might make us stumble, to be extremely careful in our interactions with those of the opposite sex, to pursue marriage tenaciously so that we will finally have an outlet for our desires, and to deny that we are sexual beings until we are married. Not only does this approach fail to recognize God's power to help single adults resist sexual temptation, but it also fails to acknowledge that sexual temptations do not disappear once you marry. Simply being able to have sex within the covenant of marriage does not guarantee that individuals will be able to resist the sexual temptations that they will inevitably continue to encounter after marriage.

Singles are not being challenged to deal with the complexities of our situation in a manner that will help us mature as Christians and prepare us either for marriage or for a life of celibacy. Instead, we are given simplistic answers that not only make us feel like failures when we don't have either a spouse or the gift of celibacy but also cause us to wonder why we have seemingly been denied God's blessing. And when we turn to the dangerous messages we receive involving sex and marriage, the situation becomes even more frustrating.

6

Happiness & Maturity
Dangerous Messages about Sex and Marriage

Family is the most important thing, isn't it? One's own family, I mean—
not anyone else's for god's sake.

Midas, *Metamorphoses*

Happiness? Good God! One must never expect that from marriage. A
few quiet moments, if you are lucky, and an occasional date that doesn't
incite you to murder.

Lily, *The Summer House*

Not too long ago, a close friend once again found herself at the end
of a relationship. Before entering into the relationship she had prayed,
"God, guard my heart. Show me your will. If this relationship is not
from you, show me now. I don't think I can survive another broken
heart." She entered the relationship cautiously, and the more she learned
about the man, the more she thought the relationship was indeed from
God. They both had a heart for missions, and they had compatible life
and ministry goals. Then six months later he ended the relationship.
Although they were perfect for each other on paper, enjoyed being
together, had a physical attraction for each other, and had the support
of their families, for some reason he "just wasn't feeling it." Her heart

was broken, and her mind was filled with questions. How could God do this to her? Why didn't he answer her prayer and spare her this pain? Didn't God know how much she longed to be married? Of course he did. So why didn't he care? He had promised to give her the desires of her heart, and marriage is a good desire. Why did God keep dangling potential mates before her only to snatch them away? Is God really that cruel? No loving earthly parent would do that. Why would her heavenly father? Is that really the kind of God she wants to serve?

These are difficult questions but ones that many older singles have asked themselves, and it is no wonder considering the messages we often receive regarding sex and marriage. When sex and marriage are upheld as signs of God's favor that are promised to all who desire them and live in God's will, older singles who have not yet received this sign of blessing are bound to question their own walks with God, as well as the truth of his love and faithfulness. As we saw in previous chapters, Christian singles are receiving many negative messages about singleness and celibacy that make it difficult to affirm our decisions to remain sexually pure outside of marriage. When these are combined with the strong emphasis on marriage that Christian singles receive from the evangelical church, the struggle to maintain our commitment to sexual purity becomes even more difficult, for these messages about sex and marriage not only affect our feelings about ourselves, but they also affect our understanding of God.

Dangerous Message 1: Great marital sex is the reward for being chaste

In chapter three we briefly discussed a group of twentysomething singles in New York City who had banded together to support each other in their quest to remain abstinent until marriage. Their frank discussions of the expected joys of sex clearly reveal a disturbing message that often surrounds discussions of abstinence, marriage, and sex in the evangelical church. Jeff Sharlet, who interviewed members of the group for an article in *Rolling Stone Magazine*, noticed that these singles viewed sex as "the Holy Grail for those who wait," "A 'sexual payoff,' according to the authors of *Every Man's Battle*, that will 'explode off any known scale.'" As support, Sharlet recounts a phone call he received from one of his contacts within the group: "'Robin read a statistic . . . that men who have sex before marriage are something like 600 percent more likely to experience a drop-off of sexual passion once they are married.' If you accept that number, the incentive for premarital chastity is stunning: a post-wedding life of sex that's 600 percent more awesome." While these singles had other reasons for remaining abstinent, the one that they returned to repeatedly was that it was insuring them amazing sex once they got married. Interestingly, as Sharlet remarks, "To the biblical austerity of chastity, they add the promise of mind-blowing sex, using the very terms of the sexual revolution they rally against."[1] Rather than focusing on celibacy as an important spiritual discipline in itself, they conceive of abstinence as a different type of foreplay that will ultimately enhance sexual pleasure.

And it isn't only sexual pleasure that will be enhanced. In *The Thrill of the Chaste: Finding Fulfillment While Keeping Your Clothes On* Dawn Eden offers the female corollary to this idea, focusing a bit more on the romance of marriage than the physical pleasures of sex. Eden argues that casual sex does not lead to marriage, but chastity does. She mentions that even though she did not have a potential boyfriend at the time she wrote the book, she believes she is closer to being married than she ever was before. Her reason for this belief is that "chastity relies on faith that God, as you pursue a closer walk with Him, will lead you to a loving husband."[2] Although she never actually says that marriage is the reward for chastity, it is implied throughout her book. And Eden is, by no means, the only one who embraces this message. The assumption often is that if we are really good, then God will reward us with a great marriage and, of course, great sex. Of course the flip side to this reasoning is that if God has not given us a wonderful spouse, then we are not very good Christians.

Ramifications and Response

This thinking often manifests itself in the common advice and supposed reassurance that once we are content in our singleness God will provide us with a spouse. While some like Al Mohler, Debbie Maken, and Candice Watters argue that we should not be content in our singleness and should relentlessly pursue a spouse, others like Henry Cloud and John Townsend focus on the need to achieve contentedness and spiritual maturity as important preparation for a spouse. While this advice to be content and focus on your relationship with God is excellent and should be embraced by everyone, the problem arises when we see this as something that should be done in order to get a mate. Camerin Courtney puts it this way:

> I have a hard time synching up this conditional distribution of gifts—this idea that we need to achieve a certain mindset before the blessing of marriage will be bestowed upon us—with the God of unconditional love. I love that we have a come-as-you-are God. A God who loved us and sought us when we were yet sinners (Romans 5:8). A God who doesn't expect us to clean up our mess before we come to him but who meets us right in the mess. I fear we lose that beautiful reality when we start assigning benchmarks to his blessings.[3]

This kind of thinking doesn't hold up to experience either. Not everyone who marries is spiritually mature and content in the state in which God has placed him or her. And not everyone who is single is spiritually immature and discontented.

Of course there are those who acknowledge that some have to wait longer than others before finding that "special someone." But once again, there is the assumption that it will eventually happen for everyone. All too often even the wait itself becomes the reason for expecting a great marriage. We tend to assume that the longer the wait, the better the prize. As Shakespeare writes in *Cymbeline*, the gift is "the more delay'd, delighted" (V.iv.105), and many contemporary writers attest to this idea. For example, Leslie Ludy, cowriter of *When God Writes Your Love Story: The Ultimate Approach to Guy/Girl Relationships*, draws on this idea when she testifies that her gift of marriage was indeed worth the wait. She writes, "[God] wanted me to trust Him enough to bring that special man to me in His perfect time. Guess what? In His perfect time, that's exactly what He did. Eric is my gorgeous and gallant knight in shining armor. I am *so* glad I didn't settle for second best."[4] What is problematic about this story, however, is that she was only sixteen when she met Eric. The language Ludy uses to describe her time of waiting and trusting implies a difficult and long struggle that is finally rewarded by God. The implication is that older singles reading her book will also be granted this miraculous intervention eventually. But how convincing is this argument for singles who may be more than twice Ludy's age when she met her prince? For older singles in particular, this kind of testimony rings hollow when matched up with the reality of our situation.

Derek Prince in *God Is a Matchmaker* does a better job acknowledging that God's timing is different for everyone and that while some don't have to wait for their mate, others have to wait a long time. Prince discusses the importance of waiting when he writes:

If you are one of those whom God requires to wait, be encouraged by the fact that God has required many of His choicest servants to wait long periods for the fulfillment of His promise or purpose . . .

God uses waiting to work out various purposes in our lives. First, waiting tests our faith. Only those who really believe in God's provision are prepared to wait for it. The apostle Peter warns us that just as gold is refined by fire, so faith must be refined by testing (see 1 Peter 1:6–7). Only faith that passes the test is accepted by God as genuine.[5]

This passage has been quoted by other authors as confirmation that God will eventually provide each of us with a mate. It seems to imply that God makes some of us wait in order to test our faith, and if we pass the test, we can get married. However, those who quote Prince rarely follow his argument all the way through. In just the next paragraph he tells us that waiting gives us the opportunity to examine our motives for wanting to marry. He stresses the importance of examining whether God really wants us to marry or if marriage is just something we want for ourselves. Unfortunately, this message often goes unheard as those who are desperate to marry cling to the hope that God is a matchmaker.

Throughout history, many good, God-fearing individuals have not been granted the spouse they longed for. Are we really to conclude from this evidence that God was punishing them for spiritual immaturity or lack of faith? Or are we to conclude that God's love and favor simply didn't extend to them? What does it say about our theology if a romantic marriage and mind-blowing sex are seemingly the supreme evidence of God's favor? By promoting ideas about sex and marriage that imply they are the rewards for serving God, the evangelical church is not only making singleness more difficult for Christian singles to accept but also creating a skewed perception of God.

Dangerous Message 2: Sex is sacred and necessary for spiritual maturity

Not only is spiritual maturity often seen as a prerequisite and guarantor of marriage, but it is also often seen as developing even more intensely through marriage and sex. Many books that provide a positive Christian understanding of sex focus on its sacredness and its connection to spirituality. There are two strong and different motivators behind these discussions, depending on the intended audience, and both reveal important truths.

First, there is the desire to fight against the world's message that sex is a basic animal instinct and that it shouldn't be taken too seriously. In contrast, Christians should recognize the seriousness of sexual relationships: sex is good and created by God for marriage. Within this discussion, many acknowledge that sex is not the "reward" for getting married, but it is a physical symbol of the spiritual covenant made between a husband and wife. This is a powerful message that needs to be emphasized, but, as we will soon see, it can also be blown out of proportion.

The second motivator is the desire to redeem the church's historically negative perception of sex. While many of us have been receiving the message that marital sex is the Holy Grail we must seek, others, especially Roman Catholics and Protestants attracted to the traditions of Catholicism, seem to have grown up with the idea that celibacy is the preferred way of life. They have had to struggle with feeling inferior because they are married. In *Sacred Marriage*, Gary Thomas writes, "As far back as I can remember, I was fully aware of the long-standing tradition of celibacy—monks and nuns who lived out their dedication to God by pledging to abstain from marriage and sex. Part of me wished I could embrace this; I wanted to be sold out for Christ."[6] Growing up, we certainly knew about the tradition of celibacy, but we were always taught that those who encouraged celibacy got it wrong and that Scripture commands us to marry. If anything, we saw people go to great lengths to explain away Paul's preference for celibacy—that is, if they addressed it at all. We don't know how to account for the discrepancy in messages. It doesn't necessarily seem to be based on denomination or church affiliation. Maybe the guys were getting the "celibacy" talk while we girls were getting the "marriage and motherhood" talk. Whatever the reason, though, the message that married Christians are not inferior to those who are celibate is certainly true and important.

The problem that arises from these attempts to redeem the church's view of sex is that they are often taken too far so that marriage and sex become the means of spiritual maturity. Singles are thereby doomed to be second-class citizens within Christianity. In his discussion of the connection between sexuality and spirituality, Gary Thomas, who is a regular contributor to *Christianity Today* and Focus on the Family, argues that "marriage is the preferred route to becoming more like [Christ]."[7] Not only does this argument neglect Christ's own example as a single and celibate man, but it also puts undue emphasis on marriage. Thomas's primary message that the purpose of marriage is not to make us happy but to make us holy is a very good one and one that more couples need to embrace. Too many people go into marriage expecting it to solve all of their problems, and they become disenchanted when marriage doesn't live up to their expectations. However, this message becomes problematic when people begin to believe that marriage is the *only* or even the *primary* means through which God makes us holy. Are not *all* Christians "being transformed into [His] image from glory to glory, just as from the Lord, the Spirit" (2 Cor. 3:18)? Yes, marriage is designed to make us holy, but so is singleness. And for the most part, many of the principles discussed in Thomas's book can be applied to the single life.

But singles seem to be excluded from the transforming work of Christ when we place too much emphasis on the sacredness of sexual intercourse itself. Gary Thomas makes it very clear that while sex can point us to God, it can never replace God.[8] But this message runs the risk of getting lost in the emphasis that is placed on the sexual act. Thomas goes so far as to equate sex and orgasm with experiencing God's presence through the shekinah glory:

> The ancient Jewish text *The Holy Letter* (written by Nahmanides in the thirteenth century) sees sex as a mystical experience of meeting with God: "Through [the act of intercourse] they become partners with God in the act of creation. This is the mystery of what the sages said, 'When a man unites with his wife in holiness, the Shekinah is between them in the mystery of man and woman.'" The breadth of this statement is sobering when you consider that this *shekinah* glory is the same presence experienced by Moses when God met him face-to-face (see Exodus 24:15–18).[9]

He even declares sex as a form of physical prayer. Now if we view sex as prayer in the sense that everything we do should be done in prayer unto the Lord, that's one thing, but when Thomas says that "we will be transformed in the marriage bed every bit as much as we are transformed on our knees in prayer," he runs the risk of worshipping sex rather than God. In many ways this is turning sex into another Holy Grail, this time for married couples rather than for singles. Then there is also the added pressure to have children, for "creating a family is the closest we get to sharing the image of God."[10] Many married couples without children will attest that they, like single adults, often feel excluded from many of the messages coming from the evangelical church, and Thomas's assertion clearly demonstrates why.

Such messages that glorify sex certainly suggest that singles cannot know God as well as those who are married because we are not experiencing the shekinah glory in the marital bed and we are not sharing the image of God through procreation. But one of the most disturbing aspects of this message regarding sexual intercourse is its similarity to ancient pagan attitudes toward sex that appear (most popularly) in Dan Brown's novel *The Da Vinci Code*. Many Christians have taken offense to this novel, particularly for its assertion that Jesus had a child with Mary Magdalene. While that is certainly a major point in the novel, it is part of a larger assertion that true uncorrupted religion is rooted in the worship of the sacred feminine and its connection with sexual love and procreation. The following passage, which occurs right after Sophie tells Langdon about an event that forever ruined her relationship with her grandfather, reveals the disturbing similarities to some contemporary evangelical discussions about sex. One night, after arriving home unexpectedly, Sophie witnessed her grandfather taking part in a bizarre sexual ritual that seemed like something out of Stanley Kubrick's *Eyes Wide Shut*. This is how Langdon responds to the description of the event:

> He explained that although what she saw probably *looked* like a sex ritual, . . . [it] had nothing to do with eroticism. It was a spiritual act. Historically, intercourse was the act through which male and female experienced God. The ancients believed that the male was spiritually incomplete until he had carnal knowledge of the sacred feminine. Physical union with the female remained the sole means through which man could become spiritually complete and ultimately achieve *gnosis*—knowledge of the divine . . .
> Sophie looked skeptical. "Orgasm as prayer?"
> Langdon gave a noncommittal shrug, although Sophie was essentially correct.[11]

Historical inaccuracies aside, *The Da Vinci Code* shares several similarities with some popular Christian teachings regarding sex: individuals are incomplete without marriage/sex; sex is a form of prayer; and sex is the primary means through which we experience the divine. We are by no means saying that these teachings are inspired by *The Da Vinci Code*. On the contrary, these ideas go back much further, and, as Gary Thomas acknowledges, are inspired by Jewish texts and mystical teachings such as Kabbalah. What we are saying, though, is that as Christians we need to be careful to examine where we get our ideas about sex and marriage. Are our beliefs about sex based on scripture, or are they based on contemporary society and other historical sources?

Ramifications and Response

These teachings have negative ramifications not only for singles, but also for married couples. When marriage is seen as our primary goal and the solution to all of our problems, and when sex is equated with experiencing the divine, is it any wonder so many people in the church are dissatisfied with their marriages? A quick glance at the marriage section of your local Christian bookstore will reveal how important many people find this issue. There is no shortage of books to help married Christians spice up their relationships in the bedroom. Some of these books are practically Christian versions of the Kama Sutra with their detailed descriptions of sexual positions. We are not saying that there is anything wrong with Christians talking openly about sexual issues or offering advice in this area, but sometimes it is taken so far that if you were to judge the Bible based on what is discussed in some of our churches, you would think that the Bible is a sex manual. Linda Dillow and Lorraine Pintus, the authors of *Intimate Issues: 21 Questions Christian Women Ask about Sex,* come awfully close to suggesting it is:

> The best way to put zip back into your lovemaking is to add a generous helping of creativity. But where do we go for our creative ideas? We know a book that is guaranteed to put the sizzle back into your sexual relationship. Its recipes for erotic holy sex will stimulate your creativity and stir up your passion. The good news is you probably already have several copies of the book in your home. If not, buy one immediately. In it you will find the most creative sexual advice given since the beginning of time. Ready for the name of the book? The Bible.[12]

The authors then proceed to use Song of Solomon as a reference point for discussions regarding everything from scented candles to oral sex.

The sex advice doesn't stop with the Christian bookstore. In chapter four we mentioned the popularity of the month-long sermon series on marriage that many churches seem compelled to do every couple of years. While these sermons can be frustrating for singles, we do acknowledge that they usually deal with many different aspects of marriage, and the principles can often be applied to any relationship. However, some churches go much further. Just within the last year Bonnie has encountered one church near her home that offered a women's Bible study on how to spice up your love life. Two other churches advertised a several month long series on Song of Solomon. The signage promised that the series would help you "keep romance alive." Even ChristianityToday. com has its own section on how to have better sex.

While we, like Lauren Winner, would applaud the church's move away from Gnosticism and the teaching that sex is evil, we too wonder if our obsession with the techniques of how to achieve "great" sex is going too far. As Winner remarks, "We've defined sex as something unsustainable—bodice-ripping, stupefying, and nightly. It is adventurous, not habitual, and happens best during romantic weekend getaways, after candlelit dinners that recall the restaurants you frequented on dates before you were married, before you were plunged into routine."[13] Rather than suggesting that married couples should seek the shekinah glory in the bedroom, Winner suggests that the transcendent nature of sex is its ability to reveal God's grace, and in order to do that you "must embrace life's decidedly untranscendent daily goings-on . . . Through sexual practice, we come to find each other fallible, and we come to love each other for the way we see each other creating very human lives out of those very fallibilities . . . For in household sexuality, we see the ways our daily human struggles offer the only language we have to call ourselves to God's grace."[14] Winner's perspective, however, is one that gets lost in the overwhelming amount of material that counsels Christian married couples that their sex lives must resemble those of the couples in popular romantic movies in order for them to glorify God.

Once again, we are not saying there is anything wrong with discussing sexual issues and wanting to keep romance alive. In fact, some churches err on the other extreme and shy away from any discussion of sexual issues including the importance of practicing chastity, leaving their congregations without any biblical teaching on issues such as adultery, divorce, and pornography. Our concern is with the amount of time and energy some church groups spend on helping their members spice up their love life. Christians complain about the world's obsession with sex, but it seems like some churches have given in to the obsession. It all comes down to this: what should be the focus of the church? Should the focus be getting everyone married and making sure they have great orgasms, or should the focus be living and sharing the gospel of Christ?

Dangerous Message 3: You have the right to be happy, and you must be married in order to be happy

"We just want you to be happy." These familiar words are often spoken by parents to their single children, and the implication is that we have to be married in order to be happy. Several writers go beyond implication, directly telling us that we must be married in order to be happy. In *Marriage under Fire*, for instance, James Dobson, drawing from the research of George Gilder, warns us of the dangers of not marrying, remarking, "Research consistently shows that heterosexual married adults do better in virtually every measure of emotional and physical health than people who are divorced or never married. They recover from illness more quickly, earn and save more money, are more reliable employees, suffer less stress, and are less likely to become victims of any kind of violence. They find the job of parenting more enjoyable, and they have more satisfying sex lives."[15] From Dobson's perspective, singles are doomed to live unhealthy, unhappy lives.

Now that we are all thoroughly depressed, perhaps we should ask ourselves if it is simply the act of marriage that makes us happy. Should we really expect that from marriage? Or perhaps the even deeper question is whether or not our ultimate goal should be happiness. Many Christians today teach that not only do we have a right to be happy but also God wants us to be happy. Joel Osteen, for instance, frequently preaches and writes about God's desire to see us happy and fulfilled. To his credit, he writes that happiness is a choice and not dependent on our circumstances. However, much of his focus is on trusting God to bring you everything you want. This is not the place to debate the prosperity message taught by many televangelists, but we do want to take a look at how this basic philosophy influences our expectations for marriage.

We have already discussed the tendency to believe that once an individual reaches a certain undefined level of spiritual maturity, often characterized by contentment with being single, God will provide a mate. Osteen takes this in a different direction and tells us what to do in order to see our dreams come true. He writes, "To live your best life

132

now, you must start looking at life through eyes of faith . . . You must have an image on the inside of the life you want to live on the outside. This image has to become a part of you, in your thoughts, your conversation, deep down in your subconscious mind, in your actions, in every part of your being."[16] From this perspective, all we need to do is embrace positive thinking, seeing the reality we desire to achieve, and it will come to pass. Yes, he begins by invoking the "eyes of faith," but what are we expected to have faith in? God's goodness despite our circumstances, or his capitulation to our desires?

Ultimately, Osteen's vision sounds a bit like obsession. Should we, single adults, really spend all of our time thinking, dreaming, and talking about a future potential marriage? A relationship that isn't promised to any of us? Or should our focus be on glorifying God whatever the state in which we are living? By equating marriage with happiness and then placing marriage as our ultimate goal, we risk turning our eyes from God. As Carolyn Mc-Cully remarks, do we really want to respond to God when he asks us what we have done with our time here on earth by replying, "We've attended lots and lots of singles meetings looking for a husband"?[17]

But many people, even those who may not embrace Osteen's overall theology, believe that God *does* promise us marriage, so we should be pursuing it as the key to our ultimate happiness. They often use scripture to support this assertion. Jeramy Clark, for example, tells us, "God knows the desires of your heart. Even better, he wants to fulfill those desires when you walk with Him." Like many others who counsel singles, he constructs his argument from Psalm 37:4: "Delight yourself in the LORD; and He will give you the desires of your heart." Clark does caution us that "this verse isn't an assurance that your every wish will come true; just because you desire to date a certain person doesn't mean God will send him or her knocking on your door. But God *does* want to see you contented and fulfilled. And He knows better than you what you need and should want in a mate."[18] While Clark doesn't believe Psalm 37:4 says that God will give us the particular person we may want right now, he does believe that God will give all of us the best mate designed for us. In *What's a Girl to Do While Waiting for Mr. Right?* Janet Folger looks at this same verse and comes to a conclusion similar to Clark's:

Many people never marry. We all know that. Some people don't *want* to . . . But what does God have to say? 'Delight yourself in the LORD and he will give you the desires of your heart' (Psalm 37:4). I've been trying to delight myself in Him ever since. Want to know my prayer? God, if the desires of my heart don't match Yours, then please change my desires. I've prayed that and meant it. But as of today, I still want to be married. That gives me hope that God will fulfill that desire.[19]

For both, the assumption is that if we have the desire for something good like marriage, God will provide it. But is this really what scripture is telling us in this passage? Or are we perhaps ignoring a deeper issue as we focus so intently on God fulfilling our desires for love, sex, and companionship here on earth? While we believe both are correct that God wants us contented and fulfilled, we would argue that God wants us to be contented and fulfilled in *him*. If we are truly delighting ourselves in the Lord, *he*, not a potential mate, will be the desire of our hearts. Of course this doesn't mean that we will necessarily stop desiring marriage, but it does mean that we will realize that a spouse will not provide true fulfillment.

The problem with discussions like Clark's and Folger's is that they tend to focus solely on a contemporary application for a particular verse without seeing that verse both in the context of the entire passage and also in the context of God's overall plan for humanity as it is revealed in the Bible. If we look at this verse and others like it within the context of the rest of the Bible,[20] surely we need to realize that the focus of the desires of our heart should not be simply for a spouse but rather for God, for he is the one who will mold us into the Christians he wants us to be by helping us to place all of our other desires in subjection to his will. Ultimately, the question revolves around our definition of happiness here in this world. Should we search for happiness through the medium of marriage, or should we determine what role happiness plays in God's plan for us?

Ramifications and Response

As we explore this issue, Eugene Peterson provides us with an interesting starting point. He references John Calvin's commentary on the Psalms when he asserts that "we must develop better and deeper concepts of happiness than those held by the world, which makes a happy life to consist in 'ease, honours, and great wealth.' "[21] For many of us the desire to marry would fall under "ease." While marriage certainly is a lot of hard work (a truth to which all our married friends would attest) and it certainly has its share of trials, most singles think being married would make life easier. We would have companionship and someone to turn to in a time of need; we would have an outlet for our sexual desires; we wouldn't have to worry about whom to bring to the company Christmas party; we would be accepted by the church. But is this truly all that God has in store for us? Peterson writes,

> We live in a time when everyone's goal is to be perpetually healthy and constantly happy. If any one of us fails to live up to the standards that are advertised as normative, we are labeled as a problem to be solved, and a host of well-intentioned people rush to try out various cures on us. Or we are looked on as an enigma to be unraveled, in which case we are subjected to endless discussions, our lives examined by researchers zealous for the clue that will account for our lack of health or happiness.[22]

Peterson's description of how people often react to those whose lives aren't "normative" and happy sounds remarkably like how the church reacts to those who are not married and even how society at large reacts to those who are not in a romantic relationship.

As the earlier quotation by Dobson illustrates, the Christian community often turns to marriage as a quick fix to all of these problems. But in *The Wounded Healer: Ministry in Contemporary Society* Henri Nouwen suggests that perhaps God never intended that we always be happy: "Many people suffer because of the false supposition on which they have based their lives. That supposition is that there should be no fear or loneliness, no confusion or doubt. But these sufferings can only be dealt with creatively when they are understood as wounds integral to our human condition."[23] Throughout scripture, God repeatedly works through suffering as a means of refining his children. If we desire to be molded into the Christians he wants us to be, shouldn't we be willing to relinquish these desires for marriage and what we think will bring us happiness in order to place ourselves completely in God's control? This is not to say that we should be fatalistic. Nor is it to say that God will never fulfill those desires but rather to remind ourselves that they cannot be our main source of hope.

So how do we find the balance between recognizing a desire for marriage and children and also avoiding unrealistic expectations that can only bring pain and discontentment? Many contemporary discussions of singleness do not make this distinction. The assumption is that if you hope and dream hard enough and long enough, God will fulfill your desire. Eugene Peterson, however, reminds us of important distinctions. He remarks,

> And hoping is not dreaming. It is not spinning an illusion or fantasy to protect us from our boredom or our pain. It means a confident, alert expectation that God will do what he said he will do. It is imagination put in the harness of faith. It is a willingness to let God do it his way and in his time. It is the opposite of making plans that we demand that God put into effect, telling him both how and when to do it. That is not hoping in God but bullying God.[24]

How often do contemporary authors on singleness ask us to "bully" God by reminding him that he must fulfill our desires in exactly the way we believe they should be fulfilled?

DIVORCE

Ultimately, our attitude toward happiness and the role that marriage and sex play in it does not only affect traditional singles, it also greatly affects the church's attitude toward those who are divorced. It is amazing, for instance, to see how this assumption that one must be married in order to be happy can rapidly change one's views on divorce and remarriage. A good friend of ours who is actively involved in the singles group of a mega church in her city developed a friendship with a woman, whom we will call Penny, who had been divorced three times. As she neared thirty, Penny felt the pressure to find husband number four. Our friend had always believed that scripture does not allow for remarriage. While we do not intend to debate that issue here, we do find it interesting that our friend's views on the subject radically changed because of this friendship with Penny. When asked why her views changed, she replied, "Why should Penny be denied happiness just because she made a mistake?"

Now, we are not advocating that the church become antagonistic toward those who are divorced. On the contrary, the church needs to show more love and support of those who are divorced. Not only do many divorced Christians feel rejected by their spouse, but they also feel rejected by their church. In the midst of their pain over their failed marriage, they need the loving support of a strong church family. Interestingly, though, the support that divorced Christians receive often focuses on getting them remarried. Without a positive message of celibacy and without a church that knows how to minister to their true needs, divorced Christians often see no other option but to seek relief from their pain in a new relationship.

A quick look through the relationship and self-help section of your local Christian bookstore reveals an alarming trend. A large percentage of these books are at least in part about helping those who are divorced to remarry. For instance, while Edward Tauber and Jim Smoke begin by cautioning those who are divorced from rushing into another marriage, their reasoning is basically the familiar advice to fix yourself before getting married: "When we are still adrift in blame-shifting, stigma-fighting, and emotion-sorting, we do not make great mates—and we are not in a good position to select one. Unfortunately, we forget that having gone through a divorce means we need to take some time to re-empower ourselves."[25] They, then, proceed to explain how their readers can ultimately find the "right one after divorce." Once again we have the assumption that once you have worked through your problems you will be ready to marry again. This leads to the belief that if you do not remarry, you must still have issues and are not *ready* to marry.

What seems to be lacking in many discussions of divorce is a positive understanding of abstinence and celibacy. Even those like Gary Thomas, who believes that Matthew 19:9 forbids remarriage in most cases, don't generally see celibacy as a real possibility for individuals who are divorced. Thomas, for example, sees what he believes to be the impossibility of celibacy as a reason to stay married: "Too many Christians enter the process of divorce assuming they can automatically remarry as soon as the divorce papers are finalized. But let's say we were to accept the biblical view (and our civil laws and church leaders were to support this), which would in most cases declare something like this: 'You may opt for a divorce, but you cannot ever engage in sex again with anyone else for the rest of your life.' Most, if not all, of the men would find or create a way to be reconciled. They would not choose celibacy."[26] While he may have a point that if remarriage were not an option, there would probably be fewer divorces, his dismissal of celibacy leaves those in the aftermath of divorce, particularly an unwanted divorce, in a precarious situation. Without a proper understanding of celibacy, many Christians see no other option but to remarry. And when marriage is seen as the source of happiness, many find themselves on an endless path of failed marriages in search of the one that will make them truly happy.

Homosexuality

These problematic ideas about happiness and marriage also affect those Christians who struggle with homosexual desires, for they imply that those homosexuals who cannot reorient themselves and enter into a heterosexual marriage are doomed to unhappiness. And, again, this idea that happiness should be our ultimate goal often leads individuals to relinquish deeply held values in favor of happiness. A good example of this occurred several years ago when a woman in Bonnie's Bible study asked for prayer for her daughter, who had just announced to the family that she was a lesbian. This woman strongly believed that what her daughter was doing was wrong, but she ultimately concluded that she would rather have her daughter live in sin and be happy than be alone. For her, happiness was more important than avoiding sin.

In *Sexual Character: Beyond Technique to Intimacy*, Marva Dawn addresses this precise issue when she explores the common argument that it's not fair for the church to "deny homosexuals any possibility for sexual fulfillment." Underlying this argument she sees four basic issues: (1) we idolize sex; (2) the Christian community does not offer proper support for those struggling with homosexuality; (3) we have the right to be happy and sexually fulfilled; and (4) we shouldn't have to suffer because of something that isn't our fault. In response to these issues Dawn draws from her own experiences with suffering. Because of her severe physical limitations, she cannot enjoy the music she loves, she cannot see to do the reading required by her work, and she cannot engage in athletic activities like she used to. As someone who has experienced both the joys of marriage and the difficulties of celibacy, she states that she would gladly give up sex in order to regain her vision. Her argument may seem harsh, but there is great truth in it. As she writes, "It is not too great a suffering to ask of homosexuals [or anyone else who is not married] that they remain celibate for the sake of the Kingdom of God. All of us have to bear certain sufferings in this broken and sinful world. And the grace of God makes them all bearable, whether they are physical, sexual, or other."[27]

Unfortunately, most of those struggling with homosexuality do not have a church community that is prepared to equip them with a positive understanding of celibacy, let alone the support to practice it. Far too many Christians think the only option is for homosexuals to reorient themselves and enter into a heterosexual marriage, but how many are able to do this? In a recent study, Stanton Jones of Wheaton College and

Mark Yarhouse of Regent University reveal that groups such as Exodus which offer help to those seeking freedom from homosexuality claim a 38% success rate: 15% enter into heterosexual relationships while 23% practice chastity.[28] What is particularly interesting about these statistics, however, is how the terms are defined. The 23% who practice chastity are at least considering heterosexual dating. If people still experience homosexual desire and do not see any increased attraction to the opposite sex, they are not classified as either a success or a failure. Rather, they are classified as "Continuing." Interestingly, this is the largest group, consisting of 29%.[29] Don't the people who fall into the 52% of individuals desiring change but not entering into heterosexual relationships need a strong, positive conception of celibacy to help them?

Rather than being seen as a wonderful opportunity to serve God, celibacy is seen repeatedly not only as second best but also as a guarantee of an unfulfilled, miserable life. How do we expect those who struggle with homosexuality or those recovering from divorce to see celibacy as a positive option when it is not seen as a valued alternative for other singles? As long as we live within a church that emphasizes marriage and happiness as the ultimate desires of our heart rather than reminding us that our ultimate desire should be for God, we risk not only alienating traditional singles, those dealing with divorce, and those struggling with homosexuality but also (and perhaps more importantly) reducing the truth of the Gospel to a simple vending machine that readily supplies all of the good things we desire as soon as we demand them.

Dangerous Message 4: Marriage is God's primary institution on earth

As justification for their focus on marriage, many contemporary Christian writers repeatedly insist that the primary importance of marriage for Christians is affirmed in scripture. James Dobson, for instance, in his zealousness to uphold traditional marriage and speak against homosexual unions writes, "First and foremost, the Holy Scriptures set forth the Creator's plan for marriage and family . . . This 'marriage' [between Adam and Eve] was the very first institution that God created, and it continues to be the primary institution of society to this day. God designed marriage between a man and a woman . . . as the means by which spiritual teaching is passed down through the generations."[30]

Joshua Harris expresses a similar sentiment in *I Kissed Dating Goodbye*: "Marriage is the first institution (Gen. 2:22–24). It was ordained before the family, before civil government—even before the church."[31] While writers like Dobson and Harris are certainly correct that marriage was the first institution established by God, this does not necessarily mean that it is the most important institution. Fortunately, Harris acknowledges this in his 2004 book *Stop Dating the Church!* when he writes that "the church is the only institution God promised to sustain forever" and that God created marriage to point to the church, not the other way around.[32] As we will explore in the next chapter, when Jesus begins to institute his church on earth, he challenges previously held ideas about family, asking his followers to devote themselves to him completely.

The assumption of some, though, is that because of marriage's primary importance to Christians, the church must conceive of its essential duty as a support system for the family. Debbie Maken, for instance, not only affirms the marriage of Adam and Eve as God's primary institution and repeatedly declares its continuing importance by arguing that the Christian faith grows through strong Christian families as parents pass on their values to their children, but she even goes so far as to admire the Puritans who with their "contempt" for single men encouraged them to marry.[33] For Maken, the church has the responsibility not only to support families but also to encourage (or shame) Christian singles into starting families. Should the church's primary goal really be supporting the family? Or is it the families (and singles) that should support the church and the Gospel of Christ? This issue will be discussed more fully in the next chapter, but here, we would like to focus on how this view of the primacy of marriage, whether conscious or subconscious, has influenced behaviors in the church. Generally, it leaves singles feeling excluded and searching for the support of Christian community.

Ramifications and Response

NEED FOR COMMUNITY

Without a spouse and children, single adults have an intense need for community, and the reality is that many churches have difficulty providing a nurturing community for them. While Christian authors often present contemporary singles as selfish loners who simply desire to achieve as much pleasure as possible, the evidence (both secular and

Christian) often demonstrates otherwise. Think about television shows such as *Friends*, *Seinfeld*, *Will and Grace*, and *Sex and the City*. Yes, these characters do live lives focused almost entirely upon themselves, but underneath it all they desperately need a community that loves and supports them. The characters in all of these shows form surrogate families with the other singles in their lives. They celebrate holidays with each other; and, as the theme song from *Friends* tells us, they are always there for each other, through good times and bad.

From a Christian perspective, John Stott attests to the importance of friendship and community when he remarks, "Single people are wise to develop as many friendships as possible, with people of all ages and both sexes. For example, although I have no children of my own, I have hundreds of adopted nieces and nephews all over the world, who call me 'Uncle John.' I cherish these affectionate relationships; they greatly lessen, even if they do not altogether deaden, occasional pangs of loneliness."[34] Stott's example provides a wonderful model for what Christian community might look like if we acknowledged the value of relationships beyond the biological family. How many Christian singles have this type of community, however? While it is true that some Christian singles have a large support network, this does not seem to be the norm.

For many Christians, loneliness rather than sexual desire is the most difficult problem with which they struggle, and this loneliness may stem in part from the lack of nurturing relationships that a true community of Christians would foster. In *I'm Lonely, Lord—How Long?: Meditations on the Psalms*, Marva Dawn addresses this issue directly when she discusses Psalm 68:6: "God sets the lonely in families." Unlike others who have used this verse as a promise that God will provide marriage and children, Dawn asks,

> What do our churches do for the lonely? How have God's people learned to love better so that we might be one of the primary families into which lonely persons are set? More and more as I travel throughout the country to teach, I grieve over the lack of concern in our churches, evidenced by the small number of single persons participating in congregations ... Consequently, I plead with you to be active, out of your own aloneness or out of your concern for a lonely person, to encourage deeper caring in your parish. Out of the healing that we experience can come a powerful ministry of sensitivity to the needs of others around us who also long to be enfamilied.[35]

141

Those of us who are single must accept some of the responsibility for being lonely in the church. As Dawn recommends, we should use our loneliness as an opportunity to reach out to others who are lonely, and we should use our singleness as an opportunity to become more involved in our church communities rather than as an excuse to feel sorry for ourselves because others are not reaching out to us. But the families in the church have a responsibility as well to embrace the lonely rather than exclude them.

INVOLVEMENT IN COMMUNITY

But how often are Christian singles able to become productive members of their local church communities? Many Christian singles run into one of two difficulties: either becoming overcommitted and burnt out or longing to be involved but finding that their church doesn't seem to want their participation. People often assume that single adults have a lot of free time and may, therefore, be called upon for any and all church duties. After all, isn't that what Paul says in 1 Corinthians 7:32–34?

> But I want you to be free from concern. One who is unmarried is concerned about the things of the Lord, how he may please the Lord; but one who is married is concerned about the things of the world, how he may please his wife, and his interests are divided. The woman who is unmarried, and the virgin, is concerned about the things of the Lord, that she may be holy both in body and spirit; but one who is married is concerned about the things of the world, how she may please her husband.

In this passage, however, Paul never says that single adults have more time. He says that the married have divided interests. In addition to the concerns of the Lord, they have to consider their spouse and children. While single adults generally do not have to work their schedules and priorities around someone else's, this does not necessarily mean they have more time. When most married people look back on the amount of time they had when they were single, they generally think of a time right out of school when they had few responsibilities. They associate responsibilities and busy schedules with marriage.

For older singles in particular, the idea that they automatically have more time than the married couples around them can be frustrating. As Laura Smit remarks, "A responsible single adult living alone may actually have less time than many married people, since he or she has no partner with whom to share the many chores of maintaining a home

142

and organizing daily life."[36] As Smit recognizes, singles may not always be in the position to do all that might be asked of them, and they may become frustrated with a church community that expects that their freedom as singles means an automatic "yes" to every request.

While this danger of being overcommitted may be the experience of some singles, others experience the exact opposite. Some single adults find it difficult to integrate into church ministries. It is as if the church just doesn't know what to do with "those singletons." In a response to a poll conducted by ChristianSinglesToday.com, one reader expressed his frustration with trying to serve in a church after his wife passed away:

> I'm an ordained minister and have pastored churches and taught at a Bible college. But that was when I was married. Now that my wife has died and I'm single again, it seems all I'm allowed to do is lead the singles ministry—and only as a volunteer.
>
> I get very little response when I send my résumé for positions of pastor, associate pastor, or even singles pastor. Most churches seem to be looking for a married person to lead their ministries, including the singles ministry. This doesn't make sense with today's demographics. Single adults constitute at least 52 percent of the adult population. When the church doesn't recognize this and make adjustments to their paradigm, they're missing more than half the potential people who might come to church.[37]

For single women, this exclusion may also become an issue because a woman's sphere of ministry is often seen to revolve around the family and home. When many women's ministries and activities are focused on being good wives and mothers, single women often feel out of place and may wonder where they should go to use the talents God has given them.

Exclusion from Community

Why are singles excluded from so many church ministries? One reason might be that the requirements for leadership in 1 Timothy 3 list being the "husband of one wife."[38] Interestingly, though, while some churches do take this literally and only allow men who have been married once and are currently married to hold positions of leadership, many do not, allowing much more flexibility in this point by including women and remarried individuals. But even in these churches, singles often have a difficult time assuming leadership positions. The question, then, is why? Interestingly, the idea that a married Christian is more suitable for these roles seems to stem, at least in part, from the assumption that single adults are inherently immature and selfish. In his discussion of the need to integrate singles into the church, Paul Peterson records a conversation with a senior pastor that reveals the stereotypes that often circulate around single Christians. After mentioning that he was involved in "single adult ministry," Peterson asked the pastor if there was a ministry to singles in his church. The pastor replied, "No way! Those single people only take and never give. They don't go to church and they don't pledge. Besides, they're all promiscuous and will cause our counseling load to increase too much."[39] Granted, this pastor's response is probably extreme, but there does seem to be a sense in many churches that singles don't have the spiritual maturity to be in church leadership. The perception is that they are far too selfish to commit to a church (perhaps because they have not yet committed to a spouse).

Selfishness is a real temptation for Christian singles. As John Stott explains, "Apart from sexual temptation . . . the greatest danger which I think we face is self-centeredness. We may live alone and have total freedom to plan our own schedule, with nobody else to modify it or even give us advice. If we are not careful, we may find the whole world revolving around ourselves."[40] Yes, single adults struggle with selfishness, but let's not forget that married adults do as well. It is a human problem, not a singles problem. We are often told that marriage and parenthood teach us selflessness and unconditional love. To some extent this is true. There is no love like parents' love for their children, but that doesn't mean that they don't struggle with selfishness in their other relationships. Some of the most selfish people we know are married. This doesn't mean that they wouldn't do anything for their children, but how much would they sacrifice for someone else's child?

Selfishness is a problem, particularly when it keeps us from doing what God commands us to do as we focus on our own desires rather than his. But as we discussed in chapter four, some Christians take this idea even further to argue that simply being single is inherently selfish, for singles have refused to obey God's "command" to marry. What is ironic is that this idea of selfishness can work in reverse as well. The intense pressure to marry can actually make singles selfish, for rather than focusing on God and his work in their lives, they may focus almost exclusively on their own desires for a spouse. When we were in our twenties, we had a mutual friend in her forties who fit this stereotype perfectly. We can't count the number

144

of conversations where she would breathlessly tell of the new, "hot," single guy who had made an appearance at the church singles group. She would obsessively plot how she was going to capture his attention and compulsively daydream about the perfect marriage and family they would have one day. Of course, once this relationship never materialized, she would be devastated—at least until the next single guy grabbed her attention. This woman was a professional with a good job and myriad opportunities to use her talents to serve God, but she spent so much of her time acting like a silly teenager that she never seemed to mature spiritually.

Focusing on marriage as God's primary institution on earth and urging all Christian singles to marry as quickly as possible might be a means of trying to protect the sanctity of marriage in the midst of a secular culture that often devalues marriage, but this message has some very dangerous ramifications not only for singles but also for the church as a whole. Not only does it make true community within the church difficult as marrieds and singles are increasingly segregated, but it also tends to keep singles from demonstrating their God-given gifts within the church as much as they should. Rather than asking singles to participate fully within God's community and compelling them to mature in their walks with God, it creates an excuse for those who aren't married, allowing them to persist in their immaturity until they are granted a spouse. Surely, the church should be a place that welcomes all into community and then challenges all individuals no matter what their marital status is to grow in their relationships with God and with others. The truth is, however, that this is too rarely the case.

Coping with These Dangerous Messages

Any older single within the evangelical church has probably experienced at least one of these dangerous messages—if not all of them. And most singles have developed coping mechanisms to deal with them. They may find themselves accepting the messages and then doing anything possible to get married and escape the dreaded state of singleness. They may jump from church to church trying to find one where they can avoid these messages. They may endure the messages in public and then gripe to their single friends in private. They may sequester themselves in a large singles group so that they don't need to interact with the married members of the church. Some, we fear, may leave the church entirely, for while dealing with these messages individually is difficult enough, confronting them all can be overwhelming.

Unfortunately, rather than addressing these negative messages and helping Christian singles to negotiate the complexities of singleness, many churches either actively promote these negative messages or don't even realize that they exist, leaving singles without any coherent way to combat them. Because they have rarely heard any different messages about singleness, and celibacy is something that only seems to apply to Catholics, many singles are left feeling that something is not right, but they aren't sure what. Is it only wishful thinking, or is there another way to approach singleness? Is there, perhaps, an empowering message of singleness and celibacy in scripture that has been overshadowed by the contemporary emphasis on family values? We believe that there is, and through the next few chapters, we will explore what scripture, the early church, and contemporary Christian writers have to say about celibacy and singleness within God's plan of Christian community. Perhaps Christian singles don't have to be condemned to feeling like outsiders in the church. Perhaps they may, instead, embrace their singleness, submitted to what God wishes to teach them through it.

Part 3

Searching for a New Direction

7

Covenant & Inclusion
Views of Celibacy in Scripture

As Christians we believe that every Christian in one generation might be called to singleness, yet God will create the church anew.

Stanley Hauerwas, *After Christendom*

My family name might perish when they put me in the grave
But I've learned it's not the family name that matters anyway
There's a stronger Name that covers me on every single day
I'm a man who's never married; I will give that Name away

Allen Levi, "Love to Give Away"

Recently Skye Jethani, one of the pastors at Christine's church, preached a sermon entitled "What Child is this who came not to bring peace?" This sermon was part of an advent series that challenged Christians to grapple with the complexities of scripture surrounding the person of Christ rather than simply accepting the traditional Christmas image of the sweet, nonthreatening Baby Jesus who came to make us all peaceful and happy. By drawing attention to Matthew 10:34–37, Pastor Jethani reminded the congregation that this Prince of Peace also declared, "Do not think that I came to bring peace on the earth; I did not come to bring peace, but a sword." Interestingly, as the verses continue, Christ reveals that his truth will divide family members from each other, for "a man's enemies will be the members of his household" (v. 36). As Pastor Jethani pointed out in his sermon, this is not the "family values" message of Christmas that we usually receive. Instead, it is a challenge that reminds us where our ultimate loyalty must lie. As Christine listened to this message, she was struck by how radical it seemed, particularly in the context of Christmas, for in today's evangelical church, it is not a message that is often emphasized. In the late twentieth and early twenty-first centuries, the emphasis on family in most evangelical churches has almost completely overshadowed this truth—that we must not allow any human ties to come between us and our Savior. For single Christians, this is a powerful message, for it reminds us that our identity needs to be fully grounded in Christ rather than in a (potential or actual) spouse.

As we have seen in previous chapters, however, this truth is often overshadowed by all of the problematic messages about singleness, sex, and marriage that singles receive from the church. How, then, do we deal with all of the dangerous implications of the ideas we have already explored? We must do what Pastor Jethani challenged his congregation to do in his sermon: turn directly to scripture, acknowledge the complexities that we find there, and recognize that the God we serve transcends our own cultural ideals. While it may be difficult to see in the midst of an often marriage-obsessed evangelical culture, scripture does present a positive view of celibacy, for it continually shows us that our focus should be on our mission here on earth as it prepares us for eternity with Christ rather than on the temporal realities of marriage and family. This is certainly not to say that scripture degrades marriage and family, for it does not. But it places family values in subordination to the church and its mission here on earth.

Refusing to Over-romanticize Marriage in Scripture

One of the first steps to helping us see the positive view of celibacy in scripture is refusing to over-romanticize verses on marriage, taking them out of their own biblical and cultural context to provide models for our own romance obsessed culture. Carrie Miles, for instance, recognizes that even in the midst of the important project of affirming marriage within a secular culture that often degrades traditional Christian values, we must be careful not to overemphasize the value of marriage. She remarks,

> As we begin to bring together the biblical message about marriage, sex, and family and apply it to today, the first thing to realize is that all three of these things are completely optional. There is no biblical mandate to marry or have children, and certainly none to suggest that people could not live without sex . . . In fact, the Bible tells us that despite the compelling love depicted in the Song of Songs, the key to a joyful life is found not in our family arrangements but in our relationship with God.[1]

This perspective, however, is not one that we often see. Instead, we find ourselves confronted repeatedly with messages that affirm the value of marriage over almost everything else.

For many, this discussion has become an either/or proposition: either you uphold the values of marriage and family or you prioritize singleness. Rather than accepting this polarization of ideas, we would like to suggest that the complexities of scripture present a both/and proposition in which either may be used by God to develop individuals into the Christian witnesses that he desires them to be. Marriage certainly has an important place in scripture. As theologian Stanley Grenz points out, marriage provides us with an important image of "the intimacy of relationship within the Godhead."[2] He remarks,

> Marriage is . . . intended to form a reflection of God as the One who loves. Specifically, the exclusive nature of the divine love is presented in the marital bond. As it incorporates its divinely given design to be the intimate, permanent bond arising out of the dialectic of sameness and difference, marriage reflects the exclusive relationship of love found within the Trinity, for there is no other God but the Father, Son, and Spirit. Marriage is likewise an apt metaphor for the exclusive love of God for creation.[3]

Marriage, however, is not the only image that we have of God's nature, since "singleness is indeed an expression of the divine will, for it too can be a means for the realization of the human destiny as the community of male and female and thereby a reflection of the divine nature."[4] The complexities of the Bible allow for both, and we need to keep them both in mind as we turn to interpret scripture. Yes, it is true that Jesus performed his first miracle at a wedding, but he also raised a single guy from the dead.

Too often, contemporary evangelical writers focus on only one aspect of this complexity as they use scripture to support their argument. Take, for example, Debbie Maken who argues from Genesis 2 that "as offspring of Adam and Eve, we too were made with a spouse-shaped hole that only a husband can occupy."[5] According to this logic, the story of Adam and Eve demonstrates that we are incomplete without a spouse, and only when we marry, will we be within God's perfect will. Is this the best way to interpret the passage, particularly when we think of the examples of singles in the New Testament (not only Jesus, Paul, and John the Baptist but perhaps even Lazarus, Barnabas, and many others) who manage not only to be complete but also within God's will?

In *Singles at the Crossroads: A Fresh Perspective on Christian Singleness*, Albert Hsu provides a different perspective on this passage that takes these other examples in scripture into account. He argues,

> Because it is a narrative passage, we must be careful about reading general instructions for all people when we really only have a description of what God did in the case of Adam and Eve. Clearly the first man needed a woman if the human race was to have any offspring . . . A safe conclusion one may make from reading this passage is that "if you ever discover that you are the only surviving representative of your sex in the world, and you come across your only existing counterpart, the two of you should consider marriage."[6]

As Hsu continues his discussion of Genesis 2, he acknowledges that the passage does point out the need for companionship, but he reveals through the examples of Jesus and Paul that companionship does not necessarily need to be found solely in marriage.[7] While Maken later acknowledges the example of Paul, she cannot conceive of a world in which both singleness and marriage might be equally valued. Instead, she discounts Paul's words in 1 Corinthians 7:1–2, remarking, "Some modern translations render this 'not to marry,' but if that were correct, then Paul would be undermining the first three chapters of Genesis."[8] While Candice Watters does not dismiss Paul so easily, she demonstrates a similar privileging of Genesis when she quotes Hubert Morken: " 'The creation mandate has never been rescinded. Never in Scripture did God say, "OK, I have enough people now. You can stop getting married and having babies." ' "[9] Maken and Watters are just two of many writers for whom this particular interpretation of the Genesis account of the creation and marriage of Adam and Eve becomes the lens from which we must view the rest of scripture. For them, anything that does not accord with this view of marriage must be discarded.

But where does that lead us? For Maken, it leads to several problematic interpretations of biblical passages. Take, for example, her interpretation of the stories of Isaac and Rebekah (Genesis 24) and Jacob and Rachel (Genesis 29–30), which she uses to demonstrate the way she believes courtship ought to be conducted in contemporary society. Taking these stories as a manual for courtship, she declares that they demonstrate "what God intends for us through the protection of family and an active negotiating father."[10] For Maken, just as Adam and Eve's story reveals the primacy of marriage, Rebekah's and Rachel's stories reveal the appropriate means of achieving this state. And Maken certainly isn't alone in her desire to use scripture as a dating manual. For Christian girls and young women in particular, women in the Bible have often been presented as models for them to follow, and these models are almost always connected directly to a romance narrative.[11] What is interesting, though, is what Maken and others must leave out of the stories in order for them to fit with the conception that scripture is a guidebook for courtship and marriage. Nowhere in her extended discussion of these stories does Maken mention Rachel's sister Leah or the conflicts that arise between them that result in the servants Bilhah and Zilpah also becoming part of this polygamous marriage. Is Laban truly to be our image of the good father who cares for his daughter by placing her within a loving marriage? What do we do with the fact that he tricks Jacob into marrying Leah first? By over-romanticizing this story and using it for a model of Christian courtship and marriage, Maken enacts a problematic hermeneutic in which anything that does not fit may be elided.

Seeing scripture solely through a lens which privileges marriage above all else as the crucible through which God works is problematic not only for Maken but also for others such as Gary Thomas, who in his book *Sacred Marriage* provides a problematic interpretation of 1 Corinthians

7:5. Following biblical scholar Gordon Fee's interpretation, Thomas argues that Paul reveals that "*abstinence within marriage* can distract us from prayer."[12] Taking this argument even further, Thomas remarks, "Sleeping with your spouse can leave your heart, mind, and soul free, for a time, to vigorously pursue God in prayer without distraction."[13] For Thomas, the interpretation rests on where one places the commas within the verse. While the verse could read, "Stop depriving one another, except by agreement for a time so that you may devote yourselves to prayer, and come together again so that Satan will not tempt you because of your lack of self-control," Thomas argues that it should read "Stop depriving one another, except by agreement, so that you may devote yourselves to prayer." According to Thomas, "By engaging in sexual relations within a permanent, lifelong relationship, a major temptation and distraction is removed, and our souls are placed at rest."[14] With this type of reasoning, celibate singles seem to have no hope of devoting themselves in prayer to God since they have no way of relieving the sexual tension.

But is the interpretation really an issue of where to place the commas? What about the context into which the verse is placed? Now, we must grant that 1 Corinthians 7 is not an easy passage to interpret. As David Garland remarks in his commentary on this chapter, "Paul's mention of a letter to him complicates the task because it obliges the interpreter to attempt some reconstruction of what in the letter prompted his response."[15] The fact that Paul begins with what seems to be a quotation or paraphrase of the letter ("it is good for a man not to touch a woman") suggests that he is refuting this idea, but how far does he take it? Is he truly arguing that sexual activity is necessary within marriage to clear the mind for prayer? Garland argues that the context of the entire passage suggests that "Paul cautiously agrees with the Corinthians' preference for celibacy for the unmarried, but he disagrees with any effort to coerce others to conform to what one may regard as ideal."[16] In the early verses of this chapter, Paul recognizes that prolonged celibacy within marriage is not appropriate, but as the chapter continues, Paul also affirms singleness with statements such as "I wish that all men were even as I myself am" (v. 7) and "But I say to the unmarried and to widows that it is good for them if they remain even as I" (v. 8). With statements such as this in the rest of the chapter, it is difficult to argue that Paul is trying to convey the idea that sexual activity is an important—let alone essential—component in clearing the mind for prayer.

In fact, when we turn to 1 Corinthians 7:32–33, Paul seems to argue the opposite: "But I want you to be free from concern. One who is unmarried is concerned about the things of the Lord, how he may please the Lord; but one who is married is concerned about the things of the world, how he may please his wife." When placed within the context of the entire passage, then, what Paul seems to be arguing in verse 5 is that since abstinence within marriage can lead to dangerous temptations, it cannot be imposed upon a spouse, but it may be mutually agreed upon for a time when both spouses devote themselves to prayer. As Garland remarks, "Because abstinence is not to be the norm in marriage, Paul allows only a temporary withdrawal from sexual intercourse."[17] For Thomas, however, the idea of abstinence (even for a brief time while in marriage) seems so problematic that he must explain it away through reconfiguring the verse and taking it out of the context of the passage. His emphasis on marriage and a proper sexual relationship within it has ultimately led him to devalue singleness and celibacy.

Debbie Maken takes this idea of the primacy of marriage even further as she repeatedly explains away examples of righteous celibacy. Not only does she discount Paul's words in 1 Corinthians 7 as being impossible to reconcile with Genesis, but she also offers a very narrow interpretation of Jesus's words in Matthew 19:11–12:

> But He said to them, "Not all men can accept this statement, but only those to whom it has been given. For there are eunuchs who were born that way from their mother's womb; and there are eunuchs who were made eunuchs by men; and there are also eunuchs who made themselves eunuchs for the sake of the kingdom of heaven. He who is able to accept this, let him accept it."

Maken asserts that "the only exception Jesus acknowledged is for those who have received a clear direction from God to be single . . . or those whose physical design, whether by birth or injury, precludes their participation in marriage."[18] While Albert Hsu, among others, sees these verses as being empowering for singles since "Jesus' teaching in Matthew 19 . . . affirms that *single persons are no less whole people for lack of marriage*, in contrast to Jewish thought,"[19] Maken asserts just the opposite: unless a single person has a clear call from God (which is seemingly manifested in a lack of sexual desire) or is physically incapable of sexual activity, he or she must be married. While the implications of these particular verses on their own may be debated, what is not up for debate is where these interpretations lead. Ultimately, Maken declares, "There is not a shred of evidence in Scripture that God is *willing* to fill the spouse-shaped void with himself."[20] Single Christians, then, are doomed to be incomplete, containing within them an emptiness that even God will not fill.

Does this truly accord with scripture, though? Isaiah 54:4–5, which tells the widows to "Fear not, for you will not be put to shame; and do not feel humiliated, for you will not be disgraced" and then declares, "For your husband is your Maker, whose name is the LORD of hosts," seems directly to contradict this assertion. Even when you place these verses within the context of a prophecy to the nation of Israel rather than a promise to a particular single woman, it reveals that our true love and loyalty need to be given to the one Spouse who will ultimately fulfill our needs. The issue, then, is deeper than simply the question of whether or not God will provide an individual with a spouse or whether he will fill that particular desire with himself. Instead, it is a question of where our needs ultimately lie. When in Philippians 4:19, we receive the promise that "my God will supply all your needs according to his riches in glory in Christ Jesus," should we assume that all of our needs will be satisfied by temporal provisions here on earth? Or is Paul speaking of deeper needs for God and the fact that ultimately our "needs" here on earth pale in comparison to our great need for God which is ultimately fulfilled only through our communion with him?

Perhaps Jeremiah 29:11 may give us some insight on this issue. This verse will probably be very familiar to anyone whose life has not met their expectations, for it is often invoked to provide hope to those in desperate situations. In this verse, the Lord declares, "For I know the plans that I have for you . . . plans for welfare and not for calamity to give you a future and a hope." Single Christians are often given this verse to provide them with hope that God's plans for our welfare will include a spouse and that we must simply live in faith until that moment arrives. The problem with this interpretation of the verse is that it not only ignores the realities of God's work on earth but also the specific context of this promise. Does God truly prosper every Christian in this world? Are every single Christian's sexual desires miraculously fulfilled? We all know of godly Christians who have not been healed of cancer, or who have not been given the child they so ardently long for, or who have not been provided with a spouse. How, then, do we interpret this promise, which seems to guarantee Christians a prosperous life full of all the good things that will give them a future and a hope?

Perhaps the answer lies in the context of the verse. This is not a word to an individual Israelite or an individual Christian. Instead, it is spoken to the Jewish exiles who have been carried off to Babylon. And it is prefaced in the previous verse by the recognition that the deliverance that they long for will not occur for seventy years. The reality is that in seventy years, most of the individuals who are now hearing the promise will be dead. The promise, then, is not for prosperity in our own individual lifetimes but rather for the hope that God provides for the Jewish nation and his work through them. Commenting on this passage in Jeremiah, Lisa Graham McMinn remarked in a chapel message at Wheaton College, "The redemption that you long for does not always come in your lifetime."[21] The real issue is not whether we are good enough Christians so that God will supply our needs here on earth, but rather whether we have our priorities straight so that we can recognize that our ultimate need for God will not be completely satisfied until we are with him in heaven.

We are reminded of this in Hebrews 11. Twice in this chapter detailing great examples of faith throughout the Old Testament, the author of Hebrews tells us that "all these died in faith, without receiving the promises" (v. 13, and repeated in different words in v. 39). Yes, Abraham and Sarah received their child, Moses led God's people out of Egypt, and Rahab was spared when Jericho was destroyed; but all of these great men and women of faith were waiting for something more, something that would not be granted in their lifetime: the appearance of the Messiah. Verse 16 tells us that they had their eyes fixed on their heavenly home not their earthly one, and as many of the later examples demonstrate, this earthly home was often filled with many difficult trials (vv. 35–38). The point of this great chapter of faith is not that God will give us everything we want if we have enough faith. Hebrews 12:1–2 tells us what the point of this chapter really is, that we follow their examples of faith and "run with endurance the race that is set before us, fixing our eyes on Jesus."

In our eagerness to emphasize the importance of marriage in a society that often seems to devalue it, we must be careful not to lose sight of the central focus of scripture: God reconciling us to himself through Christ's work on the cross. Those who focus on the primacy of marriage in scripture often remark that the Bible not only begins with a marriage, but it ends with one as well. And it is true that in Revelation 21:1–4, we are presented with a glorious vision of "the holy city, new Jerusalem, coming down out of heaven from God, made ready as a bride adorned for her husband" (v. 2). But what type of marriage is this? It is certainly not a glorification of individual marriages here on earth that simply become more perfect visions of our connection with God in heaven, for we are told in Matthew 22:30 that marriage as we understand it will not exist in heaven. Rather, it is a radically new vision of marriage in which God brings his church into complete union with himself. As Doug Rosenau and Michael Todd Wilson remark, ". . . although true sex in marriage completes the earthly metaphor [of intimacy between Christ and his Bride, the church] it too remains an incomplete and 'dimly reflected' mirror of the *ultimate* intimacy . . . that will be fully satisfied only by God *himself* at the end of the divine love story in heaven."[22] This new intimacy not only takes the place of marriage here on earth but also allows singles to participate joyfully even if they never received a spouse.

Recognizing the Shifts That Occur from the Old Testament to the New Testament

In addition to refusing to over-romanticize marriage as it is presented in scripture, we must also keep in mind the shifts that occur from the Old Testament to the New Testament, for they provide important contexts for our interpretations of marriage and celibacy in scripture. In Galatians 4:1–7 Paul points out just how transformative the coming of Christ is:

> Now I say, as long as the heir is a child, he does not differ at all from a slave although he is owner of everything, but he is under guardians and managers until the date set by the father. So also we, while we were children, were held in bondage under the elemental things of the world. But when the fullness of the time came, God sent forth His Son, born of a woman, born under the Law, so that He might redeem those who were under the Law, that we might receive the adoption as sons. Because you

are sons, God has sent forth the Spirit of His Son into our hearts, crying "Abba! Father!" Therefore you are no longer a slave, but a son; and if a son, then an heir through God.

In these verses, Paul reveals that the transformation from slave to son is not simply a transformation from an individual unredeemed sinner to a redeemed Christian, but rather it is also a historical shift from a world in which relationship with God was measured by the Law to one in which Christ's redemption frees us from the bondage of that Law. As these verses indicate, Christ's birth, death, and resurrection are a radical turning point in history, and this radical transformation must be kept in mind as we view marriage and celibacy in the Bible.

In the Old Testament marriage is the norm. In fact, as Rodney Clapp points out in *Families at the Crossroads: Beyond Traditional & Modern Options*, "Marriage was so taken for granted that biblical Hebrew has no term for bachelor."[23] In order to be part of society, individuals needed to be members of a family. Those who were not were considered outsiders or outcasts, and particularly for women, the exclusion from family meant destitution. The book of Ruth with its representation of the kinsman redeemer clearly reveals the important role that family played in Jewish culture. As a widow, Ruth was destined to live a precarious life, existing on the little that she could glean from the fields of landowners around her. The tradition of the kinsman redeemer, however, was allowed so that women in Ruth's predicament could be integrated back into the family and back into a secure position within society. It was also allowed so that men could be assured of heirs to carry on their name even if they died before having children. Deuteronomy 25:5–10 clearly sets out this practice whereby the dead husband's brother had the responsibility to "go in to [his brother's wife] and take her to himself as wife and perform the duty of a husband's brother to her. It shall be that the firstborn whom she bears shall assume the name of his dead brother, so that his name will not be blotted out from Israel" (vv. 5–6). As Clapp points out, "The Hebrews did not have a highly developed notion of the afterlife."[24] For them, the genealogical line was the only way to insure their legacy. While the story of Ruth is often discussed as a romantic fairy tale in which Ruth, by being a faithful daughter-in-law, gains a good husband, it is also a good representation of the high position that marriage and family held in Jewish culture. By acting as the kinsman redeemer, Boaz not only integrates Ruth (and by extension Naomi) back into the culture, but he also allows the line of Naomi and her husband Elimelech to continue, leading not only to the birth of King David but also to the Messiah.

As God establishes his covenant with Israel in the Old Testament, then, he works through these cultural traditions, using the family as the means through which his covenant will be manifested. In Genesis 12:2, God promises Abram, "I will make you a great nation, and I will bless you, and make your name great." Later in Genesis 15, when Abram questions how this will happen since he and Sarai are childless, the Lord reaffirms his promise, declaring, "Now look toward the heavens, and count the stars, if you are able to count them . . . So shall your descendents be" (v. 5). With the miraculous birth of Isaac, God sets in motion this plan, which eventually leads to the twelve tribes of Israel, the establishment of the kingdoms of Israel and Judah, and the birth of the Messiah. As the genealogies in Matthew 1 and Luke 3 demonstrate, the family connections that lead to the Messiah are extremely important. In the Old Testament, then, the hope for the nation of Israel is wrapped up in the continuance of the family line. We do have a few examples of individuals who remain celibate in order to serve God such as Jeremiah, who in Jeremiah 16:2 is told, "You shall not take a wife for yourself nor have sons or daughters in this place." But, for the most part, God's covenant with Israel is manifested through family connections.[25]

This emphasis on God's work being accomplished through marriage and family in the Old Testament has led some to conclude that God continues to work this way throughout the New Testament and even today. Maken, for instance, argues that "marriage is the pool from which the Covenant continues and the number of the elect is completed."[26] From her perspective, Christian singles, just like those in the Abrahamic line of the Old Testament, have the responsibility to marry, for "[singleness] produces fewer members for the kingdom of heaven than if singles married young and produced more children during their most fertile years."[27] Others like Laura Smit see an important shift that occurs with the coming of Christ that radically changes how God's work is manifested in this world. According to Smit,

> Christians recognize the coming of Christ as a turning point of history and his second coming as the culmination of history. Everything

in the world is measured in relationship to these two events. Jesus was the fulfillment of all the promises that preceded him in Scripture, but he also inaugurated a new way of life. The people of Israel, a biologically defined nation, were replaced by the church, a called-out people in whom the barriers of tribe and race are transcended. The kingdom of God broke into history with the coming of Jesus, and that kingdom will be fulfilled when Jesus comes again. From now on our orientation must be toward the future, the promise of the New Jerusalem. The changes that Jesus introduced are far reaching, and one area that was changed forever was marriage.[28]

The question that arises is how do we view this shift from the Old Covenant to the New Covenant? And most importantly for this discussion, how does that shift influence our views of marriage and celibacy?

John Piper provides important insights on these questions. Like Smit, Piper sees a radical shift from the Old Testament to the New where "the family of God grows not by propagation through sexual intercourse but by regeneration through faith in Christ."[29] Piper turns to Isaiah 56:1–7 to demonstrate how this incredibly countercultural idea is actually foreshadowed in the Old Testament. In a world where family connections were everything, Isaiah's statement in this passage is remarkable: "Nor let the eunuch say, 'Behold, I am a dry tree.' For thus says the LORD, 'To the eunuchs who keep my Sabbaths, and choose what pleases Me, and hold fast My covenant, to them I will give in My house and within My walls a memorial, and a name better than that of sons and daughters; I will give them an everlasting name which will not be cut off'" (vv. 3–5). As he explores this passage, Piper places it within the context of Isaiah 53, which prophetically describes Christ's death for our transgressions. In verse 10, Isaiah prophesies, "But the LORD was pleasedto crush Him, putting Him to grief; if He would render Himself as a guilt offering, He will see His offspring, He will prolong His days, and the good pleasure of the LORD will prosper in His hand." As a celibate, single man, Jesus had no physical offspring; so, as Piper remarks, the reference to his offspring in this verse must refer to the church that is inaugurated in the New Testament. For Piper, this verse sets the stage for an important transition from the Old Covenant to the New, where loyalty to Christ supersedes family connections and allows for singles to become part of the new family of the church. With this context in mind, Isaiah's affirmation of those who are denied children, whether they are the barren women described in chapter 54 or the eunuchs of chapter 56, makes much more sense, for as his prophecy of the Messiah makes clear, the time was coming when becoming a spiritual child of Christ would be much more important than being part of the actual Jewish lineage of the Messiah.

When we turn to the New Testament, we find this idea reaffirmed again and again, for throughout the Gospels, Jesus continually reminds his followers that loyalty to him must take precedence over loyalty to family. As we have already noted, in Matthew 10:34–37 Jesus remarks that he has not necessarily come to create harmony in families, for "he who loves father or mother more than Me is not worthy of Me; and he who loves son or daughter more than Me is not worthy of Me" (v. 37). This is echoed in Matthew 12:47–50 where Jesus, when told that his mother and brothers wish to speak to him, asks, "Who is My mother and who are My brothers?" (v. 48) and then gestures to his disciples, declaring, "Behold My mother and My brothers! For whoever does the will of My Father who is in heaven, he is My brother and sister and mother" (vv. 49–50). The realities of this new loyalty are made quite clear in Luke 9:59–60, where Jesus responds to a young man's request to be allowed to bury his father before following him with the statement, "Allow the dead to bury their own dead; but as for you, go and proclaim everywhere the kingdom of God" (v. 60). Later in Luke's gospel when Peter remarks that the disciples have left their homes to follow Jesus, Jesus replies with words that sound very similar to the promise given to the eunuchs in Isaiah: "Truly I say to you, there is no one who has left house or wife or brothers or parents or children, for the sake of the kingdom of God, who shall not receive many times as much at this time and in the age to come, eternal life" (Luke 18:29–30). In contrast both to the patriarchal culture of the time and to the realities of the Old Covenant, Jesus emphasizes repeatedly that family ties no longer take precedence. As Lauren Winner remarks, "This is not the stuff of 'family values.'"[30]

The New Testament, then, presents a world in which participation in the covenant is dependent upon an individual's relationship with Christ, setting up a new type of family connection, not one based upon biological ties but one based upon spiritual connections to Christ and his church. In a sermon entitled "United through Christ's Suffering," Skye

Jethani reveals how one brief moment on the cross clearly demonstrates this transformation. In John 19:26–27, Jesus places his mother in the care of "the disciple whom He loved" whom scholars have taken to be John, himself. As Pastor Jethani points out, Jesus had relatives who, culturally, would be expected to care for his mother, but rather than depending upon those biological ties, Jesus turns to one of his disciples, essentially asking that she be cared for by the Christian community that would rise up around John and the other disciples. With this statement Jesus places this Christian community above the nuclear family.

In her discussion of this shift that occurs between the Old and New Testaments, Laura Smit reflects upon the significance that it holds for our ideas about marriage and singleness. She remarks,

> Reformed theologian Max Thurian summarizes the discontinuity between the old and the new covenant on this subject. He points out that in the Old Testament the primary purpose of marriage was to have children who would carry on the tradition of Israel. In the New Testament, however, marriage is understood primarily in terms of the relationship that reflects the union of Christ and the church. This shift occurs because under the new covenant we become members of the community of faith through baptism, signifying our adoption in Christ, rather than being born into the nation of Israel . . . The coming of Jesus changed the meaning of marriage and raised the possibility of celibacy, that is, intentional abstinent singleness. On the one hand, marriage is no longer necessary, having become one of two possible ways of obedient life, the other being celibacy. On the other hand, marriage is now sanctified (or resanctified) as a model of the relationship between Christ, the bridegroom, and his bride, the church.[31]

As Smit points out, the shift does not devalue marriage, but it does allow celibacy to become a valid option for Christians. No longer is the covenant dependent upon biological heirs. Instead, as Stanley Hauerwas mentions, "As Christians we believe that every Christian in one generation might be called to singleness, yet God will create the church anew."[32] The amazing work of Christ's salvation means that our family is redefined. We no longer have to search for a kinsman redeemer to provide a physical heir to keep the family line intact. Instead, we are called to make disciples of others, creating spiritual heirs that will allow for the continuation of the church.

Realizing a Place in the Church for Those Who Are Not Married

With this shift in mind, we can then turn to passages in the New Testament that deal with celibacy and individuals who are celibate and take them seriously, realizing that there is indeed a place in the church for those who are not married. Jesus provides a good place to start. Maken discounts Jesus's example as a celibate single by saying, "Let's not justify being single just because Jesus was! There are a lot of things Jesus was and did that we are *never* going to be or do."[33] The issue, however, is not justifying singleness or determining exactly how much we can mold our lives to Jesus's model but rather exploring what Jesus's singleness reveals about the truths of his kingdom. We have already seen how Jesus repeatedly reminds his followers that their loyalties need to shift from their families to him. As a single man existing in a culture where marriage and heirs were the primary goals, Jesus's lifestyle as well as his words testifies to a radically new way of thinking about family and inheritance. As Winner mentions, "Jesus's singleness is not simply a reminder that life can be lived well as an unmarried person; it is rather a way into Jesus's radical teachings about marriage and families."[34] Jesus's singleness reminds us that our ultimate loyalty needs to be devoted to him and his church rather than our biological families. In his novel *The Da Vinci Code*, Dan Brown proposes the seemingly radical idea that Jesus fathered a child with Mary Magdalene, and in the context of the truths of scripture and the traditions of the church, it is a heretical idea. But perhaps what is even more radical is that Jesus remained celibate yet generated the offspring of his church, creating new family connections through which his new covenant could be enacted. Through Jesus's example, we find not only a model for living as single Christians but also a clear representation of why this singleness is now possible.

From this perspective, we can now give serious consideration to Paul's words in 1 Corinthians 7. In the first few verses of this chapter and particularly in verse 25, it is clear that Paul is not setting up celibacy as a new law that displaces marriage. He acknowledges that there is an important place for marriage, but throughout the chapter, he also recognizes that singleness is not only a valid option but also at times a more preferable option. Particularly in verses 32 through 35, Paul emphasizes that singleness may allow for more "undistracted devotion to the Lord" (v. 35). While Gordon Fee may conclude that this section of

1 Corinthians 7 "is not your standard Paul,"[35] the primary message of the passage found in verse 27 ("Are you bound to a wife? Do not seek to be released. Are you released from a wife? Do not seek a wife") is very standard Paul in its admonition to be content. And the passage as a whole sounds remarkably similar to the message about family loyalty that we receive from Jesus throughout the Gospels. Jesus continually asks his followers to break their ties with family in order to serve him fully, and, as Paul recognizes, this is much easier to do when you are not married.

What makes this passage even more fascinating, though, is that the world of the newly established church is so different from the patriarchal culture from which it emerged that this singleness is now an actual possibility not only for men but also for women. In the culture of the day, women, in particular, had to be connected to a particular family in order to be protected.[36] Paul, however, counsels both the unmarried and widows that "it is good" to remain single (v. 8), and he warns women as well as men that the realities of marriage may distract them from devoting themselves entirely to God (vv. 32–35). But how will these single women be able to devote themselves to God if they are condemned to live as outcasts, desperately trying to find a way to provide for themselves without the protection of a family? For the answer we must return to Jesus's statement defining who his true brothers and sisters are: "whoever does the will of [His] father who is in heaven" (Matt. 12:50). This new family, the church, will be the family that allows these single women to survive in a wider culture that has no place for them, for as James 1:27 reveals, "Pure and undefiled religion in the sight of our God and Father is this: to visit orphans and widows in their distress, and to keep oneself unstained by the world." In fact, Acts 6 reveals just how seriously this issue was taken, for when there was a complaint that widows were being neglected by the church, the leaders of the early church chose seven men to address the problem. Singleness is now a valid option because the church will be the family and support system that these singles need to survive.

But do Paul's words even apply to Christians today? There are some who would argue that since we are no longer in "the present distress" that Paul mentions in 1 Corinthians 7:26, we have no reason to heed his words about celibacy in this chapter. While "the present distress" may refer to circumstances particular to the Corinthian church, Paul's statements about needing to find the best way that we can serve God, whether in marriage or in singleness, resonate not only with Jesus's earlier words but also with messages we receive throughout the New Testament regarding the importance of keeping our focus squarely upon Christ and the eternity we will share with him rather than being carried away by the pleasures of the temporal world. While we may not live in the same urgency that the early church did, continually looking for the return of the Lord, we are reminded in 1 Thessalonians 5 that we should be living this way, for "the day of the Lord will come just like a thief in the night" (v. 2). Paul's advice, then, does seem to transcend the world of the Corinthians.

Therefore, what we have in the New Testament is a different conception of singleness and marriage than the view that we receive throughout most of the Old Testament, and this difference rests squarely upon the formation of the church as the family of Christ. While the covenant of marriage that was established in Genesis with Adam and Eve is still important, it is now placed side by side with the possibility of celibacy as an equally valid means of serving God. By widening the conception of family from biological relationships to spiritual connections, Christ reminds us to look to the eternal rather than the temporal, for, as Hauerwas remarks, "our true home is not the biological family but the church."[37]

Rediscovering a Positive Theology of Singleness

Taking these verses on celibacy seriously allows us to begin to craft a theology of singleness as we explore what its purpose is in the kingdom of God. Most Christians in the evangelical church in America are probably familiar with discussions of marriage that present it as an important metaphor for God's powerful, exclusive love for the church. In his discussion of marriage in *Sexual Ethics: A Biblical Perspective*, Stanley Grenz reveals that the metaphor of marriage may actually work in three different ways. In the Old Testament, marriage is "employed as a metaphor for Yahweh's relationship to the nation Israel."[38] Throughout the prophets in particular, we see that God remains faithful to his chosen spouse despite her continual infidelity. In the New Testament, the metaphor shifts to reveal "Christ's union with the church,"[39] which will ultimately be fulfilled in the church's final redemption at the end times. Finally, the metaphor of marriage as a symbol "of the triune nature of

God" persists throughout scripture and demonstrates the intimacy of "three persons who share the one divine nature but who are distinct from each other."[40] Marriage, then, has a deeper spiritual significance than simply a union of two human beings, for it also reveals important spiritual truths about God and his relationships within the trinity as well as with humanity. But what about singleness? Are there spiritual truths that may be revealed by those who live in a state of celibacy? We would argue that, yes, there are important truths revealed by celibacy.

In *Sexuality and Holy Longing: Embracing Intimacy in a Broken World*, Lisa Graham McMinn comments on the vastness of God who cannot be explained completely by one metaphor. She remarks,

> The fullness of God's nature cannot be captured in one human who bears God's image, or in marriage as a model of God's love for the Church, or in one of Christianity's traditional emphases on evangelism or holiness or contemplation. God's nature is most fully represented in the diversity of community—male, female, married, single, Protestant, Catholic, young, old, Asian, African. We are incapable as individuals of carrying or experiencing the fullness of God. Yet as we come to understand and validate different elements of God's diversity, we see our own distortions and false assumptions. We become aware of our own incompleteness.[41]

With her discussion of the importance of diversity, McMinn reveals an important truth: we come to understand God better as we see various representations of his nature in the models around us. Relying solely on one metaphor diminishes the richness of God's character. It is important to realize that we are not upholding celibacy as *the* way to understand God but rather as one aspect of the myriad ways God has allowed us access into his divine nature and plan for us: an important metaphor that is generally ignored in our contemporary evangelical culture.

In his eighteenth sonnet, the seventeenth-century English poet John Donne attempts to capture a seeming paradox of the church by comparing it to a bride "Who is most true and pleasing to [God] then / When she is embraced and open to most men." While recognizing the loving, exclusive nature of the relationship between the church and God that is repeatedly described as a marriage, Donne also reminds us that the church must remain open to seekers who long to join in this communion. The church, then, is both the faithful bride and the seemingly unfaithful wife who invites many to participate in this "exclusive" relationship.

The paradox that Donne creates reveals that there is far more to a Christian's relationship with God than is captured by the traditional metaphor of a good faithful marriage, for while God's love for us is in one way exclusive, it is also available to everyone.

While Donne's image of the unfaithful spouse is one way of approaching this idea, celibacy or singleness may also help us to comprehend God's love and the realities of the church in a way that acknowledges the complexities of this seeming paradox. In his discussion of singleness, Grenz highlights the important aspects of this image, remarking,

> Singleness . . . constitutes an equally powerful imagery of yet another dimension of the divine reality as the One who loves, namely, the universal, nonexclusive, and expanding nature of the divine love . . . The "family" formed by the love of single persons is not the product of the intimate sexual acts shared by two people, but arises more spontaneously out of a dynamic of love that is open beyond exclusive boundaries. As such, the less formal bonding of singles reflects the openness of the divine love to the continual expansion of the circle of love to include within its circle those yet outside its boundaries.[42]

While the metaphor of marriage gives us insights into the permanent, exclusive relationship between God and us, the metaphor of singleness captures a different aspect of this relationship that reminds us of God's intense love for everyone and his desire that all will have fellowship with him. Both metaphors are necessary to help reveal the complexities of God's love for us.

In addition to revealing an aspect of God's love for us, singleness also testifies to realities of the freedom that we have in Christ. In *Families at the Crossroads*, Clapp highlights several of the freedoms that singles bear witness to, including "freedom from biological compulsion," "freedom to acknowledge and live within limits," true "freedom to marry" now that the compulsion to marry is removed, and "freedom to be a whole self rather than a schizophrenic self."[43] As Christians, our devotion to Christ should free us from the standards and values of the world around us, and in his list of freedoms, Clapp emphasizes how singles can be a radical testimony of the ability to withstand social pressures. As we have seen in previous chapters, contemporary American society and, occasionally, even the evangelical church present us with dangerous messages that do not accord with the truths of scripture. Celibacy stands as a powerful testimony against many of these messages and affirms God's truth.

If we look at the examples of freedom that Clapp presents, we can see how they clearly present a lifestyle that is counter to the images we are bombarded with. For example, contemporary American society tells us that sex is a biological need that we cannot resist. If we do not give in to our desires, we become stunted and repressed. Celibacy reveals this to be a lie, for by placing our bodies under subjection to God, we may discipline the flesh, choosing to refrain from having sex but still living complete lives as we witness to the power of God's love and redemption. Choosing to place limits on our desires also demonstrates the reality that true freedom under God comes from respecting limits rather than living in unrestrained "freedom" to do anything and everything. As our society is gradually beginning to recognize (particularly in terms of the environment), complete freedom may create serious problems. In a recent episode of the Oprah Winfrey show entitled "Go Green," Oprah's guests challenged her viewers to place limits on their consumption, asking them to change one light bulb, to refrain from using one napkin out of the five or six they may use a day, or to begin to recycle. By voluntarily limiting their freedom to consume, Oprah's viewers could help contribute to a better environment. While society is gradually beginning to realize this truth in terms of the environment, it is far from embracing it in terms of sex, which is no longer placed solely within the context of marriage. Celibate Christian singles testify to the fact that God may work through these limits to accomplish the goals that he has for them.

We are also frequently told in the secular media as well as in the church, that we cannot be complete without a partner. Christian singleness testifies to the truth that ultimate completeness is found in God, not in a human companion, leaving us free to marry or to remain single, for in both states we find our ultimate fulfillment in God. Finding our fulfillment in God also allows us to ground our identities in him rather than being controlled by what Clapp calls the "schizophrenia of the postmodern age" that asks us to be open to all possibilities so that consumer capitalism may continually create new needs and desires that must be fulfilled by some new product.[44] In chapter two we saw how Carson Brown approaches this issue from a secular perspective, acknowledging the challenge that virgins or celibates may pose to our consumer culture that uses the pursuit of sex to market goods. Christian singles may remind us that rather than being controlled by the whims of the market, we must be grounded solely in God.

In addition, harkening back to Paul's words in 1 Corinthians 7, Christian singles testify to the freedom to pursue God wholeheartedly and embrace the wider church community. This is certainly not to say that married Christians cannot serve God with their entire hearts, but by remaining free of the demands of marriage, Christian singles often have more flexibility to do God's work wherever he calls them and more opportunities to spread their love more widely. In fact, for singles the need to exist within a wider Christian community is often much more intense than it is for married Christians because they cannot find the Christian community that they long for in a spouse or children. Rather than being confined by the nuclear family, Christian singles are compelled to go out into the church and into the world to find and make brothers and sisters in Christ. Christian singles remind us that we all need to be ready and willing to do whatever God calls us to do, even if that occasionally requires finding our priorities in God rather than in our families.

Celibacy, then, should have an important place in our discussions of our relationship with God and with the world, for it not only provides an important metaphor for God's love for us but it also gives us examples of the countercultural aspects of Christianity that compel us to find our identity and purpose in God rather than in anything else. But these are not the only aspects of celibacy that are important for today's evangelical church, for celibacy also reminds us that, as Christians, our hope lies in Christ and our eternity with him rather than in this temporal world of spouses and heirs. For those who have no hope of resurrection, this earth is all that there is, and the best hope that many people have for their memory living on after their death is their children and grandchildren. Building upon Hauerwas's ideas in *A Community of Character: Toward a Constructive Christian Social Ethic*, Clapp powerfully summarizes the witness that Christian singles have in this area:

> The married Christian ultimately *should* trust that his or her survival is guaranteed in the resurrection; the single Christian ultimately *must* trust in the resurrection. The married, after all, can fall back on the passage of the family name to children, and on being remembered by children. But singles mount the high wire of faith without the net of children and their memory.

170

If singles live on, it will be because there is a resurrection. And if they are remembered, they will be remembered by the family called church.[45]

As we experience both the joys and the sorrows of this world, it is easy to forget that we and this world will eventually pass away. What seems so important to us now will pale in comparison to the realities we experience in eternity with God. Christian singles are an important reminder of the truth of the resurrection that should compel us to remember where our ultimate loyalty lies.

We have all probably heard sermons that refer to the metaphor of marriage as an important image of God's love, but how many of us have ever heard a sermon discussing what celibacy may reveal about God and the truths of our Christian faith? If it is true that God in his infinite majesty cannot be confined by one image or metaphor but must be experienced through a diversity of images, then perhaps it is time to bring these images of celibacy into the discussion. As almost anyone who attends a suburban, evangelical church will tell you, singles are often in short supply. The chairs or pews tend to be filled with families. Is this because of a lack of singles in American society? Certainly not. As we mentioned in chapter four, the 2006 national census revealed that 46% of American adults are single, and as Carolyn Koons points out in her discussion of the realities of singleness in America, "Never again will America be a 97 percent married and 3 percent single adult population."[46] The number of singles in society is growing, but, for the most part, they are not making it into our churches. We wonder if one reason why today's evangelical church has such a difficult time drawing in singles is its intense focus on marriage and the nuclear family. And this is not simply an issue of alienating those who do not fit into the church's demographic. Instead, it may actually indicate that by focusing on the marriage metaphor of God's exclusive love, we have neglected the celibacy metaphor of God's all-inclusive love that invites everyone to participate. As Hauerwas remarks, "Singleness reminds the church we grow not through biological ascription but through witness and hospitality to the stranger."[47] Perhaps by accepting this metaphor more fully and living out its implications, our churches may become more welcoming to those who exist outside of the nuclear family.

8

Monks & Martyrs
Views of Celibacy in the Church's Past

God wants celibacy because He wants to be loved . . . I need something majestic to love . . . In the world I found nothing of this majesty for which I yearned.

Søren Kierkegaard, *The Journals* XIA 154

We are still living with the old romantic illusion that the highest happiness, the great significance, the only romance in life, consists in our relationships with women and in the sensual satisfactions we derive from them. We forget only one thing: that the soul and the spirit are just as real and strong and demanding as the flesh—they are so much more so!

Paul Claudel, *Correspondence*, Paris 1926

For most single women, turning thirty can be difficult. It's not so much that you feel old; after all, they say thirty is the new twenty. But it is a time when you start to realize that your life is not following the schedule you thought it would. Most of us assumed that by this time we would be married and have children. Not that we all expected to be housewives, but even the most career-minded of us assumed that we could have both a career and a family. But then thirty hits, and our biological clocks start ticking. Sure, we might have another ten years before we *really* have to start worrying, but we now know how quickly ten years can go by. It's time to get serious about getting married, right? Some start trying multiple singles groups, and others start trying the internet. When we turned thirty, online dating was not yet in vogue, and we didn't want to change churches simply in the off-chance we might meet eligible single men. Instead, we started to face the fact that we might not get married—ever. Since we grew up without any positive single role models, this was be a terrifying thought. We knew the apostle Paul valued singleness, but no one in the Protestant Church seemed to. We knew Jesus advocated celibacy "for the sake of the Kingdom of Heaven," but we weren't exactly sure what that meant, especially for those of us who weren't called to a traditional full-time ministry that could be better served by not having a family.

Since the Protestant Church didn't offer us much guidance, we began to look to the Catholic Church for help. While we never seriously considered it, there was some appeal in converting to Catholicism and becoming nuns, for then there would at least be some *reason* for being single and celibate. It would provide a way to serve God full-time without having to worry about paying the bills as well. To the surprise and concern of her family, Bonnie even attended an Introduction to Catholicism class at a nearby Franciscan Renewal Center. Although the class was interesting, it didn't provide any insights into a life of celibacy. Even the nun leading the class couldn't think of any value to leading a celibate life unless you have taken a vow requiring it. The Protestant Church excluded us from their messages of abstinence because we were over eighteen, and the Catholic Church excluded us from their messages of celibacy because we weren't nuns. But at least the early church fathers had a long history of valuing celibacy. Maybe we could glean some insights from them for our lives.

Misogyny in Early Views of Celibacy

The Nature of Sex

One of the first things we discovered when we turned to the early church fathers was that we needed to sift through many negative messages in order to find the positive. The most obvious negative message

173

was found in the misogyny that characterized so much of the discussion of celibacy. When exploring the early church fathers' teaching on celibacy, it is difficult to overlook their teachings on women. While some argue that they were merely the products of their time and culture, other critics have gone so far as to blame Augustine for over a thousand years of sexism in the Catholic Church. Either way, it is difficult not to let their condemnation of all sexual desire and their mistrust of women color the way we read their praise of celibacy. One even begins to wonder if it is possible to value celibacy without fearing sexual desire and mistrusting women.

When it comes to the essential nature of sex, the early church had a very different perspective from the contemporary church. For the most part, the church today views sex as something good that was created by God. It only becomes sinful when it is taken out of its proper context: marriage. In direct contrast to this, the early church fathers generally viewed sex and sexual desire as shameful, carnal, of the flesh, in a word—evil. While concession was made for sex within marriage, the act itself was still considered suspect. Tertullian (c. 145–c. 220) wrote that the only difference between marriage and fornication is the laws governing the degree of illicitness. The nature of sex itself does not change.[1] While we might agree that the essential nature of sex does not change (seeing sex as something that is essentially good that is only corrupted when taken out of the context of marriage), Tertullian would argue that sex is essentially bad, even if it is allowed within marriage. Writing almost 200 hundred years later, Jerome (c. 347–c. 420) echoes this idea, using Paul's words in 1 Corinthians 7 to support his argument: "If it is good not to touch a woman, it is bad to touch one: for there is no opposite to goodness but badness." He argues that according to Paul marriage was only allowed in order to avoid the even worse sin of fornication and that "surely a thing that is allowed because there may be something worse has only a slight degree of goodness."[2] For Tertullian and Jerome, sexual activity even within marriage is a shameful manifestation of humanity's sinful desires.

In addition, while procreation was often seen as good, the means of procreation was still seen as problematic. Because many like Jerome believed that Adam and Eve did not have sex until after the fall, procreation was inextricably linked with an act that emphasized humanity's fallenness.[3] For some, in order for procreation to occur without sin, it would have to be an act of the will alone. Sexual desire could have no part in it. Augustine (c. 354–c. 430), however, highlights the difficulties of this, remarking, "Whenever it comes to the actual process of generation, the very embrace which is lawful and honourable cannot be effected without the ardour of lust."[4] While procreation might be necessary and good, the sexual desire inherent in the act of sex made the activity shameful.

The Nature of Women

This questionable view of sexuality reflects not only the early view that sex was a result of the fall but also the early church's view of women. Throughout the writings of the early church fathers we see repeatedly the negative conceptions of women as evil temptresses who can easily lead men astray. Jerome, for example, argues that "[Paul] did not say, it is good not to have a wife: but, it is good not to touch a woman: as though there were danger even in the touch: as though he who touched her, would not escape from her who 'hunteth for the precious life,' who causeth the young man's understanding to fly away."[5] But why are women so dangerous? As Tertullian reveals, it is not simply the power that they have to seduce men that makes them hazardous. The real danger lies in an inherent sinfulness that they received from their mother Eve. In *On the Apparel of Women* Tertullian implies that Eve was single-handedly responsible for the fall, and that all women are Eve. He tells women, "*You* are the devil's gateway: *you* are the unsealer of that (forbidden) tree: *you* are the first deserter of the divine law: *you* are she who persuaded him whom the devil was not valiant enough to attack. *You* destroyed so easily God's image, man. On account of *your* desert—that is, death—even the Son of God had to die."[6] Tertullian's condemnation of women ultimately may go back to 1 Corinthians 11:7 and the belief of many at that time that man was created in the image of God, but woman was not. Writing two hundred years later, Augustine emphasized this point that women do not bear the image of God as men do: "But in the sex of their body [women] do not signify [the renewal of mind in which is the image of God] . . . The part, namely, which they signify in the very fact of their being women, is that which may be called the concupiscential part."[7] In other words, men represent the mind and soul while women represent sexual desire and lust. If a man truly believes that women only represent sexual desire and lust and are the devil's gateway, of course he should seek a life of celibacy. Why would he align himself with such a deplorable temptress as woman? But what does that mean for a woman, or a man for that matter, who believes that women were also created in the image of God?

Even when the early church fathers have something positive to say about women, it is often presented in a way that ultimately devalues them. While the early church fathers often praise virgins or celibate women, they must find a way to explain how a woman could be worthy of high esteem. In order to be praiseworthy, a woman must, in essence, cease to be a woman. In *The Banquet of the Ten Virgins* Methodius (c. 826–c. 885) demonstrates this problematic perspective when he has Thecla, a first-century virgin martyr who reputedly traveled with Paul and preached the gospel, argue that Christ replaces the "passions and weakness of women" with Christ's "manly virtue."[8] This idea is also developed by Jerome who argues that under the new rule of Christ the virgin is no longer a woman, for "the distinction of sex is lost."[9] He writes to Lucinius, who with his wife Theodora took a vow of celibacy, that Theodora was "once a woman but now a man; once an inferior but now an equal."[10] While this loss of the "distinction of sex" might be a way for some women to gain more power within a patriarchal society, what is ultimately the cost? Women must abandon their femininity to keep from being a threat to male purity. It is no wonder that many today agree with controversial Catholic theologian Uta Ranke-Heinemann who wrote, "Celibate hatred of sex is hatred of women."[11] Recovering a positive view of celibacy from this discussion is a difficult proposition.

Responding to the Misogyny

It would be easy to become angry and dismiss everything the church fathers have to offer. But if we reject anyone with whom we don't agree one hundred percent of the time, we would end up rejecting everyone. In *The Cloister Walk* Kathleen Norris provides us with a model of how we might begin to approach some of these issues productively. As a Protestant with a growing interest in Catholicism, Norris recounts her impressions of various Catholic doctrines and practices. In one section of the book, Norris reflects upon several of her encounters with sexism in the church. First, she mentions a friend of hers who had to work through a time of resisting his call to celibacy. His resistance often manifested itself in anger toward his abbot but occasionally revealed itself through misogyny. Her next example is another friend who was taught that as a monk he should avoid women. When he then encountered women as students and colleagues on a college faculty, his fear manifested itself as misogyny. For both men, misogyny was the sign of their struggles with celibacy. As they matured in their calls, however, they learned to value women as friends rather than to see them as sexual temptresses who might lure them from their vows.[12]

Norris's examples remind us just how common it is for us to lash out at those we believe to be thwarting our desires. Is the monk who speaks negatively about women because of his own sexual frustration really that different from the woman who speaks negatively about men because of a failed relationship or an unfulfilled desire to be married? Is seeing all women as sexual temptresses really that different from seeing all men as perverted sexual predators? A bitter woman may argue that society supports her conclusion—just watch an episode of *Law and Order: SVU* if you doubt it. But Tertullian probably could have argued that society, likewise, supported his view of women. Thinking about the potential fears and frustrations of the early church fathers and seeing how, often, we are no different in our own frustrations might help us to put this misogyny in perspective.

In addition, it may help to see how the contemporary Catholic Church has dealt with this issue. Though some still may question their position, in recent years Catholic teaching on celibacy has been kinder to women. Raniero Cantalamessa, a Franciscan Capuchin Priest and Preacher to the Papal Household since 1980, addresses some of the church's historic teaching regarding celibacy when he writes that "we need [not] to make demons of the other sex, especially of women, or scorn or insult beauty simply because it is 'visible' and 'transitory'. Beauty, as we know, comes from God, even if it can be wrongly used. Since in the past, in this and in every other area, things were always seen from a man's point of view, it is not surprising that the ambiguity of sex . . . was translated into ambiguity about women and into misogyny."[13] Rather than promoting fear and suspicion of the opposite sex, he encourages fellow celibates to view their attraction to the other sex as something good that has been offered to the Lord.[14] This perspective not only acknowledges the potential goodness of sexual desire, but it also recognizes that it is possible for a single and celibate Christian to experience sexual desire in a God-honoring way that does not demand physical gratification.

Both Norris and Cantalamessa provide us with examples of productive ways to look at church history, acknowledging the dangers of misogyny but also recognizing that these beliefs and feelings don't have to overshadow the positive messages of celibacy that were also promoted by the early church fathers and the Catholic Church. Yes, the misogyny expressed by the early church fathers is troubling, but we must remember that the positive view of celibacy did not arise with them. We have already seen how scripture presents us with positive images of celibacy, particularly in connection with the New Testament church. We may, therefore, affirm celibacy without affirming the negative ideas about sex and women that permeated the early discussions regarding celibacy.

The Virgin Martyrs

Another difficult topic to negotiate is that of the virgin martyrs. For many women who were raised Catholic, these tales stir up anger and frustration, for they seem to imply that the only worth women have stems from their virginity. In *Cloister Walk*, for example, Norris recounts the reaction of a Benedictine nun upon discovering that Norris was writing about the virgin martyrs: "They set women back! As if in order to be holy you had to be a virgin, preferably a martyr, and that's not where most women are."[15] We, however, did not grow up with tales of the virgin martyrs. Because these tales are relatively new to us, we don't have the years of baggage and hurt that some have who have been encouraged to aspire to an unrealistic ideal that few achieve. Although we can understand why many women hate the virgin martyr tales, we can also see within these tales messages of empowerment for women (and perhaps even men) who wish to define themselves by God's standards rather than those of the world.

By AD 200, celibacy was considered the ideal for both women and men in the Christian church, and this message stood in direct contrast to the world around them. The Roman government penalized the unmarried and the childless, and Judaism still maintained that the survival of Israel depended on marriage. Although there is debate over the historical veracity of the virgin martyr narratives, they certainly reflect some of the dominant beliefs of the early church and testify to the social position of women in the Greco-Roman world. Many of these women found freedom in Christianity: not just spiritual freedom but also social freedom. Under Roman law a woman's refusal to marry and procreate for the sake of the empire was an act of treason. The implicit or even explicit rebellion in the acts of the virgin martyrs these women, however, is often ignored. Norris, in particular, bemoans the fact that the virgin martyrs are often turned into pious clichés, portrayed as powerless women willing to die for their virginity, which is seen as a passive physical state. But Norris argues that their virginity was anything but passive: "It was a state of being, of powerful potential, a *point vierge* from which they could act in radical resistance to authority."[16] For women, maintaining their virginity before God allowed them a powerful voice that asserted that they belonged to God.

The story of the typical virgin martyr goes like this: A young Christian girl refuses an arranged marriage to an unsympathetic pagan nobleman. For this she is subjected to various forms of torture. Throughout her ordeals she remains strong, articulate, intelligent, and loyal to Christ. In some accounts, God intervenes and rescues the virgin from her torturers. Thecla, for example, is to be burned on a pyre, but God sends a heavy thunderstorm so she can escape unharmed. Later, when she is condemned to fight the "wild beasts" in the arena in Antioch, God intervenes by turning the beasts against each other. Through Thecla, many come to Christ. Not only is she given the gifts of preaching, evangelizing, and healing, but she is able to continue her apostolic work even without Paul's assistance. In those cases when God does not intervene and spare the virgin's life, she always maintains a strength which defies the conventions of accepted female behavior at the time. When virgin martyrs were beheaded outside of the city, they would often pick up their heads, march back into the city, and keep preaching. Mahya, a sixth-century servant girl, runs through the streets shouting, "Men and women, Christians, now is the moment to pay back Christ what you owe him. Come out and die for Christ, just as he died for you . . . This is the time of battle!" When she is publically stripped naked and tortured, she maintains her dignity and boldly states, "It is to your shame . . . that you have done

179

this; I am not ashamed myself . . . for I am a woman—such as created by God."[17] These women are far from the asexual, veiled virgins spoken of by many of the early church fathers!

Unlike many of today's women who seek empowerment through the freedom to engage in sexual activity outside of marriage, these women found empowerment and freedom through celibacy. They testify to the fact that virginity is not passive, safe, and weak. Instead, it can be a strong countercultural statement of resistance. While some may suggest that the message left to us in the virgin martyr tales is one in which women are exhorted to value virginity above all else, leaving those who are no longer virgins feeling ashamed and unworthy of respect, the issue really isn't one of physical virginity. In fact, as Norris points out, many of these women were probably sexually violated. The issue instead is one of power and control, where women refuse to sacrifice their commitment to God to the pressures of their families and their societies. And, as Norris reflects, this is an important message for women who are often told by contemporary media that being an attractive woman means objectifying yourself and relinquishing your values. Norris asks,

> What might it mean for a girl today to be as the early virgin martyrs were and defy the conventions of female behavior? She would presume to have a life, a body, and identity apart from male definitions of what constitutes her femininity, or her humanity. Her life would articulate the love of the community . . . that had formed her, and would continue to strengthen her. And she would be virgin in the strongest possible sense, the sense that Methodius had in mind when he said of St. Agatha: "She was virgin, for she was born of the divine word."[18]

Virginity, then, becomes a symbol of much more than sexual purity. It is an acknowledgement that we have offered ourselves to God completely and that we refuse to submit to those who wish to supersede this commitment. A Benedictine sister interviewed by Norris expresses this idea well: "Virginity is a state that returns to God in wholeness. This wholeness is not that of having experienced all experiences, but of something reserved, preserved, or reclaimed for what it was made for. Virginity is the ability to stay centered, with oneness of purpose."[19] Wow! How would our churches, our *world*, be different if single adults, young and old, had this view of celibacy and singleness instead of the view that they need to spend all of their energies looking for a mate so they can have sex and thereby experience the "divine"?

The virgin martyr tales provide us with a powerful example of what it might look like to see what is potentially powerful in the traditions of the early church and apply it to our situations today. Rather than simply ignoring these tales or ridiculing them as remnants of a patriarchal culture that strived to enforce female virtue and virginity at all cost, we can instead see the truth of virginity and celibacy that lies behind these trappings: a truth that gives women (and men) value as unique individuals before God who, through his power, can resist the world around them in their commitment to their Savior. In today's world where controlling one's sexuality generally means feeling free to engage in sex with no strings attached, the virgin martyr tales remind us that succumbing to the pressures of the world around us to display our sexuality in the way that society deems appropriate is not necessarily freedom.

Monasticism

With the growing acceptance of Christianity in the third century, the practice of celibacy gradually became more popular, and the number of virgin martyrs decreased. At first, celibates remained part of the general population of Christians. In addition to the order of widows, which some believe Paul references in 1 Timothy 5, consecrated virgins who lived with their families were active members of their local congregations. By the fourth century, however, celibate men began to join monastic orders or prepare for ordination to the priesthood. Some, like Augustine, did both. Over the next few hundred years celibate men and women gradually withdrew into separate communities, finding that these communities provided them with more support for their chosen vocation and gave them the added prestige of a separated, consecrated life. While the earliest tradition incorporated celibates into the wider Christian community, more and more celibates left the local congregation for the monasteries and convents. Therefore, by the seventh century very few unmarried celibate Christians were a part of the local congregations.[20]

Monasteries provided a supportive community in which celibates could devote their lives to prayer and contemplation. Unfortunately, as

181

the power of the monasteries grew, the abuses of the system did as well. In *A History of Celibacy*, Elizabeth Abbott comments on some of the more flagrant abuses of the monastic system: "Many [monasteries] . . . degenerated into cesspits of political intrigue, money-mongering, and power-brokering, and—antithetical to the core reason for monasticism— libertine venues for sexual scandals on a breathtakingly vast scale."[21] However, despite these abuses, monastic life was often still seen as the best option for those seeking to live a life totally devoted to God.

While today we may not see seclusion within a monastery as empowering, for many men and women it was, for it gave them freedom from the daily drudgery experienced by most of society and it gave them access to literacy, which was denied to almost everyone else. For many medieval men and women, in particular, monasteries provided them with the opportunity to serve God and to develop their own talents in a way that would not have been possible in a life outside the monastery walls. In addition, monasteries often allowed individuals to experience an important sense of purpose as they worked together to help the surrounding community. As Mary Skinner relates, "Religious houses helped keep the peace, provided lodging for travelers, and protected the poor. They governed many people and administered the economy of extensive lands . . . Women's monasteries provided education for girls, offered second careers for widows and wives, and an alternative to marriage for young girls. They were centers of liturgical revival and religious renewal for entire provinces."[22] As the members of these communities banded together to serve God, they were also meaningfully employed in serving others. For them, celibacy was not a curse but rather it was a blessing that enabled them to assume important roles within their societies. Although monastic life is not an option for most Protestant single adults today, perhaps we can discover important truths from the model of communal Christian service found within it.

Some may be surprised to learn that this idea of Christian celibates living together in community for a higher purpose is not completely foreign to the Protestant Church. In fact, centuries after England abandoned its Catholic heritage, the idea was still so appealing that various writers proposed plans for a Protestant form of monastic living. In the late seventeenth and early eighteenth centuries, for instance, writers such as Mary Astell argued for a type of female monastery where women would come together to educate themselves so that they would become productive members of society. Rather than imitating the fashionable women of the time period who were educated only enough to become beautiful and alluring wives for important men, these women were to devote themselves to God and education so that if they did leave and get married, they would be able to educate their children wisely and help build a stronger society that was devoted to God rather than to wealth and fashion.

While Astell's ideas remained theoretical, in the nineteenth century Anglican sisterhoods became a reality in Britain. The census of 1850 revealed that Britain had far more women than men, and the British had to discover something to do with these "redundant" women. While some women chose to emigrate in hopes of finding a husband elsewhere, others turned to the Anglican sisterhoods as a way of finding meaningful work. Anna Jameson who was a vocal supporter of these sisterhoods discusses their importance in *Sisters of Charity, Catholic and Protestant, Abroad and at Home*. She remarks, "We require in our country the recognition—the public recognition,—by law as well as by opinion, of the woman's privilege to share in the communion of labour at her own free choice, and the foundation of institutions which shall train her to do her work well."[23] By providing a way for young, single, Protestant women to engage in meaningful work, these Anglican sisterhoods allowed them to share in "the communion of labour" that Jameson believed was so necessary in order for society to develop.

Today, women don't need to marry in order to survive in society. We are not excluded from the workforce, and we have the freedom to get an education and earn a living. We have the opportunity to find meaningful work that was denied to many women who lived before us, but we do not necessarily have meaningful community. And this is true not just for women but also for men. This reality may explain why, even today, there are individuals who, while not wanting to become monks or nuns, are attracted to living in community with fellow celibates. For instance, the Catholic lay movement Focolare, which developed in Italy during the Second World War and continues until today, encourages members to live in celibate communities with other members. According to an article in the *Chicago Tribune*, Focolare currently has "thousands of members in the Midwest" and "nearly 90,000 members worldwide."[24] While not all of the members are celibate, the most devout are, living in single sex residences. They have jobs outside of these residences, but they come together to live and to strive for unity between Christians and non-Christians. Stephen Schubert, one of the residents of a Focolare house in Oak Park, Illinois, describes it as "being married to God . . . I've got hundreds of brothers and sisters and mothers and fathers."[25] These residents see the unity within their community as a model for the type of unity they hope to bring about in the rest of the world.

And it is not only Catholics who are interested in these ideas. Throughout the twentieth century several Protestant and ecumenical monasteries have developed across the world, one of the most notable being the Taizé Community. This community developed during the 1940s out of Brother Roger's desire to provide refuge to those fleeing the atrocities of World War II. A few years later, he and six other men committed themselves to live in life-long community, practice celibacy and simplicity, and share God's love with others. Today the community has over a hundred brothers and is a place of pilgrimage for visitors from all over the world.

Similar movements such as New Monasticism and the New Friars are gaining popularity with young single Protestants. Rob Moll describes this trend:

> These communities are the latest wave of evangelicals who see in community life an answer to society's materialism and the church's complacency toward it. Rather than enjoy the benefits of middle-class life, these suburban evangelicals choose to move in with the poor. Though many of the same forces drive them as did earlier generations—a desire to experience intense community and to challenge contented evangelicalism—they are turning to an ancient tradition to provide the spiritual sustenance for their ministries.[26]

Even these young evangelicals, probably still in the most social and passionate time of their lives, recognize how content many of our churches are to live without true Christian community. They look to the monastic tradition for ideas of how to enact Christ's love to the poor. We wonder if it is possible to implement any of these monastic ideals within the suburban church. Or does such commitment to one another and to the community require moving out of the old community and forming a new one?

Perhaps Kathleen Norris provides an insight into this issue. At a monastic funeral Norris attended, she had a conversation with a young monk who, "gesturing back at the cemetery" remarked on "one of the strengths of the monastic life": "My friends are there, my mentors and guides in the religious life . . . and one day I'll join them."[27] Those in the monastic tradition find comfort in a community that transcends the temporal world. A friend of Norris describes it this way: "Monastic funerals always blur the line between this world and the next; one feels that the present is just a moment in the continuum between this community, and the community of the saints."[28] How many people in our churches view community in the same way? Those of us who are single are in great need of community, but unfortunately many of us feel excluded from our church families. If we take an honest look at our churches, this isn't a problem that affects just singles. Too many married couples and families, although they may be affirmed from the pulpit and the various ministries, also lack the community they desire. Perhaps we need to model our church communities more on the monastic tradition—not necessarily by withdrawing from the world but rather by providing a family rooted in the eternal rather than the temporal. How might our churches be transformed if we truly saw them as the first stage in developing family relationships with fellow Christians that would exist throughout eternity?

The Relationship between Celibacy and Friendship

The monastic tradition can offer a beautiful picture of community and celibate friendship; however, it is also full of stories of monks who disappear into the desert or some other lonely place to escape from the temptations of their fellow men and commune solely with God. While there is certainly a place for solitude and contemplation, negotiating the relationship between the extremes has been problematic for monks and nuns, and contemporary Protestant singles must negotiate these difficulties as well. In *The Imitation of Christ*, one of the classic works of spiritual guidance, Thomas à Kempis (c. 1380–c. 1471) repeatedly warns his readers that solitude is far better than cultivating close friendships. He counsels, "Desire to be familiar with God alone and His Angels, and avoid the acquaintance of men" and reminds his readers, "The greatest Saints avoided, when they could, the society of men, and did rather choose to live to God, in secret."[29] The fear is that close relationships with

185

anyone will distract us from our total commitment to God. Is this the only way to remain celibate and devoted to God—to sequester ourselves away not just from the opposite sex but also from everyone so that no one will distract us from serving God? As we have already discussed in earlier chapters, many Christian singles struggle with loneliness and a lack of community. Should they continue down this road in the hope that it will bring them closer to God, or is there a place for community and close friendships among those committed to celibacy?

Cantalamessa provides a more contemporary perspective on this issue, and while he does not advocate complete solitude, he does place clear restrictions on friendships among those committed to celibacy. Although he acknowledges the value of friendship, even what he calls "special friendships," he warns about the dangers of what used to be known in celibate communities as "particular friendships." He writes that these "particular friendships" are "a bane to religious communities because they are exclusive, self-seeking, clique-forming, and time-absorbing. They indeed are opposed to the universality that is to characterize the virginal way of loving." In contrast, Cantalamessa characterizes "special friendships" as those that are non-exclusive and non-possessive. They must be thoroughly immersed in God, further a dedication to celibacy, and encourage universality and community. Unlike "particular friendships" they do not require more time than other relationships.[30] For Cantalamessa the ideal is community in which "special friendships" prevail so that all may participate equally in friendship in a way that does not cause conflict or distract from the deeper purpose of serving God.

For those living in monastic communities, this advice may be useful and necessary, but for those like us who haven't taken monastic vows but are striving to live a productive celibate life in the world, this advice may be very frustrating. Cantalamessa's warning against friendships that require more time than other relationships seems to preclude the possibility of having close friends. For single Protestants who are not part of a monastic community, this can leave us feeling like we are not only denied communion with a spouse, but we aren't even allowed to have any deep, meaningful relationships. Is there anything, then, that we can draw from this Catholic tradition of celibacy and friendships?

As we explore this issue, we must first realize that Cantalmessa is not writing to single laypeople in the church. He is writing to those who have taken religious vows, or are considering doing so. Second, we must realize that his views of friendship are not representative of every religious order. In *Unveiled: The Hidden Life of Nuns*, Cheryl Reed examines the lives of nuns in various religious communities across the United States. She includes in her discussion two communities with very different views of friendship. The Trappistines in Crozet, Virginia, believe that their vow of chastity includes the denial of close friendships and any form of emotional intimacy. In a manner reminiscent of Thomas à Kempis, one of the nuns explained, "When I'm not attending to my relationship with Jesus, and I'm seeking friendship or distractions, what I'm doing is evading my loneliness. When I'm seeking to have my needs fulfilled by other people, I am prostituting myself."[31] From this perspective, focusing completely on God demands the sacrifice of friendships.

This, however, is not the only perspective. *Spiritual Friendship* by Aelred of Rievaulx (c. 1110–67) reveals a tradition that values the closeness of friendship within monastic communities. For Aelred, friendship is not a dangerous distraction from devotion to God; instead, it "is a path to the love and knowledge of God."[32] From this perspective, learning to love others and negotiating the difficulties inherent in personal relationships may actually help Christians mature in their own relationships with God. Today, the Benedictine sisters in Ferdinand, Indiana follow in this tradition, not only encouraging friendships with each other but also openly discussing their sexual desires and frustrations in their relationships with men. They acknowledge their attraction to men and their desire for children. Unlike the sisters in some of the other communities Reed visited, these women don't believe that God gives them "special graces" that make them immune to sexual desire. Rather, they focus on supporting one another and not acting on their sexual desires. One nun who enjoys working alongside men remarked, "Just because I have [temptations] doesn't mean I go out looking for that genital satisfaction." She added, "I think it's healthy, because it calls me to womanhood and to look to the vows, and not to feel inhibited—to allow myself to have those feelings and acknowledge that I am a woman; I am sexual rather than dried up and not attractive. It energizes me."[33] Rather than seeing these relationships as distractions from her vocation, she uses the difficulties inherent in them to reaffirm her decision before God. The monastic tradition, then, is a complex one, for we have various versions from which to draw as we consider the value and importance of friendship.

Ronald Rolheiser provides us with one way of negotiating this complexity. His view of friendship is closer to that of the Ferdinand Benedictines than that of the Crozet Trappistines, and it probably has more significance for us because he is not writing specifically to those who are committed to lifelong celibacy. In his discussion of friendship, he specifically addresses the issue of platonic friendship between men and women. In chapter five we looked at some of the warnings we are given regarding heterosexual friendships and explored how some believe you should even avoid that dangerous cup of coffee with someone of the opposite sex, for it can lead you down a slippery slope. While acknowledging that such friendships require caution, Rolheiser believes they are definitely worth the risk and the effort. In fact, he states that "few things are as healing and life-giving as is friendship between woman and man, man and woman . . . I believe that, in the end, friendship survives longer than sex and spawns a wider, deeper, more life-giving intimacy."[34]

This idea that two celibate individuals of the opposite sex may have a "life-giving" intimate relationship that does not lead to sex is a radical one—one that our evangelical culture has a difficult time embracing. As we have seen in previous chapters, the evangelical church's obsession with sex often mirrors that of the secular world. Rolheiser attests that "in our culture's view, a view we have generally interiorized and made our own, to love means to make love, to be a lover. Platonic heterosexual friendship is seen as too incomplete, too empty, or as simply unrealistic . . . When to love someone means to make love to that someone, then it becomes hard to trust that simple friendship might be more life-giving than having sex."[35] But Rolheiser suggests that we do not have to be limited by that view. Perhaps, rather than being guided by cultural values, we can forge a stronger conception of friendship that enables individuals to come together in a true community where individuals may give love and be loved without always defining love in terms of sexual activity.

Ultimately, Rolheiser encourages all of us, single and married, to be "sexual in the proper sense—namely in the way Christ was." For Rolheiser, sexuality is not tied to genital activity. Instead, it is displayed in the way we long for connection and communion with others. Christ, therefore, provides us with a perfect picture of appropriate, celibate sexuality in this world, revealing "that, among other things, friendship and love, celebration and community, happiness and the kingdom, lie in the coming together of hearts." Celibate friendships, then, "can be an important way to keep alive, visible and in the flesh, that part of the incarnation which tells us that when one is speaking of love, the human heart is the central organ."[36] By actively engaging with the tradition of celibacy and demonstrating the countercultural power celibate friendships may have to remind Christians that our focus needs to be on love rather than sex, Rolheiser reveals an important truth in the midst of the complexities of this tradition. History shows that monks and nuns often had a difficult time negotiating the risks of celibate friendships with some repudiating friendship for solitude and others embracing improper forms of obsessive love and desire. While their struggles reveal the difficulties of achieving the balance Rolheiser proposes, they do not negate its underlying truth. And it is this truth that has the power to transform our ideas of Christian community in radical ways.

The Relationship between Celibacy and Marriage

Many evangelical Christians may know nothing about the misogyny of the early church fathers, the lurid virgin martyr tales, the history of monastic communities, or the controversies over celibate friendships, but they will probably know the value the Catholic Church has placed on celibacy. Although scripture indicates that both marriage and celibacy are good, there seems to be a human tendency to lift one state above the other. Just as the evangelical church tends to lift marriage above celibacy, the early church lifted celibacy above marriage.

This natural inclination to rank marital states can perhaps best be seen in Tertullian's treatise *On Exhortation To Chastity* when he writes of three degrees of perfection related to sexual activity. The highest degree is that of virginity from the time of one's birth. This is followed by virginity/celibacy from the time of one's baptism. The third and lowest degree of perfection (but, it should be noted, still a level of perfection) is monogamy in marriage and celibacy after the death of one's spouse.[37] While still preferring celibacy to marriage, Ambrose (338–397) and Jerome both make a point of saying that they do not wish to degrade marriage.[38] In fact, their discussions are actually quite similar to those contemporary evangelicals who may acknowledge that singleness is okay but assert that marriage is the preferred choice. The values are reversed, but the discussion surrounding them is essentially the same. While we are certainly not suggesting that we invert the current hierarchy and go back to viewing celibacy as superior to marriage, these words of the early church fathers remind us that single adults have not always been viewed as second-class citizens and that celibacy was once a positive choice for both men and women.

Interestingly, even today when contemporary Catholics have a much higher view of marriage than the early church did, many do still value the celibate vocation over marriage. Cantalamessa, for example, is clear that both states (marriage and celibacy) are gifts from God: "Virginity is a charism, and marriage is a charism too. Both are therefore particular 'manifestations of the Spirit.' How can they be incompatible or opposed to each other, if both come 'from the same Spirit'? . . . The one confirms the other, it does not destroy it . . . Indeed, what merit would there be in not marrying, if marriage were something bad or simply dangerous and inadvisable?"[39] He does show his preference, however, when he writes that while celibacy "is not *ontologically* (that is, in itself) *a more perfect* state, . . . it is an *eschatologically more advanced* state, in the sense that it is more like the definitive state toward which we are all journeying."[40] What is it about celibacy that makes it so valuable within Catholic theology? And is there anything from this discussion that could also apply to single Protestants?

If we discount the early church's teaching that sex is inherently sinful, as Cantalamessa does, why would anyone prefer celibacy to marriage? Perhaps surprisingly, some of the arguments for celibacy that move beyond the idea that sex is inherently sinful are arguments we have already seen proposed by Protestants for proving why marriage is the preferred state. If anything, rather than demonstrating the superiority of one state over the other, they reveal that God may work through both marriage and celibacy. But since the contemporary evangelical church focuses so intensely on the arguments for marriage, perhaps it is important to be reminded of the opposite perspective. As we saw in chapters four and six, many today believe that single adults are immature and selfish and that marriage is God's vehicle for maturing us emotionally, psychologically, and spiritually. The early church fathers taught the exact opposite. When they discuss the reasons people are attracted to marriage, the early church fathers include the same reasons we might: to satisfy their loneliness and sexual desire, to seek status and social acceptability, or to fulfill the desire to live on through offspring. But instead of seeing these reasons as natural and appropriate, they saw them as selfish and prideful. Gregory of Nyssa (335–394), for instance, may acknowledge that marriage can be good if it is characterized by "sobriety and moderation" and one's primary pursuit is heavenly things, but he also writes that marriage is "the primal root of all striving after vanities" and that it lends itself to the sin of pride through the desire to bring honor to the family name and leave historical records in the form of children.[41] Today there are those who accuse singles of being selfish and prideful, unwilling to sacrifice their own desires for the sake of a spouse and children. While this certainly may be true of some, we should acknowledge that marriage can also be motivated by selfish and prideful desires, especially if those desires are rooted in self-preservation through biological heirs. We are all guilty of these vices, regardless of our marital status.

Physical vs. Spiritual Children

In Malachi 2:15 we are told that God desires "a godly offspring," and this verse is often invoked to motivate singles to marry and procreate for God. How can one who is celibate provide God with the "godly offspring" he desires? As we saw in chapter seven, we are not limited to biological offspring. Most of the church fathers would acknowledge that the desire to have biological children is good as long as the desire is to raise children to bring honor to the Lord rather than to bring honor to oneself. In conjunction with this, they would argue that the higher aim should be to raise *spiritual* children rather than *physical* children: something that celibates may also participate in. Augustine, for instance, reminds his readers that celibacy is by no means "barren, but a fruitful mother of children of joys by [Christ] her Husband."[42] And Jerome develops this idea in his letter to Eustochium: "The old law had a different ideal of blessedness, for therein is said: 'Blessed is he who hath seed in Zion and a family in Jerusalem:' and 'Cursed is the barren who beareth not:' and 'Thy children shall be like olive-plants round about thy table.' . . . But now even to eunuchs it is said, 'Say not, behold I am a dry tree,' for instead of sons and daughters you have a place forever in heaven."[43] As we discussed in the previous chapter, this Old Testament passage prophesies the transition that occurs between the Old and New Covenant, where the spiritual family comes to take precedence over the biological one.

191

Jerome, however, does not end with his reference to Isaiah 56. He does not simply see a covenantal switch from biological children to spiritual children. Instead, he believes that there is a progression that gradually moves from sexual procreation to virginal procreation. Jerome explains that during the time of the patriarchs only those with children were considered blessed. Then, in the time of the prophets, there was a gradual introduction of "the virtue continence" which at that time was only found in men such as Elijah, Elisha, and Jeremiah. But then, just as Paul draws a parallel between Adam and Christ in 1 Corinthians 15, Jerome draws a parallel between Eve and Mary: "But now that a virgin has conceived in the womb and has borne to us a child . . . , now the chain of the curse is broken. Death came through Eve, but life has come through Mary. And thus the gift of virginity has been bestowed most richly upon women, seeing that it has had its beginning from a woman."[44] The fact that Christ is born of a virgin and will then create spiritual children of God reveals a distinct shift from the Old Testament.

Contemporary Catholic writers draw on these ideas to remind us of the relevance of celibacy to our own world. Thomas Dubay, a Marist priest, retreat master, and spiritual director, writes of celibacy anticipating a kingdom that has not yet come: "Marriage and sexual relations within it belong to this world which is passing away (1 Cor. 7:29–31), but the virgin anticipates the final age in which there is no earthly marriage (Matt. 22:30), the final enthralling fulfillment of all human life."[45] And, interestingly, this view of celibacy is an integral part of Pope John Paul II's catechesis in *The Theology of the Body: Human Love in the Divine Plan*. He teaches that when humanity was created in the image of God, the body and spirit existed in perfect communion. Therefore, male (Adam) and female (Eve) existed in a mutual relationship that was characterized by the unselfish giving of each to the other. With the fall came a division between the body and the spirit, and Adam and Eve began to see each other as objects to be possessed rather than gifts to be given unselfishly and accepted unconditionally. Thus, after the fall, their nakedness caused them to feel vulnerable and ashamed. Pope John Paul II states that shame "contains such a cognitive acuteness as to create a fundamental disquiet in all human existence."[46] Because of this sense of shame and the rupture between the body and the spirit, we fail to achieve the "mutual communion of persons" that we all seek. This communion will not be achieved until we join Christ in heaven.

At that time, Christ will be everything to everyone, and there will be perfect communion.

He explains it like this, "Eschatological man will be free from that opposition. In the resurrection the body will return to perfect unity and harmony with the spirit. Man will no longer experience the opposition between what is spiritual and what is physical in him . . . This state . . . does not signify any disincarnation of the body nor, consequently, a dehumanization of man. On the contrary, it signifies his perfect realization."[47] In the meantime, marriage signifies the original unity before the fall when Adam and Eve were able to give themselves freely to one another without shame. But celibacy also signifies the free giving of oneself—not to one other person, but to God, and therefore, to all people: "By choosing continence for the kingdom of heaven, man has the knowledge of being able in that way to fulfill himself differently and, in a certain way, more than through matrimony, becoming a 'true gift to others.' "[48] In Pope John Paul II's view, marriage reflects our original sinless condition before the fall, and celibacy foreshadows our future condition after the resurrection of the body. Both symbolize a state of perfect communion with God and others.

While it is certainly not surprising to see how contemporary Catholic thinkers draw from the tradition of the early church on this issue, it is perhaps surprising to discover that contemporary evangelical authors also echo many of these ideas. The early church fathers' ideas about the selfishness of marriage or the importance of virginal procreation may seem odd to us today, but we have already seen in chapter seven, how contemporary Protestant thinkers such as Laura Smit, John Piper, and Rodney Clapp reveal the revolutionary power of these ideas. Not only does Piper echo Jerome in his discussion of Isaiah 56, but Smit echoes the early church fathers as well as she speaks of human history being on a trajectory "moving toward a time when marriage will be obsolete."[49]

Rodney Clapp takes the discussion even further in his book *Tortured Wonders*. While addressing the early church's dangerous disdain for anything associated with the physical body, Clapp acknowledges their positive messages as well and demonstrates the significance these early ideas of celibacy may have for us today. He begins by explaining how sex and death are integrally related in the cycle of life. In a world where everyone dies, humanity must procreate in order to survive: thus, the argument that if everyone were to take a vow of celibacy, the human race would die out. Clapp writes, "To procreate was in one sense to admit and allow the overarching sway of death . . . By contrast, confident Christian celibacy, based on the hope of the resurrection of a then undying body, was a bold witness to the total defeat of death."[50] He then goes on to explain how revolutionary this is, not just for the early church, but also for the contemporary church today: "The explosive revelation of God in Jesus Christ is apocalyptic—it ends the world as it was and redefines all life and existence on its own terms. No human institution, however estimable, including the biological family, stands utterly unaffected or unshaken by the coming of the kingdom."[51] For Clapp as well as for Piper and Smit, these ideas of the value of celibacy embraced by the early church fathers are not only relevant for today but are essential reminders for the church to look beyond this world to the next. Although we may have several variations on a theme, we also have a consistent message across several different Christian belief systems. Whether it is the early church fathers, contemporary Catholic priests, mainline Protestants, or evangelicals, we have a positive message of celibacy emerging that is consistent with both Old and New Testaments—that celibacy was introduced with the coming of Christ and anticipates our final state in heaven.

The Purpose of Celibacy

This similarity of message across time periods and denominational lines suggests that celibacy is not simply an irrelevant relic of an earlier time. Instead, it might actually serve an important purpose in the Christian Church. But how has this purpose been described throughout church history? And may we gain insights from these descriptions? Some of the early writers believed that celibacy contributed to the life and ministry of the church through martyrdom and prophecy. In "Concerning Virgins" Ambrose writes, "Virginity makes for martyrs." We saw this perspective elucidated in the tales of the virgin martyrs who were persecuted and killed for practicing celibacy. This probably isn't the positive message of celibacy for which we have been searching. We doubt that any of us wish to be martyred for being celibate. If there are some who do desire to be martyrs for Christ, surely preaching the gospel is a much better reason for such a fate.

On the other hand, Tertullian and Origen (c. 185–c. 254) believed that celibacy contributes to the life and ministry of the church through the gift of prophecy. Cantalamessa also attests to the prophetic nature of celibacy when he writes, "By the simple fact that it exists, . . . this form of life shows what the final condition of men and women will be: one that is destined to last forever. It is a prophetic existence."[52] Just as marriage is a symbol of Christ's relationship with the church, celibacy is a symbol of our eternal state. This is good news for those of us who have been annoyed by the constant reminder that marriage is a metaphor for the church's relationship with Christ to the exclusion of other metaphors. The reasoning often follows that if you are single you are incapable of fully appreciating your relationship with God because you do not have a human relationship to compare it to. When celibate singleness is seen as a symbol of our future state when we are in perfect communion with God, we have a more complete view of the church. Both marriage and singleness are symbolic of our relationship with Christ. Either by itself is an incomplete picture.

In his homily on 1 Corinthians 7 John Chrysostom (c. 347–c. 407) offers yet another potential purpose for celibacy. He states that the purpose of celibacy can change throughout history. He believed that in Paul's time the purpose of celibacy was to expedite the coming of God's Kingdom, but in his own time the purpose of celibacy was to raise human beings to the ranks of angelic powers. Certainly, this conception of celibacy is problematic. As Rodney Clapp reminds us in *Tortured Wonders*, we are not angels. We are human beings with God-created bodies living on a God-created earth, and we should not adopt a Gnostic disdain for everything associated with this life. Scripture never tells us that we should aspire to be angels. In fact, the reality that Christ did not come to earth as an angel but as man in a human body should impress upon us the importance of our earthly bodies: a truth that is ultimately emphasized in the fact of the bodily resurrection. While we most certainly would not wish to embrace John Chrysostom's ideas about celibacy for his time, he does raise an intriguing idea. Are we being challenged to rediscover the purpose of celibacy for our own time period?

Like John Chrysostom, many of the early church fathers saw celibacy as having a transcendent aim. Gregory of Nyssa argues in his treatise *On Virginity* that in order to achieve this transcendence celibacy must be more than just sexual abstinence, it must be a purity of both body and soul. We would agree that celibacy based on a merely physical state holds no value.

Not only would this overvalue unintentional virginity, but it would also devalue grace, conversion, and forgiveness, which are essential elements of Christianity. But, in our view, Gregory of Nyssa takes his idea of a transcendent celibacy through a disengaged soul too far when he describes virginity as "a deadening of the bodily passions" and advocates the avoidance of all "pleasures of the senses."[53] So is there anything of relevance, then, that we can take from this idea of celibacy having a transcendent aim? Is it possible to lead a life of celibacy for the sake of the kingdom of God without denying everything pleasurable in this life?

Historically, the traditional monastic vows of chastity, poverty, and humility have certainly embraced some of what Gregory of Nyssa describes without taking it quite as far as he did. Thomas Dubay shows the link between celibacy, humility, and poverty in his analysis of Matthew 19, for after Jesus's discussion of celibacy, he welcomes the little children and then instructs the rich young ruler to sell all of his possessions and give to the poor.[54] Likewise, Pope John Paul II writes that celibacy "for the sake of the kingdom of heaven" must be characterized by "successive self-sacrifices" throughout the entire breadth of one's life.[55] While all Christians are asked to "present [our] bodies as a living and holy sacrifice,"[56] does this mean that if we desire to see our celibacy as a gift rather than a curse, we must also seek to live lives of poverty? Of course the two together do leave one with the freedom for unconditional service to God, but should we assume that God calls every older single adult to a traditional full-time church or para-church ministry that requires a commitment to poverty?

A quick glance at the chapter titles of Nancy Leigh DeMoss's book *Singled Out for Him: Embracing the Gift, the Blessings, and the Challenges of Singleness* could lead us to think that she, from a Protestant perspective, also believes singleness is linked with this type of obligation. She organizes her book according to ten commitments she believes a single adult should make in order to embrace the single life, and interestingly, they echo some of the ideas presented by Gregory of Nyssa, Thomas Dubay, and Pope John Paul II. According to DeMoss, singles should be committed to:

Receiving celibacy as a gift

Serving Christ with all [their] time, abilities, and energy

Relinquishing all [their] expectations of material, physical, and emotional security

Developing personal discipline

Being morally pure

Honoring [their] parents

Relating to families

Giving extravagantly rather than living extravagantly

Leaving a spiritual legacy for the next generation

Pursuing an intimate relationship with God above all else

While these are certainly all good commitments, and commitments to which we all (single or married) should aspire, they can seem a bit daunting. Particularly daunting is the commitment to relinquish all expectations of material, physical, and emotional security. Fortunately, DeMoss explains what she means by this, and perhaps her insights might help us to see how we might apply Gregory of Nyssa's ideas about the "transcendent aim" of celibacy to our lives as twenty-first century Protestant singles who do not have the support of a monastery. In her discussion, DeMoss reveals that she does not mean that single adults should not have any material, physical, and emotional security. Rather, she says we should have no *expectations* of such. In fact, no one should, for even marriage does not guarantee security. Many married couples lack material security. And many (dare we say most if not all) married couples lack complete physical and emotional security. [57]

Ultimately, the truth behind all of these ideas is that no object, act, or human relationship can satisfy all of our needs or longings. Only God can truly meet our needs, and in him is where our loyalty needs to be. What celibacy helps us remember is that, as Henri Nouwen writes, "No human being can understand us fully, no human being can give us unconditional love, no human being can offer constant affection, no human being can enter into the core of our being and heal our deepest brokenness." Although most of us know this to be true, we still tend to expect this fulfillment from a spouse, and as we saw in chapter six, the church all too often, in an attempt to honor marriage, encourages this false expectation. Nouwen warns us that "when we forget that and expect from others more than they can give, we will become quickly disillusioned; for when we do not receive what we expect, we easily become resentful, bitter, revengeful, and even violent." [58] We all have unfulfilled longings that will not be met until we are together with Christ in heaven, and trying to fulfill them with anything but God ultimately enslaves us to those desires. As DeMoss writes, "Part of the purpose of those longings is to cause our hearts to become more detached from this earth and more attached to our true home in heaven."[59] In a sense, this is the same "transcendental aim" Gregory of Nyssa asks us to strive for. He definitely takes it too far, rooting it in a disdain for the physical world and suggesting that we should seek to be like the angels. But that does not negate the truth that our lives are on a path from one world to the next. We need to keep our eyes focused on our eternity with Christ even while our feet are planted firmly on the earth. Rather than seeking to be like the angels, we should seek to be human beings, created in the image of God, who are becoming every day more and more conformed to his likeness.

Augustine describes our condition on this earth in his *Confessions* when he writes, "Thou madest us for Thyself, and our heart is restless, until it repose in Thee."[60] In *Forgotten Among the Lilies: Learning to Love Beyond Our Fears* Ronald Rolheiser applies this concept specifically to the celibate life. Rather than speaking of his celibacy in pious terms, he writes, "A celibate life is of itself an absurdity, pure and simple. Man without woman and woman without man is absurd."[61] This probably isn't what most single adults want to hear, but it is often how we feel. Rolheiser acknowledges that he will always feel lonely, no matter how many friends he has and no matter how supportive his community is. But he also acknowledges that this loneliness also exists within even the best marriages. So what hope is there, especially for the celibate? According to Rolheiser, the hope lies in the acknowledgement of the absurdity of our state: "Only when this foolishness is recognized does inconsummation become thirst for a wider love, then self-pity turns into hope, confusion into clarity, foolishness into beauty. Then absurdity becomes a center of peace and there, finally, things begin to make some sense and both marriage and celibacy become possible and beautiful."[62]

Unlike many of his predecessors, Rolheiser does not see celibacy as transcendent because it rejects marriage or because it is "like the angels." Rather, he states that it is "only in accepting this limit, this pathos, that we rise above ourselves and become more human, because it is then that we let go of those imaginings and unrealistic expectations which prevent us from living in advent for God's kingdom."[63] Nouwen expresses a similar sentiment in regard to loneliness. He writes, "Instead of running away from our loneliness and trying to forget or deny it, we have to protect it and turn it into fruitful solitude. To live a spiritual life, we must first find the courage to enter into the desert of our loneliness and to change it by gentle and persistent efforts into a garden of solitude."[64] What DeMoss, Rolheiser, and Nouwen manage to do is to take the seemingly impossible goals of the early church fathers and rework them for today, reminding us of the ultimate truth of our incompleteness and longing for God and showing us how this longing may propel us into a closer relationship with God even without the support of the monastic life.

Redefining Our Terms

The interaction of ideas among early church fathers, contemporary Catholic thinkers, and contemporary Protestant writers demonstrates that there are many things that we can learn from both past and present Christian teachings on celibacy. On the most basic level, it is certainly helpful to realize that there is a tradition of valuing the celibate state. In addition, it is important to realize that we don't have to discount all of the early church's ideas or the Catholic Church's teaching on the subject because of past sexism and disdain for the human body, for it is possible to value celibacy without hating marriage and fearing sexuality. But, perhaps most importantly, we can begin to see how to take these ideas that may seem strange to us on the surface and find the deeper truths we may embrace.

The fact remains, however, that without actually being part of a monastic community, we still don't have the support we really need, for those who are part of a monastic community are provided with the advantages of a clear calling and a sense of security. Rolheiser acknowledges that "unlike married persons and consecrated religious, singles in the world are rarely given a thriving set of symbols which can provide a symbolic hedge within which to understand their inconsummation." In addition, the consecrated religious have chosen their state. Most Protestant singles have not, at least not to the same extent, for most singles hope that their state will be temporary. This distinction in and of itself tends to separate us from the positive messages of celibacy available to the consecrated religious. Thomas Dubay, for instance, writes that "the very concept of temporary virginity is a self-contradiction."[65] That is difficult for us as Protestants to accept. The distinction here is that Dubay is referring to virginity as a spiritual vow one makes rather than as a temporary physical state we lose upon marriage. We tend to refer to our singleness as a "season of life": we cannot imagine it lasting forever. While Rolheiser does not try to persuade everyone to take religious vows, he does warn us of the dangers of being unable to view celibate singleness as a potentially permanent state. If we only think in temporary terms we run the risk of never fully seeing our lives as worthwhile and actually worth living.[66]

The challenge for Protestant singles who desire to move beyond the state of obsessively searching for a spouse but who don't feel called to take a vow of permanent celibacy is to see how we might redefine celibacy for the twenty-first century. Is it possible to fully embrace the state of celibacy for the time that God calls us to it without either giving up hope for marriage if God desires it or relentlessly striving to change the state into which God has placed us? While the concept of abstinence might serve for some as they commit to sexual purity until marriage, many older Christian singles need more than this message of waiting until marriage. Chastity, which is a more affirming message of placing sexual desires under God's control both outside and inside of marriage, might serve for others, but with its dual focus on both singleness and marriage, it may not provide Christian singles with a strong enough message that is specific to their unique situation. Shifting the focus to celibacy, then, allows Christian singles to reframe their position by placing it within the traditional discussions of celibacy throughout church history, giving them the opportunity to tap into truths that may empower them to live radically countercultural lives that testify to God's amazing power.

9

Discipline & Community
Views of Celibacy in Contemporary Christian Thought

Every time Christians make a fetish of the family, you can be sure they
don't believe in God anymore.

Stanley Hauerwas, "On: Dietrich Bonhoeffer
and John Howard Yoder"

A right understanding and practice of singleness is crucial to the health
of Christian family—especially in a postmodern world. To put it strongly,
there is a least one sure sign of a flawed vision of the Christian family:
it denigrates and dishonors singleness.

Rodney Clapp, *Families at the Crossroads*

Several years ago when Christine began teaching at Wheaton College,
she experienced firsthand a long-standing tradition in which new faculty
members were introduced at the fall faculty banquet by the provost of the
college who would discuss their academic credentials as they walked to the
front of the banquet hall. Married faculty members would be accompanied
by their spouses, and the provost would introduce them as well and talk
about their families as the couple stood together in front of the professor's

colleagues. For single faculty members, these introductions proved to be rather awkward, for while married faculty members were introduced both professionally and personally, single faculty members were introduced only professionally. While the intent of these introductions was certainly not to make the new single faculty feel uncomfortable, the implication was that the only personal information that was important to this community was marital status and number of children. For Christine, who had spent the past few years at a secular graduate school, these awkward introductions demonstrated just how different this evangelical community was from the rest of the academic world. She appreciated the fact that, unlike a secular institution where all that mattered were professional credentials, Wheaton College valued the personal, but she wished that it could be defined more broadly than simply the ability to acquire a spouse and children.

For many Christian singles, this tension is one that we must deal with on a regular basis. In response to many of the social changes that occurred in the United States in the late twentieth century, such as the growing acceptance of sexual activity outside of marriage, the rise in divorce, and the desire of many homosexuals to marry, evangelical churches began to speak more directly of "family values" that would counter these influences. By focusing on the family, the church could clearly separate itself from the values of the secular society that surrounded it. While many Christian singles can sympathize with this desire to uphold the value of the family, we also feel frustrated by the fact that the evangelical church has now become so closely tied to this particular social institution that it seemingly has no place for those who are unmarried. Family values have now assumed such an important place in the church that to question their prominence is to provoke quite a bit of controversy.

The response to John Piper's sermon "Single in Christ: A Name Better than Sons and Daughters" clearly demonstrates this point. For many Christian singles, this sermon was a breath of fresh air—something that we could cling to in the midst of all of the discussions of family values with which we had been inundated for years. As Christian singles e-mailed the link to the sermon to our single friends, there was a sense that finally someone was placing these family values in perspective. For many other Christians, however, Piper's sermon was an attack on all they held dear. In this sermon, Piper presents a clear call to action that challenges the prevailing discussion of family values: "I am declaring the temporary and secondary nature of marriage and family over against the eternal and primary nature of the church . . . This is not trivial; this is huge . . . I fear [we have] settled into our land and our culture and idolized the family, idolized marriage. We are here for a vapor's breath and then we are gone. What happens here is relatively minor compared to what will be after the resurrection."[1] As the many negative responses to this sermon on Focus on the Family's webzine for singles indicate, Piper struck a nerve, particularly when he went on to affirm the value of celibacy for today's Christians. Now, Piper was certainly not devaluing marriage or calling all Christians to embrace a celibate lifestyle. This sermon, in fact, was part of a larger series that dealt primarily with marriage. But the idea that marriage and family should be secondary to the church proved to be a radical concept that many refused to embrace.

But is it such a radical concept? Surely, scripture reminds us again and again that our loyalty to Christ supersedes all other loyalties even those as good as loyalty to marriage and family. Why, then, can't we see both marriage and celibacy as valid ways of serving God for the limited time that we are here on earth? What would it mean, for instance, to radically reconceive our ideas of celibacy to empower Christian singles to live our lives fully for God without remaining in stunted adolescence, searching obsessively for a spouse, or wallowing in depression and self-pity? Think of the transformations that could take place if we as singles embraced our freedoms and began to participate fully in the work of the church. Think of the powerful witness that these freedoms could be for unchurched singles who might be more willing to seek out a church community where they would feel valued as children of God and brothers and sisters in Christ. How might we begin to see celibacy in a new light?

Placing Marriage in Perspective

One of the first steps in this process must be placing marriage in a proper perspective. While we acknowledge that today's secular society may not value the family as much as it should and we recognize that the church should be a haven for families to provide the support that they need, marriage cannot be the sole focus of the church. As we have discussed in previous chapters, many evangelical leaders who speak to singles hold out marriage as if it were the Holy Grail. Marriage is our ticket into maturity as a Christian, full membership in the body of Christ, and ultimate happiness. The assumption often is that Christian singles cannot experience life fully until we are married, but is marriage really the perfect solution for every ill a single Christian might experience?

Let's begin with a discussion of Christian maturity. We have probably all observed Christian singles who refuse to grow up and choose rather to live as immature adolescents until they find a spouse. Is this a danger that Christian singles may fall prey to? Certainly. Immaturity, however, is not limited to singles. Immaturity is a human condition: one that we must all confront as we work to develop into the Christians that God wants us to be. Do the responsibilities of a spouse and children help many individuals to grow more mature? Yes. But so may the responsibilities of negotiating a job, a mortgage, an illness, or any other reality of life without any support from a spouse. The difference is not necessarily the outward trappings of life but how we approach the challenges that God allows us to experience. In *The Sacrament of Love: The Nuptial Mystery in the Light of the Orthodox Tradition*, orthodox theologian Paul Evdokimov addresses just this issue, remarking, "Trying to prove the superiority of one state over the other [marriage or celibacy] is . . . useless: it is an abstract, because impersonal, process. The renunciation at work in both cases is as good as the positive content that the human being brings to it: the intensity of the love of God."[2] What transforms us into mature Christians are not the externals of marriage or single-ness but rather the work that we allow God to do within our hearts. Marriage cannot be the answer to spiritual maturity.

Marriage also cannot be the ultimate cure for loneliness as so many try to suggest that it is. Do many singles feel lonely on a Friday night as they sit watching bad reality television while seemingly the rest of the world is contentedly communing with their families or experiencing blissfully romantic dates? Yes. But so do many married men and women who discover, often to their surprise, that their spouses do not fulfill all of their deepest needs. In their essay, "From Conduct to Character—A Guide for Sexual Adventure," Stanley Hauerwas and Allen Verhey refer to what they term " 'Hauerwas's law': 'You always marry the wrong person.' "[3] Rather than supporting the romantic ideal that marriage will live up to the intense, fairy-tale excitement that is so often portrayed in literature, movies, television, and music, they remind their readers that "the adventure of marriage is learning to love the person to whom you are married."[4] And often that process is a difficult one of realizing that a spouse may never understand the deepest feelings or yearnings of your heart. Only God will ever truly know the deepest recesses of each of our hearts, so, ultimately, each of us will remain, to one extent or another, lonely in this world as we come to recognize again and again that only in eternity with Christ will we ever feel completely known and loved. As Ronald Rolheiser declares, "We are always in some way frustrated, in some way sleeping alone, whether we are having sex or not."[5] Marriage may be an image of Christ's love for his church, but it cannot fulfill our deepest longings completely.

Neither does it always contain the amazing, transcendent sexual experiences promised to many teenage abstinence pledgers. While the leaders of many abstinence campaigns often highlight the glories of sex that will automatically be theirs if they just wait until marriage, the reality is that, as Hauerwas and Verhey remark, "Sex is as frequently messy and boring as it is spiritually fulfilling."[6] In many cases, the church has simply accepted the world's construction of love as demonstrated solely by a passionate, emotional connection, which is revealed through intensely erotic sexual encounters. In *Real Sex*, Lauren Winner reminds her readers, "Married sex is a given. It is solemnized and marked in ritual. It is established. It is governed by vows. It becomes a ritual in itself; it becomes a routine."[7] The idea of marital sex as routine is one that many Christians and most non-Christians would reject. Doesn't routinized sex demonstrate that there are problems in the marriage? Perhaps the problem lies not in the routine sex but rather in the overly romanticized view of sex that many Christians have come to accept. Rather than seeing sex as part of the covenant of marriage that will go through various stages and transformations in the course of the marriage, many mistakenly believe that if they aren't reveling in a sex life that is as exciting as the couple in the latest romantic movie something must be wrong. Sexual satisfaction becomes the barometer for every other aspect of life, and we come to believe that sex is the solution for all of our issues of intimacy and community. Theologian Marva Dawn provides an interesting perspective on this issue, declaring, "It seems to me that much of the sexual behavior in U.S. society today is grounded in the failure to distinguish between our profound needs for support on the level of social sexuality [building nurturing non-romantic relationships with people of both sexes] and the attraction of exciting genital stimulation."[8] Have we overemphasized sex to such an extent that we expect a good sex life to resolve all of our other issues? At times, we do, and as Dawn suggests this overvaluing of sex leads many to inappropriately seek for support in sexual activity.

Speaking particularly about sex, Hauerwas and Verhey argue that if we told the truth, "extravagant expectations could be lowered, the possibility and plausibility of saying 'no' could be nurtured as well as commanded, and the harm of unfulfilled expectations lowered."[9] And this applies not only to truth about the sexual act but also to marriage as a whole. Marriage and sex are blessings given by God, but by overemphasizing them, we place huge pressures on Christian married couples to live up to these unrealistic expectations, encourage individuals to use sex as a means of trying to find fulfillment for other aspects of their lives, and leave singles feeling like second-class citizens who will never be fully functioning humans, let alone Christians, if they don't get married.

Acknowledging the Complexities of the Single Life

In addition to placing sex and marriage in perspective, we also need to acknowledge the complexities of life for contemporary Christian singles. Too often Christian singles are defined simply as teenagers who need to be encouraged to abstain until their perfect partner comes along. Older singles in particular need much more complex discussions to help us confront the confusing realities of our lives. Simply glancing through the chapter titles of Camerin Courtney and Todd Hertz's book *The UnGuide to Dating* provides a glimpse of just how complex this world is. Today's older Christian singles must confront "The Dating Drought," "Men in the Church: O Brother, Where are Thou?" "Changing Gender Roles," "Dating Non-Christians," "Internet Dating," "Matchmaking," "Sexual Temptation," "Body Image," "Biological Clock," and "Intergender Friendships." These older Christian singles cannot be satisfied with the simple, romantic tale of just trusting God until he brings Prince or Princess Charming to the door. Many of us have already had to encounter the idea that God may not have this partner in store for us. In addition, the world of the church may also become more difficult for us to navigate as we begin to realize just how far our singleness sets us apart from the rest of the congregation.

Perhaps one of the first steps in acknowledging these complexities for singles lies in reformulating our ideas of celibacy. For most, celibacy is an antiquated word associated solely with the Catholic Church: priests, nuns, and monks take vows of celibacy, but it certainly has no part in contemporary Protestant society. Even those such as Stanley Grenz who have a much more nuanced view of singleness than most do not necessarily define celibacy in a way that acknowledges the complex realities of today's older singles. In *Sexual Ethics*, Grenz divides singleness into four categories: "youth and early adult," "unchosen," "willed celibate," and "postmarriage."[10] Many older Christian singles today are caught between the "unchosen" and "willed celibate" categories. We have remained single, waiting for the right partner, but may now be beginning to realize that this partner may not actually arrive. We don't necessarily feel called to celibacy in the traditional sense of that calling, but we also do not want to live the rest of our lives focused solely on looking for a spouse. The problem is that there is too large a distinction between these two categories. We need an intermediate category here to bridge the gap.

According to Grenz, "An individual can never be celibate in a de facto manner, that is, simply because he or she is not yet married or was previously married. Rather, the celibate person has chosen the single life as the best option for the fulfillment of a personal calling."[11] For many older Christian singles this is a problematic definition, for it seemingly offers us only two alternatives: to be dissatisfied and frustrated with our single state or to make an official vow of celibacy, similar to that embraced by the Catholic Church, as a means of fulfilling some radical calling in which marriage would be a hindrance. In her book *Get Married* Candice Watters gives some very specific examples of how she believes this type of celibacy should (or should not) manifest itself in the evangelical church. She writes, "If you're going on a missions trip once a year, volunteering at church twice a week, and holding down a traditional job, and on top of it all, dating the cute new guy in your singles group, you're not following the celibate job description."[12] So what does constitute the celibate job description? Watters asserts that a celibate life should aspire to Paul's level of devotion as expressed in 2 Corinthians 6:3–10:

> . . . giving no cause for offense in anything, so that the ministry will not be discredited, but in everything commending ourselves as servants of God, in much endurance, in afflictions, in hardships, in distresses, in beatings, in imprisonments, in tumults, in labors, in sleeplessness, in hunger, in purity, in knowledge, in patience, in kindness, in the Holy Spirit, in genuine love, in the word of truth, in the power of God; by the weapons

of righteousness for the right hand and the left, by glory and dishonor, by evil report and good report; regarded as deceivers and yet true; as unknown yet well-known, as dying yet behold, we live; as punished yet not put to death, as sorrowful yet always rejoicing, as poor yet making many rich, as having nothing yet possessing all things.

While Watters is correct that we all should strive for this level of devotion, whether we are single or married, it is problematic to assume that there are only two options—get married or be persecuted as a celibate witness for God. The reality of our world is that Christian devotion does not usually lead to torture and imprisonment, even for those who serve in full-time overseas missions. While it certainly can and does for some, this is not the norm, and defining celibacy by this standard implies that unless you are actively experiencing persecution as a celibate warrior for God, you must be married.

What we need is another category: those who are committed to celibacy until God reveals a different plan for them. Laura Smit is one of the few to present this idea. In her discussion of Paul's view of singleness in I Corinthians, she remarks,

> It does seem . . . that singleness must be the default choice for a Christian, given the clear preference for singleness expressed in this text and in Jesus' teachings. In other words, the burden of proof is on the decision to marry, not the decision to remain single. Christians should assume that they will be single unless and until they have a godly reason to marry. Christians should never marry out of insecurity, fear, a desire to escape the parental home, a need for affirmation, or a search for financial stability. Christians should only marry those who enhance their ability to live Christlike lives, those able to be true partners in Christian service, those who give them a vision of the image of God and the glory of Christ.[13]

This type of celibacy does not necessarily require an official vow or a special vocation for which singleness is essential. Instead, it is a powerful recognition of the truth that Paul expresses in Philippians 4:11: "I have learned to be content in whatever circumstances I am."

By thinking of celibacy in this way, perhaps we can begin to move away from the terms "gift of singleness" or "gift of celibacy" that are so frustrating to many singles. As Lauren Winner remarks, "Perhaps we ought not fixate on *the call to lifelong singleness*. Some people, of course, are called to lifelong singleness, but more of us are called to singleness for a spell . . . Often, our task is to discern a call to singleness for right now, and that's not so difficult. If you are single right now, you are called, right now, to be single—called to live a single life as robustly, and gospel-conformingly, as you possibly can."[14] By defining celibacy in these terms—being called by God to live chaste lives as strong, single Christians for as long as he desires us to fulfill this role—perhaps we can begin to affirm the many older Christian singles who have decided to accept the challenge of Philippians 4:11.

Negotiating Single Sexuality and Sex

Celibacy as a Spiritual Discipline

But what about sex? If singles embrace this new definition of celibacy, what happens to our sexuality and our desire for sex? Debbie Maken addresses this issue in her response to Piper's sermon. She remarks, "Singles will fail the goals advanced by Piper, not only because there is no increased Scriptural acceptance for New Testament singleness, but because their sexual nature was never changed or altered in the New Testament. Until we figure out the obvious—see Old Testament sex drive, see New Testament sex drive (hmmm, no difference)—we are going to be engaging in imaginary possibilities."[15] For Maken, as for many others, the sexual drive is one that cannot be controlled; therefore, Christians who have sexual desires and wish to live in God's will must be married. If not, they live their lives on a powder keg of sexual desires that will inevitably explode into inappropriate sexual activity. What is interesting about this conception of sex is not only that it ignores how much of sexual desire is actually constructed by the society around the individual (did the Old Testament Hebrews really think of sexual desire in exactly the same way as twenty-first-century Americans do?), but also that it assumes that sexual desire is the one thing that, as Christians, we cannot bring under God's control. We can placate it through marriage, but we cannot control it as Christian singles.

In his book *The Spirit of the Disciplines: Understanding How God Changes Lives*, philosopher Dallas Willard presents an alternative perspective, remarking, "The vitality and power of Christianity is lost when we fail to integrate our bodies into its practice by intelligent, conscious choice and steadfast intent. It is with our *bodies* we receive the new life

209

that comes as we enter his Kingdom."[16] Rather than holding the body to a separate standard, Willard reminds us that spiritual disciplines are enacted precisely through this body. The call, then, to bring our lives in conformity to Christ is not simply addressed to our intellect or our spirit but also to our bodies. Theologian Richard Foster applies this concept specifically to single sexuality in *The Challenge of the Disciplined Life: Christian Reflections on Money, Sex, and Power*:

> Donald Goergen [in *The Sensual Celibate*] has noted that "feelings are meant to be felt, and sexual feelings are no exception." When we try to deny these feelings we cut ourselves off from humanity . . . But to accept them does not mean to act upon them. Sexual feelings are not to control us; we are to control them. It is an illusion to think that sexual desires are uncontrollable. Just because we may feel angry enough to want to murder someone does not mean that we will do so. We control our feelings of anger so that we do not kill, and in the same way we bring our sexual feelings under our authority.[17]

Controlling our sexual desires (both inside and outside of marriage) is part of our development as Christians. And celibate, single Christians can testify to the truth that this self-control of sexual desires is possible.

Now, it may be possible, but it is certainly not easy. We do not want to make the mistake of assuming that all singles who are celibate have received a miraculous gift from God whereby our sexual desires have entirely disappeared. Celibacy is, ultimately, a spiritual discipline: one in which we train our minds and bodies by placing them in subjection to God's commands. As Lauren Winner remarks, "[Spiritual disciplines] are ways we orient our whole selves—our bodies and minds and hearts, our communities and rhythms and ways of being in the world—toward God . . . practicing spiritual disciplines helps align your feelings, your will, and your habits with God's will."[18] Thinking of celibacy as a spiritual discipline helps us to understand the value of controlling sexual desires in the midst of a world in which this practice seems at best ridiculous and at worst dangerous. We are not giving up sex because we think it is evil or because we wish to punish ourselves or because we desire to prove that we are more holy than our sexually active brothers and sisters. We refrain from sexual activity because it helps us to place God, sex, and Christian community in the right perspective. Celibacy is a way of enacting through our bodies our belief that God, not us, is in control. It reminds us that he desires us as Christians to build relationships with others that are not based solely on sexual attraction nor on biological connections but rather on our communion with him and our concern for our neighbors.

Celibacy also compels single Christians to grapple with important issues of the faith. As Richard Foster remarks, "The classical Disciplines of the spiritual life call us to move beyond surface living into the depths,"[19] and celibacy certainly has the potential to allow single Christians to grow much more mature in our faith. For many older, Christian singles, celibacy is, by far, the spiritual discipline that has most forcefully compelled us to confront the realities of the Christian faith. In an evangelical Christian world that so easily promises that God will give everyone "the desires of their hearts," celibate Christian singles who have not received the spouses for whom we so desperately long must come to terms with this seeming discrepancy. Are we simply bad Christians whom God has chosen to punish, or is God's love a fraud? Or is there another answer in which we come to realize that the deepest desires of our heart need to rest not in the temporal realities of marriage and family but rather in our eternal relationship with God? While this is a reality that all Christians should be grappling with, many celibate Christian singles have to deal with it much more directly and vividly in our personal lives.

Christian singles often must deal with the issue of Christian vocation in a much more direct way as well. Those married Christians who are not called to a traditional full-time Christian ministry, often see their role in the Christian community as raising good, Christian children who will provide a strong foundation for the next generation of the church. Christian singles, however, cannot find much comfort in this biological ministry. We must discover the unique plan that God has for us in the development of his church and the spreading of his gospel beyond the walls of the local church congregation. We must also negotiate the difficulties of being part of a church that many times doesn't seem to have any place for us. As we explored in chapter four, it is often difficult for single Christians to feel connected to local church congregations that overlook us in their zealous attempts to care for the families that make up the majority of the church. Christian singles must wrestle with these realities in the context of scripture, which commands us not to isolate ourselves but to be part of the body of Christ. While these issues are not necessarily unique to celibate Christian singles, they are common to many of us, and the discipline of celibacy compels us to look beyond the surface of a comfortable, complacent Christianity to the deeper realities of God's truth.

But how is celibacy possible? Even if we recognize that controlling sexual desire is an important spiritual discipline that allows us to place ourselves in subjection to God and to learn important truths about the Christian walk, how do we do it? Well, the first thing to recognize is that it is not an easy process. As Willard remarks, "The one lesson we learn from all available sources is that there is no 'quick fix' for the human condition. The approach to wholeness is for humankind a process of great length and difficulty that engages all our powers to their fullest extent over a long course of experience."[20] Celibacy is not simply flipping a handy switch in the brain labeled "sexual desires" from the "on" position to the "off" position. Instead, it is a process of conforming our will to God's will even if we don't necessarily understand why God has chosen this particular state for us right now. In this, however, celibacy is no different from other aspects of our lives that we need to place in subjection to God, and as such it begins with immersing ourselves in scripture and in prayer, acknowledging the truth of God's right to our bodies, and asking for his help to overcome our fleshly desires.

In her discussion of chastity, Winner demonstrates why thinking of chastity (or celibacy according to our redefinition) as a spiritual discipline is so important, for "[it] helps us quiet that nagging voice in our heads that says, 'I'm being made to give up something that is totally normal and natural!' Of course, the desire for sex is normal and natural, but many spiritual disciplines . . . center on refraining from something normal . . . The unmarried Christian who practices chastity refrains from sex in order to remember that God desires your person, your body, more than any man or woman ever will."[21] Seeing celibacy in this way allows us to place it in perspective. We are not being tortured or asked to do something that is completely impossible. We are being asked to obey God, and he is able to transform us from the flawed human beings we all are into the images of Christ he asks us to be.

Sexuality vs. Sexual Activity

As Christian celibates engage in this process of transformation, one of the key components that we must recognize is that sexual activity is not the same as sexuality. While being celibate means that we do not engage in sexual activity, it does not mean that we cease to be sexual. In the introduction to *Soul Virgins*, Doug Rosenau recounts an experience of telling a friend that he was going to lead a workshop on singles' sexuality. His friend's response is revealing: "Two hours on single sexuality? How many ways can you say *don't*?"[22] While "don't" may be an appropriate response to singles' sexual activity, it is certainly not an effective response to the many complexities involved with singles' sexuality. Unfortunately, it is as far as many speakers and churches get in their discussions. As Lisa Graham McMinn reveals, "A challenge of the contemporary Church is to claim a theology of sexuality that names, validates, and embraces the sexuality of singleness."[23] One place to start is to realize that singles, like all humans, are sexual beings. Sexuality for Christian singles isn't magically ignited when the wedding ring hits the finger.

In *Sexual Ethics* Stanley Grenz presents a good discussion of sexuality that moves beyond its representation in sexual activity and reveals not only how single Christians may be considered to be sexual but also how we may enact this sexuality appropriately. In his definition of sexuality, Grenz argues,

> To be human means to exist as male or female, to be an embodied being. And embodiment means sexuality. Singles, then, are sexual beings. And they remain so whether or not they engage in genital sexual acts, for affective sexuality is not dependent on genital expression. Even voluntary participation in a celibate lifestyle does not necessitate a denial of one's fundamental sexuality. On the contrary, it can actually comprise a concrete way of expressing it.[24]

From the Christian perspective, this construction of sexuality has important ramifications, for as Grenz reveals, the fact that we are created male and female reminds us that "as isolated individuals we are unable to reflect the fullness of humanity and thus the fullness of the divine image."[25] Sexuality, then, provides us with our drive to connect with others, for "our existence as sexual beings gives rise to the desire to enter into community, and thereby to actualize our design as human individuals. Sexuality, then, is an expression of our nature as social beings . . . This need to find fulfillment beyond ourselves is the dynamic that leads to the desire to develop relationships with others and ultimately with God."[26] When we look at it from this perspective, sexuality has a much larger purpose than simply compelling individuals to find a mate.

Our culture, however, tends to deny this larger purpose, equating sexuality almost entirely with the sexual act. While we tend to think of sexuality as a biological drive that transcends time and culture, Grenz reminds us that "it is our culture, not biology, that places such great emphasis on genital involvement as the only means whereby we can find the closeness we all quite naturally desire."[27] Yes, the sexual drive is biological, but the emphasis that we place upon it, the way we describe it, and our beliefs in the way that it is aroused are strongly influenced by our culture. The response of Rosenau's friend to the idea of a workshop on single sexuality reveals just how much the secular emphasis on sexuality as represented solely through the act of sex has come to permeate the church. Reclaiming this wider definition of sexuality, however, is essential to maintaining a strong conception of celibacy. If sexuality is essential to defining who we are as human beings and if sexuality is defined simply as having a vigorous sex life, then celibates are inevitably flawed or warped. If, however, we define sexuality more widely, we can begin to conceive of a world where strong, positive sexuality may be productively displayed even by those who are committed to celibacy.

Ronald Rolheiser, in his book *The Holy Longing*, provides us with this wider definition that takes into account sexuality's purpose in drawing us toward each other and to God. According to Rolheiser, "In its maturity, sexuality is about giving oneself over to community, friendship, family, service, creativity, humor, delight, and martyrdom so that, with God, we can help bring life into the world."[28] When we see sexuality in this light, we can begin to understand how sexual intercourse is only one example of how sexuality may be lived out in this world. Celibates, then, are not forced to repress our sexuality because we refuse to have sex. Instead, we are challenged to enact our sexuality in other ways to the glory of God.

Building upon this wider definition of sexuality we may begin to see how celibate, Christian singles may manifest our sexuality appropriately. Marva Dawn points us to the example of Jesus as one to follow as we embrace single sexuality. She reminds us, "Jesus gives us the perfect model for social sexuality. His gentleness and concern for the marginalized smash the stupid stereotypes of male machismo. His strength and courage overturn the sticky sentimental notions of 'Jesus meek and mild.' He kept his social sexuality distinct from his genital sexuality by relating in powerfully wholesome, upbuilding, nongenital ways with persons of both sexes."[29] While we will never reach the perfection of Christ here on earth, we must strive to be more like him, and for Christian singles, his celibacy may encourage us to move beyond our narrow focus on sexual desires to see how we may relate to those around us within this wider definition of sexuality.

Doug Roseneau and Michael Todd Wilson echo these ideas, ultimately proposing that single Christians need "to master the skills for *going beyond their sexual longings to a larger capacity for love*,"[30] and this challenge is one that celibate Christians need to embrace not only for ourselves but also for a wider witness in the church. Instead of becoming lost in depression or consumed with finding a spouse, Christian singles need to look around and see what needs we might be able to address as we channel our desires for community into love for our neighbors. How might we effectively "be" Christ in the lives of those around us? Can we drive an elderly neighbor to the doctor? Can we babysit for our friends' children? Can we invite friends and newcomers over for a meal after church? Can we serve at a soup kitchen over the holidays? Can we take the time to do mission work overseas? Can we mentor younger singles in the church who are struggling to find a meaning in their singleness?

Developing this "larger capacity for love" is essential for today's evangelical church, which, too often, is so concerned with preserving its families that it ignores many who desperately long for the Christian community that the church has the potential to provide. In her discussion of this issue, Laura Smit equates today's Protestant church with an example she draws from Langdon Gilkey's book *Shantung Compound* in which the author records his experiences in an internment camp during the Japanese occupation of China. She states,

> Most of the missionaries were detained with their families, and their care for their families trumped their sense of obligation to the rest of the community. No one had enough space to live with much privacy, but some families who had arrived earlier than others had two small rooms for their family of four or five people, whereas the later arrivals had only one. Gilkey was in charge of housing assignments, but when he tried to get some of the missionaries who had two rooms to rearrange themselves to make the space allocation more fair, he met complete resistance. No family was willing to sacrifice anything for the good of the community, and several parents appealed to their moral duty to look out for the good of their families as a defense for such selfishness.[31]

What stands out to Gilkey and to Smit is that in contrast to the Protestant missionaries who separated themselves into distinct family units and placed their families above everything else, the Catholic priests who, as Gilkey records, "*mixed* . . . made friends with anyone in camp, helped out, played cards, smoked, and joked with them. . .were a means of grace to the whole community."[32] Without family ties, the priests had the freedom to express their love beyond family boundaries to include everyone within this newly formed community.

What would it mean for our churches to express love in this manner? Marva Dawn provides a glimpse of what might happen, declaring, "I am convinced that, if the Church could provide more thorough affection and care for persons, many would be less likely to turn falsely to genital sexual expression for the social support they need."[33] Perhaps by embodying this wider sexuality, celibate Christian singles can provide the rest of the church with a model from which they too may begin to live out the call to community that transcends family boundaries. And by doing so, the church as a whole may begin to be transformed into a community that provides so much love that genital sex may assume its proper place rather than becoming the ultimate focus of so many within our society. After all, is sex really the most important issue here? In *Sex for Christians*, Lewis Smedes questions that assumption:

> Actually, in my judgment, most single people place physical sex itself in some category beneath their highest priority. While it is true that sexual intercourse has lost its moral specialness, it is also true that sexual intercourse is not single people's most basic need. What takes top priority is the hunger for close personal relationships. It is, I think, a mistake to suppose that single people are all lustfully rushing to get into bed with someone. What is happening is that single people are infected with a terrible loneliness, and the filling of that closeness gap is uppermost in their needs and desires.[34]

From what we have experienced and noticed in others, Smedes is correct. Sex is being used to fill other needs: needs that should be provided for when we live within a strong Christian community but, too often, are not.

Lisa Graham McMinn's interview with a man named Gary provides an interesting perspective on this topic. When reflecting upon his wife's desertion of him and the dissolution of their twenty-five-year marriage, he remarks, "I had a number of years in my marriage where my sexual needs were being met but not my intimacy needs. Now I have intimacy needs being meet [sic] and not sexual needs. I prefer this; I feel more complete with this. My soul has been enlarged. My completeness is more in community now, in meaningful relationships. My friends affirm that I seem healthy and stable, and I feel that, too."[35] Gary's experience is a powerful reminder that our needs cannot be wrapped up simply in the desire to have sex, and his affirmation that he "feels more complete" in his community even though his sexual desires are unfulfilled is a strong testimony to the fact that we need to place sex within its proper context. Broadening our definition of sexuality allows us to do this, for it helps us see that there is more to us as sexual beings than simply our desires for sex, and by expanding the ways that we may express our sexuality, it compels us to create the kind of Christian community that works to meet each other's needs for love and intimacy.

Recognizing the "Holy Longing" for God that Resides within All of Us

As we consider the needs of single as well as married Christians, we must also recognize that there resides within all of us a need that will never be satisfied here on earth: a holy longing, as Rolheiser calls it, that ultimately should drive us to God. In contemporary American society we are used to thinking that every need that we have will be satisfied if only we work hard enough or pray hard enough, but the reality is that we all experience dissatisfaction. As Rolheiser reminds us, "It is no easy task to walk this earth and find peace. Inside of us, it would seem, something is at odds with the very rhythm of things and we are forever restless, dissatisfied, frustrated, and aching. We are so overcharged with desire that it is hard to come to simple rest. Desire is always stronger than satisfaction."[36] As much as we try to search for satisfaction with work, money, relationships, pleasures, or sex, we discover that we cannot completely silence the yearning that is always in our hearts. Even as Christians, who have confidence in a God who "will supply all [our] needs according to His riches in glory in Christ Jesus" (Phil. 4:19), we realize that all of these needs may not be supplied here on earth. As Paul tells us a few verses earlier in Philippians, he has "learned to be content in whatever circumstances [he is]" (v. 11). Learning to be content in the midst of whatever circumstances we are in is essential precisely because of these feelings of restlessness. We will not be completely whole until we are with Christ in heaven, but we can learn to be content even in the midst of the difficulties we face here on earth.

But why do we have this dissatisfaction? In his poem "The Pulley," the seventeenth-century poet George Herbert provides us with an intriguing explanation. he imagines the scene of God creating the earth and pouring out his blessings upon it. God bestows beauty, wisdom, honor, and pleasure, but then just as He is about to pour his last blessing upon the earth, he decides to keep it. Rest remains in heaven with God. In the last two stanzas of the poem, God explains this decision:

> "For if I should," said he,
> "Bestow this jewel also on my creature,
> He would adore my gifts instead of me,
> And rest in Nature, not the God of Nature;
> So both should losers be.
>
> "Yet let him keep the rest,
> But keep them with repining restlessness:
> Let him be rich and weary, that at least,
> If goodness lead him not, yet weariness
> May toss him to my breast."[37]

As Herbert recognizes, God cannot allow us complete rest here on this sinful and fallen earth, for if he did, we would have no need to turn to him. More recently, McMinn has described this process and its ramifications for human relationships, reminding us that "in our fundamental longing for unity, communion, and consummation, we simultaneously reflect *imago Dei* and, whether or not we know it, we are yearning ultimately for the One who can satisfy our deepest longing to be known and loved."[38] This restlessness is what draws us to God, compelling us to recognize our deep need for his rest and for himself. It is important not only for conversion but also for the recognition that this world is truly not our home. Rather than becoming complacent here, we must continually remember that we are growing and developing to prepare us for eternity with God.

Unfortunately, we too often try to satisfy this yearning for God with the temporal things of earth, believing that if we can just find the perfect job or the perfect home or the perfect spouse, we will finally be content. This endless searching for satisfaction not only blinds us to the truth that rest is found only in God but also leads to frustration and desperation as we begin to realize that nothing else will bring perfect contentment. But what, then, do we do with this restlessness? How do we use it to draw us closer to the God who provides the wholeness we are all so fervently searching for? For Rolheiser, this is the key question, for "spirituality is, ultimately, about what we do with that desire."[39] Rather than trying to assuage this desire with the seeming solutions in the world around us, we need to discover how to use that desire to turn us to God.

Rolheiser (drawing on Henri Nouwen) provides perhaps the most specific discussion of this issue, listing four clear steps in this process of negotiating our restlessness:

1. Own your pain and incompleteness.
2. Give up false messianic expectations . . . We must stop expecting that somewhere, sometime, in some place, we will meet just the right person, the right situation, or the right combination of circumstances so that we can be completely happy.
3. Go inward . . . sitting still long enough for restlessness to turn to restfulness, compulsion to freedom, impatience to patience, self-absorption to altruism, and heartache to empathy.
4. It is a movement that is never made once and for all.[40]

While these steps are relevant for all Christians struggling with feelings of incompleteness, they are particularly applicable to Christian singles who may feel this incompleteness more intensely than those who have a spouse and children. In the first two steps, we are challenged to recognize the reality of our situation rather than trying to deny it or cover it up with the busyness of our lives. We acknowledge the truth of our pain and then in the third step wait for God to transform us in the midst of that pain. The key element here is that we are not asking God to remove the pain of incompleteness that we all must struggle with, but rather we are asking Him to use this pain precisely as it was intended: to draw us closer to him and to help create the empathy that allows us to be witnesses for him in the rest of the world. This is certainly not an easy process, and it is one that most of us would rather avoid, which is why we search for satisfaction any other way. But it is necessary in all of our lives, and as Rolheiser points out in the final step, it is a process that we have to enact time and time again as we continually ask for our restlessness to make us more like Christ.

Finding Support within the Church Community

This process of becoming more like Christ in the midst of our loneliness and restlessness is not an easy one, particularly when it is linked with flawed secular and even "Christian" ideas about sex and celibacy. In her book *Real Sex*, Lauren Winner records a conversation between a nun and a group of college students. When one of the college students asks, "What's the deal with not having sex?" Sister Margaret responds with an interesting statement: "I think we have an easier time of it here together in our community than you unmarried young people do out there, alone, in the world."[41] Sister Margaret's insightful comment reveals an important truth about today's evangelical church: we do not have a community in which those experiencing celibacy find the support that we need. Certainly, we are encouraged to refrain from sex outside of marriage, but we are generally not provided with the support (either socially or theologically) that we need to sustain this decision.

What would it mean for the evangelical church to begin to support Christian singles in our celibacy? Firstly, churches would need to recognize the power that they have to help individuals struggling with sexuality. Now, as Rolheiser reminds us, "One shouldn't go to church looking for a lover."[42] The role of the local church is certainly not to find or become a single Christian's spouse, but as McMinn remarks, "Communities of faith can be powerful agents of change and redemption for broken ideas about sexuality."[43] By creating a community in which individuals may be vulnerable with each other and then be held accountable to the truths of scripture, churches may help to transform lives and support individuals in these transformations. Many churches have begun to deal with some of these issues, providing support networks for young teens who desire to remain abstinent, married couples who are dealing with sexual issues, abused men and women who must confront the damage done to them in the past, and individuals who struggle with sexual sins such as pornography. While a support group for celibate singles might be one answer to the problem, perhaps what the church really needs to do is place all of these issues within the wider framework of what God says in scripture about singleness, marriage, and sexuality, bringing everyone together in brokenness before the Lord. As Winner mentions, "It is not enough for individual Christians to decide to be chaste; the church must be a community that works toward chastity, a community whose structures and rhythms make chastity seem plausible and attainable."[44]

But what would this type of community look like? A few years ago, Christine had the opportunity to be part of an adult Bible community at her church in which women of all ages came together to discuss issues of sexuality within the framework of scripture. What was amazing about the experience is that it demonstrated just how powerful Christian community could be at providing the support and insights women needed at the various stages of life that they were in. As they looked at various passages of scripture together and revealed personal experiences that demonstrated how God could work through various issues, community was built as women began to support their fellow sisters in Christ. But how often do individuals make themselves vulnerable to their brothers and sisters in Christ and allow true community to occur? While it may occasionally happen in small groups, it is certainly rare for an entire church to embody this type of community.

For Christian singles, in particular, this type of community is essential. Married couples cannot sequester themselves with our spouses and children and find strength from them; we all need the support of our Christian brothers and sisters. Unfortunately, the church rarely sees community as anything wider than supporting the individual nuclear families that make up the majority of the congregation. While we recognize the value of the family, we must also realize that Christian community within the church is ultimately more important. As Hauerwas remarks, "Christians do not believe marriage and the family exist for themselves, but rather serve the ends of the more determinative community called church. The assumption that the family is an end in itself can only make the family and marriage more personally destructive. When families exist for no reason other than their own existence, they become quasi-churches, which ask sacrifices far too great for insufficient reasons."[45] By shifting our perspective and recognizing the potential power of community within the church that can bridge gaps between single and married, male and female, child and adult, ethnic minority and white majority, rich and poor, we can begin to embody the truth of the diversity of the body of Christ, and we can begin to support each other in the unique difficulties of all of our Christian walks.

The church, however, does not exist solely to provide support for the Christians within it. Instead, it is given the charge of going out into the world to make disciples. And, interestingly, by taking this command seriously, the church may also begin to support singles within and outside of the church more effectively. Too often, our churches are so internally focused that they fail to interact effectively with the world around them. Conceiving of community as stemming almost solely from the nuclear family, churches may provide strong support for the children in the congregation, hoping that they will be church leaders of the next generation, but they may not look outside of the biological family to try to bring others into the family of God. A church that intentionally creates a community based not on biological ties but on spiritual ties may be more open to outreach to others who may not fit the particular demographic of the church. And as Hauerwas reveals, the treatment of singles within the church plays an important part in demonstrating what type of community it is, for "singleness in the church must become the occasion for friendship as we know we are linked by a communion that allows our differences to become the occasion for recognition of the other as other. If singleness should play the role I say, then Christians must surely be a people with a genius for friendship."[46] Surely, we would all like our churches to be characterized by "a genius for friendship" that not only involves every individual within the church but also proves to be appealing to our neighbors outside of the church, drawing them into this unique community that clearly reflects God's love for all.

A proper view of singleness and celibacy, then, is important not solely for older Christian singles who need support in the complexities of our lives but also for the church as a whole so that it may truly embody the community and love that make it such a powerful force of transformation in this world. As Winner relates, "Singleness prepares us for the other piece of the end of the time, the age when singleness trumps marriage. Singleness tutors us in our primary, heavenly relationship with one another: sibling in Christ."[47] This is not to say that every Christian must remain single, but by restoring singleness to its proper place within the church and grappling with the realities of celibacy, we can remind ourselves that this world is not our final destination. As we exist in community with each other here on earth, we are preparing for an eternity within the family of God, reminding ourselves of the importance of these spiritual ties and embodying the love that will draw others into this family.

Afterword
Where Do We Go From Here?

We cannot even honestly preach the Gospel when we cannot offer community to those to whom we are preaching.

Ronald Rolheiser, *Forgotten among the Lilies*

When we began to think seriously about writing a book on celibacy and the evangelical church, we weren't sure where we would end up. In fact, we were afraid that we wouldn't be able to find anything positive to say about celibacy beyond the idea that for some mysterious reason God had called us to remain single and we needed to accept that call. We have been amazed and blessed at what God and the wisdom of many other Christians have revealed to us in this process. While the book began with the quest of two isolated individuals, it ends in the midst of a small but growing number of Christians who recognize the value of singles within the community of the church. Both of us have been encouraged not only by the many Christian thinkers who have helped to contribute to our ideas on celibacy and the church but also by our own church bodies that have enabled us to become part of their communities and have valued our perspectives as single women. Unfortunately, not everyone has had such a positive experience in the church.

As the evidence from the previous chapters reveals, the experience of being an older single in the contemporary evangelical church is often not an easy one, and the reality is that there is no one simple solution that will suddenly solve all of the problems. It might be nice to think that if we just start a singles group or have a seminar all of the problems will immediately disappear. The truth is that each church and each Chris-

223

tian single will have different issues and different ways of negotiating them. In the midst of these complexities, however, we do believe that there are some general principles and practical ideas that will help to build stronger Christian communities in which everyone feels valued as members of the body of Christ.

Advice for Singles

Developing a More Complex Faith

As Christian singles, one of the first things we need to do is resist the temptation to think that our lives will only really start once we are married. Rather than existing in a holding pattern, waiting for marriage, and basing our ideas of God's faithfulness on whether or not he provides us with the spouse and children we desire, we must work toward developing a more complex faith. Do we give up hope that God may have marriage in mind for us? No. Do we allow that desire to control our lives? No. As Christians, we know that God desires the best for us. Problems arise, however, when we begin to define that "best" according to our desires and will rather than his. Too often, our faith is based on the assumption that God wants whatever we think will make us happy. We conveniently ignore the fact that God may actually be more concerned about our eternal souls and our witness to those around us than he is in whether or not we have someone to cuddle up with on a cold Saturday night. Where, then, does our faith lie? Is it in the blessings of this world that we hope God will bestow upon us? Or is it in the knowledge that God's will is best even when we face the trials and tribulations of not getting every good thing that we desire?

Part of developing a more complex faith also revolves around reconceiving our ideas about our purpose here on earth. Are we simply biding time until heaven, trying to be as happy as possible during the wait? Are we simply finding godly spouses and having lots of children so that we may increase the membership of the church? Neither of these options seems to encompass all that Christ intends when he challenges us in Acts 1:8 to be his "witnesses" throughout the world. As we mentioned at the conclusion of chapter two, Jesus's parables in Luke 12 remind us that we are on earth only for a short time. Are we to be busy storing up treasure for ourselves on earth like the rich man in Luke 12:16–21, or are we rather to be like the good steward in Luke 12:42–44 who works for his master even when the master is absent? A quick survey of the evening newscasts reveals the world of evil and pain that exists outside our fairly comfortable existence as Christians in the United States. Perhaps this reality suggests that our focus needs to be taken off ourselves and our desires and turned instead to supporting our brothers and sisters in Christ, to working to bring others into the community of the church as they too experience God's salvation, and to addressing the great evils of the world around us that often make God's truth difficult for non-Christians to perceive. Frankly, none of this is easy, for it asks us to move beyond a simplistic faith based upon the idea that being a Christian merely involves partaking in the blessings God doles out from heaven to one that acknowledges that there is far more to the Christian faith than individual blessings. This change in mind-set is, however, essential. Singleness is not an excuse for immaturity. We can't wait until marriage to grapple with the complexities of our faith.

Embracing Christian Community

Neither can we wait until marriage to commit to being part of the Christian community. As singles, it is too easy to come up with reasons to avoid going to church. Whether it is because of the frustration of feeling excluded from a congregation that seems to focus solely on families, or the jealousy of looking around at happy Christian families that seem to have everything that we desperately desire, we often decide that it is far easier to commune with God on our own rather than working through these challenges. Ellison's post on ChristianSinglesToday.com reveals that it is often easier to avoid community than to deal with the pain involved in attending church: "After a few weeks of 'good excuses' for missing church, I started more and more easily talking myself out of attending. I didn't want to walk in alone. I didn't want to look around and feel jealous. I'd found myself crying during baptisms or student affirmations of faith, longing to have a baby to commit to the Lord or a teenager to hear profess faith before the congregation. My self-pity was distracting me from worshiping God. So I just didn't go to church."[1] Unfortunately, this is a reality for many Christian singles, but rather than giving up and abandoning the church, we need to move through the pain, acknowledging that God desires us to be in community with other Christians and allowing him to help us mature through these trials.

Managing this task is not an easy one, but it is a challenge to which God calls us as Christian singles. Rather than giving in to the frustration, anger, or self-pity that may be our natural responses to our experiences in the church, we must release these emotions to God, trusting that his love will sustain us and reminding ourselves that even in the midst of what seems to be evidence to the contrary, he loves us and wants the best for us. With this assurance as our foundation, we must then commit to fulfilling our roles as members of whatever Christian community he has called us to. Rather than existing on the outskirts of the church, we must discover and fully embrace our place within the body of Christ. We need to get involved and stay involved, finding the ministries and small groups that will allow us to serve and be served. And these connections must involve more than simply hanging out with other singles. True community does not consist of different groups coexisting under the same roof but never interacting. While there may be times for groups to divide off from each other for specific ministries, we need to work to bridge the gaps, particularly between the marrieds and singles. What ministries or groups can we be involved with that will allow us to develop relationships more widely across the church? How can we work on building upon the relationships that we already have with others in the church?

Rather than waiting for the rest of the church to come to us, we need to be proactive about developing relationships with them. And once we have started to develop these relationships, we need to be willing to be vulnerable to our brothers and sisters in Christ as we express our needs and ask for their support. Too often, Christian singles feel that they must "put up a good front" so that they don't fit into the stereotype of the lonely, pathetic loser who can't find a spouse. By making ourselves vulnerable, we allow true relationships and community to develop. In addition, for those of us who have managed to negotiate some of the difficulties of being single in the evangelical church, we must be an encouragement to other singles who are still in the midst of their overwhelming pain and frustration, becoming a bridge for them so that they may move from their loneliness into Christian community.

Advice for the Church

While singles must take responsibility for themselves and resist the temptation to avoid the difficulties of entering into community, the church must also recognize its part in helping singles to become fruitful members of the body of Christ. In her article entitled "Integrating Single Adults into the Life of the Church," Mary Graves remarks, "Whether articulated or not, every church has an attitude toward singles and singles ministry."[2] Are singles simply ignored? Are they relegated to the ghetto of the singles group? Or are they an important and essential part of the church? Each church must reflect upon the realities of how singles are treated within the church, and part of this reality must include the fact that not all singles have the same needs or concerns. The young single man right out of college, the thirtysomething single mother raising two children on her own, the fortysomething man struggling with homosexuality, the fiftysomething never married woman, the sixtysomething divorced man, and the seventysomething widow will all have different challenges when it comes to being integrated into the body of Christ, and each church must be sensitive to the varieties of these challenges.

Embracing a Balanced Biblical View of Singleness and Marriage

How, then, may churches address the varied needs of the singles in their midst? Perhaps the best place to start is to make sure that the church embraces a balanced biblical view of singleness and marriage. Without this foundation that affirms both marriage and celibacy as equally valid ways of serving God, the church may find itself slipping into patterns that emphasize the value of one state over the other and implicitly or explicitly alienating those who do not fall into the norm for that particular church. As we have seen, singles in the church often feel the pressure to marry as we are told to focus on abstinence (just holding on until the right person comes along) rather than celibacy (living fully in the state of singleness until God calls us to a different state). Having a positive view of celibacy will allow singles to focus on our walks with God in the present, developing spiritual maturity and living our lives to glorify him now rather than simply putting our lives on hold until marriage.

Affirming celibacy as well as marriage may also compel the church to present a stronger, more nuanced discussion of sexuality, singleness, and marriage to teenagers. While abstinence campaigns have had a certain amount of success, many Christian teenagers need to have a deeper understanding of why God wants them to say no to premarital sex. Warnings of pregnancy, STDs, heartbreak, and loss of self-esteem or promises of amazing sex after marriage can only go so far. As young people mature, they need a theology of sexuality that not only reveals God's purpose for sex within marriage but also acknowledges that single adults may learn to embrace their sexuality fully in a way that honors God and brings them into community with others. By honoring celibacy just as much as marriage and reminding teenagers that God's love for them is not wrapped up in whether they get married or not, churches can empower their teenagers not only to say no to premarital sex but also to begin to wrestle with some of the issues that prove to be so difficult for older singles. While most of these Christian teenagers will probably be married in their twenties, this type of education will provide a strong foundation for those who remain single into their thirties or beyond, and it will also help nurture a generation of married Christian adults who are more attuned to the value of celibacy within the church and will be able to provide greater support and understanding to their single brothers and sisters.

In addition to upholding a biblical view of celibacy and marriage, churches must work to create a definition of community that moves beyond the nuclear family. Since the norm in many of our evangelical churches tends to be marriage and family, churches need to pay particular attention to those who are not in this demographic. If we truly believe that as Christians we come together as the body of Christ, we need to think about the realities of how we live this out. Do we simply come together on Sunday morning, exchange a few pleasantries, listen to a godly sermon, and retreat back to our homes? Or do we come together as brothers and sisters in Christ to share each others' burdens, encourage each other in the faith, and challenge each other to move out into the world to demonstrate God's love to non-believers?

What would it mean for our church family truly to be our family? Would there be messiness and conflict as we move beyond the surface pleasantries to the realities of our lives? Of course. The Epistles are full of the difficulties that arise when church members are closely involved in each other's lives. But there would also be a chance of true community as we open ourselves up to serve and be served by others. And there would also be the chance of truly living out the metaphor of the body of Christ that we receive in 1 Corinthians 12 as we all learn to value each other for the unique contributions that we bring and to "have the same care for one another" (v. 25). Too few churches today live out the truths of this passage, for it is rare that "if one member suffers, all the members suffer with it; if one member is honored, all the members rejoice with it" (v. 26). Too often, we don't even know of the suffering or rejoicing of the members of our own church bodies, and if we do hear of their pains and joys, we often don't know the individuals well enough to truly cry or laugh with them.

Enacting Biblical Ideals in the Life of the Church

With a strong biblical foundation on marriage, singleness, and Christian community, churches may, then, begin to address the practical aspects of church life that often make it difficult for singles to become part of the community. One of the most visible places for this to occur is in the pulpit where a balanced view on marriage and singleness and a radical reconception of the family may provide an important framework for how pastors frame their sermons. For some pastors, this might mean addressing some of these issues directly from the pulpit. For others, it might mean challenging their congregations to have more complex views of God, hope, faith, love, community, and outreach. For still others, it might mean consciously remembering that singles make up a percentage of their congregations and that illustrations focusing solely on marriage and family may not be the best way to speak to this part of their audience. Now, we are certainly not saying that pastors should avoid all references to marriage and children so that they do not offend singles, but perhaps they should think twice before resorting to generalities that assume that everyone in the congregation is married. Christian singles searching for community certainly don't expect the subject of Christian singleness to be the main focus of any church. Nor should it be, for singleness is simply one of many different states to which God calls us and from which God uses us. What we are looking for is a church community whose commitment to inclusion of marrieds and singles is evident from the pulpit.

Singles are also interested in churches where this commitment to inclusion is revealed through the approach to leadership positions within the church. Are singles asked to become participating members of the church who help to take responsibility for supporting various ministries? Are singles discipled to help them prepare for leadership roles to which they might be called? Are singles in these leadership roles supported so that they may do their work effectively? Few enter the church ready to assume positions of leadership, and singles just like marrieds must be encouraged, trained, and supported so that we may mature spiritually and participate fully in the work of the church. Having singles in leadership may also help provide a different (and necessary) perspective. Often, married individuals don't even recognize how much of a focus evangelical churches place on the family, for they are generally part of the demographic the church is trying to support. Without singles in leadership churches run the risk of inadvertently excluding singles throughout the church as they neglect to see things from their perspective.

Nowhere is this problem more evident than in many church programs that seem designed to frustrate singles. For many Christian singles, a quick glance at a church bulletin will give us a clear sense of whether we will be welcomed fully into the church or not, and often simply thinking from the perspective of singles can help identify problems that may be addressed very easily. For example, are all of the Sunday school classes divided up by stage of life, and does this division assume that all members will be married with children by their late twenties? If so, perhaps adding a few topical courses that would allow singles and marrieds to mix and build community might be a good idea. What about women's and men's retreats and seminars? Are they generally focused on marriage and family? If so, perhaps varying the topics occasionally would encourage singles to attend. And what about potlucks or church get-togethers? Are they advertised as "family nights out"? Is everyone required to bring enough food to feed a large family? Thinking about how events are advertised and allowing for flexibility for those who arrive solo are important ways to demonstrate concern for the singles within the church.

But what about the issue of the singles group? Is creating one the best way to address the unique concerns of singles? According to a poll on ChristianSinglesToday.com 71% of Christian singles desire to be part of one.[3] For many younger singles in particular, singles groups may provide them with a sense of community and acceptance within the church. Many older singles, however, have become disillusioned with singles groups, having grown tired of feeling excluded from the rest of the church or annoyed with the meat-market mentality of some singles groups. In fact, some churches have decided against singles groups precisely for these reasons. When the leaders at Bonnie's church in Arizona considered starting a singles group, they received so many letters from singles begging them not to that they decided against it. Each church needs to make the decision for itself, but for churches that decide to establish a singles group, they must be careful to keep it from becoming either a ghetto or a meat market. Strong, biblical teaching, discipleship, outreach, and connection to the rest of the congregation are essential to helping singles groups be successful.

No matter what the programs of the church are, one of the key issues for singles is fellowship, and churches can help singles integrate into the community by becoming places that not only see the singles in their midst but also welcome them. Often, we think of church as the place where we can reconnect with our friends after a long week, but what about the newcomers, particularly those who might be sitting alone? Simply looking around and introducing ourselves to people we don't know is a start. That start, however, also needs to be taken further, for a quick greeting from a few people every Sunday does not equal relationship or community. Both Christine and Bonnie remember that when they were younger and living at home, their parents made a point of asking people from church over for lunch after the Sunday service. Sometimes, the invitation was extended to friends that they knew well, but other times it was given to visitors or people who had only been attending for a few weeks. How often does this happen today? Unfortunately, it doesn't seem to happen as often as it should, particularly between married members of the church and singles. We are all so busy that we tend to rush home from church to try to catch up on rest or have some family time rather than looking for those who might be open to this perfect opportunity for fellowship.

And lunch on Sunday afternoons is not the only opportunity for fellowship with singles that church members often let slip by. As any single will attest, holidays can be a very difficult time, for even if singles are used to eating alone, the thought of Christmas dinner, Thanksgiving dinner, or Easter dinner without friends to share it with is often difficult to face. A few Christmases ago, an Atlanta radio station, recognizing the plight of many singles, began advertising various places where singles could go to spend the holidays. Interestingly, most of them were bars. What does it say about Christian community when the bars seem to be a more welcoming place than the church for the holidays? While there are certainly many families within the church that welcome singles into their midst during the holidays, how many singles are ignored as families decide to spend time only with each other? A few years ago when Christmas fell on a Sunday, several mega-churches made the national news for deciding not to hold Sunday services on Christmas. Their reasoning seemed to be that the holiday was a time for families, and a Sunday morning service might impinge upon that family time. Should family time really be held as a higher priority than coming together as a Christian community to celebrate Christ's birth? Frankly, many singles far away from family may have welcomed Christmas falling on a Sunday since it gave them the chance to be in Christian community on that holiday rather than having to spend it alone. Remembering singles at the holidays is a good start at trying to think of the family of God rather than simply the nuclear family.

Of course, the real goal of fellowship is not simply to have someone to say hello to on Sunday morning or a place to eat a holiday meal; true fellowship needs to build strong relationships. And this can be difficult to do, especially between singles and marrieds. Jacqui's experience that she shares on ChristianSinglesToday.com is only too common: "One of the hardest tasks in a family-oriented church is developing close friendships with people of other marital status. I want to have a servant's heart, but I'm often the one making the effort to keep a friendship going with a married person. I do the calling, the organizing, the waiting. I understand the busyness of a parent's life; one of a married person's biggest struggles in a church community is finding time for other people. Sometimes I wonder if marrieds and singles can really be friends. But until marrieds and singles find a way to value each other, and to develop and maintain friendships, churches will always have a divide."[4] We need to work to break down this divide, finding the connections that we have with each other that extend beyond spouses and children and making the time to develop true friendships. Only when this happens will we be able to truly build Christian community.

We also need to think more creatively when it comes to addressing the needs of individuals within the church. Often, fellowship and friendship are fostered through giving help to others in need and receiving help in turn when we are suffering. In certain respects, the church can be very good at helping families in need. Many churches, for instance, have a well-developed program of offering meals to mothers who have just delivered new babies, but sometimes needs extend beyond food. When Bonnie was suffering from pneumonia, for instance, she called up her church to tell them that she wouldn't be able to help out with the audio/visual on Sunday as she was scheduled to. The person who took her message immediately asked if she needed any food delivered. Having managed to stock up on chicken soup before she crawled into bed, Bonnie didn't need any more food. What she did need was someone to mow her lawn. When she voiced her need, the response was, "Oh, I never would have thought of that." I am sure that there are many needs that both marrieds and singles never really think about that would allow us to build relationships with each other. We need to be both vulnerable in making those needs known and willing to take the time and effort to address even the unexpected needs when we can.

Striving for True Christian Community

In November 2007, Laura Miguelez, an assistant professor of theology at Wheaton College, spoke on the topic of family at a Wheaton College chapel. She had agreed the previous summer, not knowing that her mother was going to die shortly before she had to deliver that message. Even though Chaplain Kellough told her that she did not need to follow through with the commitment, she decided to speak, and her message powerfully illustrates the important role a church family may play as it meets the needs of one in pain. As a single woman, Miguelez did not have a husband or children to help her in the midst of her grief, but she did have her church family. In her chapel message, Miguelez testified to the incredible importance of family—not the nuclear family but the church family. After her mother's death, Miguelez was filled with the "desire to disappear," but she resisted that desire and attended church the next Sunday. The response that she received from her church family demonstrates the power the church has not just to comfort someone in need but also to reveal God's faithfulness to his children. Each hug, prayer, card, e-mail, phone call, meal, and offer of help affirmed God's love to her and reminded her that she needed to exist within this community rather than disappear into her own grief. Thinking of all of the love that was demonstrated toward her, she responded, "How can I disappear when I am surrounded by a family that has expressed so much love and concern for me?"[5]

Miguelez's example provides hope that this type of Christian community that affirms and supports all of its members is possible. And shouldn't it be the goal of every church? Shouldn't we in the church be asking ourselves, "How do we as the body of Christ present Christ to each other and to the rest of the world? Are we truly a model that will glorify Christ as we demonstrate his love?" The refrain of an old Christian chorus from the 1970s said, "They will know we are Christians by our love, by our love. Yes, they'll know we are Christians by our love." How many non-Christians would say that of our churches today? How many single Christians would say it?

Bibliography

Abbott, Elizabeth. *A History of Celibacy*. Cambridge, MA: Da Capo, 1999.

"The Abstinence." *Seinfeld*. Written by Steve Koren. Directed by Andy Ackerman. NBC. November 21, 1996.

Aelred of Rievaulx, *Spiritual Friendship*. Translated by Mark F. Williams. Cranbury, NJ: Associated University Presses, 1994.

"The Agony and the 'Ex'-Tasy." *Sex and the City*. Written and Directed by Michael Patrick King. HBO. June 3, 2001.

Ahbez, Eden. "Nature Boy," *Nature Boy*. Performed by Nat King Cole. Asv Living Era, 2003. Compact disc.

"Alone in the Pew." Christianitytoday.com. February 27, 2008. http://www.christianity today.com/singles/newsletter/2008/mind0227.html (accessed May 23, 2008).

Ambrose, "Concerning Virgins." *Some of the Principal Works of St. Ambrose*. Translated by H. De Romenstin, with the assistance of E. De Romenstin and H. T. F. Duckworth. A Select Library of the Nicene and Post-Nicene Fathers of the Christian Church, edited by Philip Schaff and Henry Wace, 2nd ser., 10. Christian Classics Ethereal Library. http://www.ccel.org/ccel/schaff/npnf210.iv.vii.ii.iii.html (accessed May 23, 2008).

Apatow, Judd, and Steve Carell. *The 40-Year-Old Virgin*. Directed by Judd Apatow. Universal, 2005.

"Arrival." *Smallville*. Written by Todd Slavkin and Darren Swimmer. Directed by James Marshall. WB. September 29, 2005.

Associated Press, "No easy answers in the 'Book of Daniel.'" January 5, 2006. http://www.msnbc.msn.com/id/10618884 (accessed May 23, 2008).

Augustine, *The Confessions of Saint Augustine*. Translated and annotated by J. G. Pilkington. A Select Library of the Nicene and Post-Nicene Fathers of the Christian Church, edited by Philip Schaff, 1st ser., 1. Christian Classics Ethereal Library. http://www.ccel.org/ccel/schaff/npnf101.vi.VIII.XI.html (accessed May 23, 2008).

———. "Of the Work of Monks." In *Moral Treatises of St. Augustine*. Translated by H. Brown. A Select Library of the Nicene and Post-Nicene Fathers of the Christian Church, edited by Philip Schaff, 1st ser., 3. Christian Classics Ethereal Library. http://www.ccel.org/ccel/schaff/npnf103.v.vii.xli.html#v.vii.xli-Page_524 (accessed May 23, 2008).

———. "On Marriage and Concupiscence" In *Saint Augustine's Anti-Pelagian Works*. Translated by Peter Holmes and Robert Ernest Wallis. A Select Library of the Nicene and Post-Nicene Fathers of the Christian Church, edited by Philip Schaff, 1st ser., 5. Christian Classics Ethereal Library. http://www.ccel.org/ccel/schaff/npnf105 .xvi.v.html (accessed May 23, 2008).

———. *Sermons on Selected Lessons of the New Testament*. Translated by R. G. Mac-Mullen. A Select Library of the Nicene and Post-Nicene Fathers of the Christian Church, edited by Philip Schaff, 1st ser., 6. Christian Classics Ethereal Library. http://www.ccel.org/ccel/schaff/npnf106.vii.lxxxiv.html (accessed May 23, 2008).

Barna, George. *Single Focus*. Ventura, CA: Regal, 2003.

Barna Group. "Born Again Adults Less Likely to Co-Habit, Just as Likely to Divorce." *The Barna Update*. August 6, 2001. http://www.barna.org/FlexPage.aspx?Page= BarnaUpdate&BarnaUpdateID=95 (accessed May 23, 2008).

———. http://www.barna.org/FlexPage.aspx?Page=Topic&TopicID=17 (Evangelical Christians, accessed March 9, 2008).

———. http://www.barna.org/FlexPage.aspx?Page=Topic&TopicID=21 (Gender Differences, accessed March 9, 2008).

———. http://www.barna.org/FlexPage.aspx?Page=Topic&TopicID=10 (Unchurched, accessed March 9, 2008).

"Bay of Married Pigs." *Sex and the City*. Written by Darren Star. Directed by Nichole Holofcener. HBO. June 21, 1998.

Bearman, Peter, and Hannah Brückner. "The Relationship between Virginity Pledges in Adolescence and STD Acquisition in Young Adulthood." Center for Disease Control and Prevention. http:// www.cdc.gov/STDConference/2004/PlenMiniPlen/Bearman. pps (accessed May 23, 2008).

"Best Laid Plans." *Everwood*. Written by Sherri Cooper. Directed by Jason Moore. WB. November 1, 2004.

"The Best Laid Plans." *7th Heaven*. Written by Brenda Hampton. Directed by Harry Harris. WB. September 20, 2004.

"The Big One." *Gilmore Girls*. Written by Amy Sherman-Palladino. Directed by Jamie Babbit. WB. February 25, 2003.

Brown, Carson. "The New Sexual Deviant." *Bitch: Feminist Response to Pop Culture*. 13 (2001): 68–73.

Brown, Dan. *The Da Vinci Code*. New York: Doubleday, 2003.

Brown, Gabrielle. *The New Celibacy: A Journey to Love, Intimacy, and Good Health in a New Age*. Rev. ed. New York: McGraw-Hill, 1989.

Budziszewski, J. "Called to Singleness." Boundless Webzine. http://www.boundless. org/2000/ departments/theophilus/a0000318.html (accessed May 23, 2008).

Cantalamessa, Raniero. *Virginity: A Positive Approach to Celibacy for the Sake of the Kingdom of Heaven.* Translated by Charles Serignat. New York: Alba House, 1995.

Carlson, Allan C. "A Revolutionary Theology of Sex: Martin Luther on Sex, Marriage and Family" Family Research Council. July 2, 2004. http://www.frc.org/get. cfm?i=WT04G01 (accessed May 23, 2008).

Clapp, Rodney. *Families at the Crossroads: Beyond Traditional and Modern Options.* Downers Grove, IL: InterVarsity, 1993.

———. *Tortured Wonders: Christian Spirituality for People, Not Angels.* Grand Rapids: Brazos Press, 2004.

Clark, Jeramy. *I Gave Dating a Chance.* Colorado Springs: Water Brook, 2000.

Cloud, Henry and John Townsend. *Making Dating Work: Boundaries in Dating.* Grand Rapids: Zondervan, 2000.

Courtney, Camerin. "The Problem with Platitudes." ChristianityToday.com. February 11, 2004. http://www.christianitytoday.com/singles/newsletter/mind40211.html (accessed May 23, 2008).

———. "Single on Sunday Morning." ChristianityToday.com. September 20, 2000. http:// www.christianitytoday.com/singles/newsletter/mind00920.html (accessed May 23, 2008).

———. "Singles in the Hands of a Manipulative God?" ChristianityToday.com. May 9, 2007. http://www.christianitytoday.com/singles/newsletter/2007/mind0509.html (accessed May 23, 2008).

———. "Why Aren't Christians Dating?" ChristianityToday.com. September 4, 2002. http:// www.christianitytoday.com/singles/newsletter/mind20904.html (accessed May 23, 2008).

Courtney, Camerin and Todd Hertz. *The UnGuide to Dating: a He Said/She Said on Relationships.* Grand Rapids: Baker, 2006.

Crittenden, Daniellle. *What Our Mothers Didn't Tell Us: Why Happiness Eludes the Modern Woman.* New York: Simon & Schuster, 1999.

Davis, Julie, writ. and dir. *I Love You, Don't Touch Me.* MGM, 1998.

Dawn, Marva J. *I'm Lonely, Lord—How Long: Meditations on the Psalms.* rev. ed. Grand Rapids: Eerdmans, 1998.

———. *Sexual Character: Beyond Technique to Intimacy.* Grand Rapids: Eerdmans, 1993.

DeMoss, Nancy Leigh. *Singled Out For Him: Embracing the Gift, the Blessings, and the Challenges of Singleness.* Buchanan, MI: Life Action Ministries, 1998.

Dever, Mark. "Singleness." In *Sex and the Supremacy of Christ* edited by John Piper and Justin Taylo, 133–35. Wheaton, IL: Crossways, 2005.

Dever, Mark, et. al. "Sex and the Single Man." In *Sex and the Supremacy of Christ.* Edited by John Piper and Justin Taylor. Wheaton, IL: Crossway, 2005. 133–150.

Dickinson, Amy. "Male virgin's letter inspires critics and defenders." *Chicago Tribune*, August 1, 2007. Sec. 5 Tempo.

Dillow, Linda and Lorraine Pintus. *Intimate Issues*. Colorado Springs: WaterBrook Publishers, 1999.

Dobson, James C. "Marriage on the Ropes." Focus on the Family. Newsletters. September 2003. http://www2.focusonthefamily.com/docstudy/newsletters/A000000771 .cfm (accessed May 23, 2008).

———. *Marriage under Fire*. Sisters, OR: Multnomah Publishers, 2004.

Donne, John. "Holy Sonnet 18." In *The Norton Anthology of English Literature: The Major Authors*, 7th ed., edited by M. H. Abrams et al., 624–25. New York: Norton, 2001.

"The Drought." *Sex and the City*. Written by Michael Green. Directed by Matthew Harrison. HBO. August 16, 1998.

Dubay, Thomas. *"And You are Christ's": The Charism of Virginity and the Celibate Life*. San Francisco: Ignatius Press, 1987.

Eden, Dawn. *The Thrill of the Chaste: Finding Fulfillment While Keeping your Clothes On*. Nashville: W Publishing Group, 2006.

Eldredge, John and Stasi. *Captivating*. Nashville: Nelson Books, 2005.

Elliot, Elisabeth. *Keep a Quiet Heart*. Grand Rapids: Revell, 2004.

Epstein, Julius J., Philip G. Epstein, and Howard Koch. *Casablanca*. Directed by Michael Curtiz. Warner Bros., 1942.

Evdokimov, Paul. From *The Sacrament of Love: The Nuptial Mystery in the Light of the Orthodox Tradition*. In *Theology and Sexuality: Classic and Contemporary Readings*, edited by Eugene F. Rogers Jr., Malden, MA: Blackwell, 2002. 179–193

Farmer, Andrew. *The Rich Single Life: Abundance, Opportunity & Purpose in God*. Pursuit of Godliness Series, edited by Kevin Meath. Gaithersburg, MD: Sovereign Grace, 1998.

Fielding, Helen. *Bridget Jones's Diary*. New York: Penguin, 1996.

Fielding, Helen, Andrew Davies, and Richard Curtis. *Bridget Jones's Diary*. Directed by Sharon Maguire. Miramax, 2001.

Folger, Janet L. *What's a Girl to Do? While Waiting for Mr. Right*. Sisters, OR: Multnomah, 2003.

Foster, Richard J. *A Celebration of Discipline: The Path to Spiritual Growth*. Rev. ed. New York: Harper, 1988.

———. *The Challenge of the Disciplined Life: Christian Reflections on Money, Sex & Power*. New York: Harpers, 1985.

Franck, Dennis. *Reaching Single Adults: An Essential Guide for Ministry*. Grand Rapids: Baker, 2007.

Garland, David E. "1 Corinthians." In *Baker Exegetical Commentary on the New Testament*, edited by Robert W. Yarbrough and Robert H. Stein. Grand Rapids: Baker, 2003.

Graves, Mary. "Integrating Single Adults into the Life of the Church." In *Baker Handbook of Single Adult Ministry*, edited by Douglas L. Fagerstrom, 149–54. Grand Rapids: Baker, 1997.

Gregory of Nyssa, *On Virginity*. In *Select Writings and Letters of Gregory, Bishop of Nyssa*. Translated by William Moore and Henry Austin Wilson. A Select Library of the Nicene and Post-Nicene Fathers of the Christian Church, edited by Philip Schaff and Henry Wace, 2nd ser., 5. Christian Classics Ethereal Library. http://www.ccel.org/ccel/schaff/npnf205.ix.ii.ii.iv.html (accessed May 23, 2008).

Grenz, Stanley. *Sexual Ethics: A Biblical Perspective*. Dallas: Word, 1990.

Ham, Pete, and Tom Evans. "Without You," *Music Box*. Performed by Mariah Carey. Columbia Records, 1994. Compact disc.

Harris, Joshua. *Boy Meets Girl: Say Hello to Courtship*. Sisters, OR: Multnomah, 2005.

———. *I Kissed Dating Goodbye*. Sisters, OR: Multnomah, 1997.

———. *Not Even a Hint*. Sisters, OR: Multnomah, 2003.

———. *Stop Dating the Church! Fall in Love with the Family of God*. Sisters, OR: Multnomah, 2004.

Hauerwas, Stanley, *After Christendom? How the Church Is to Behave if Freedom, Justice, and a Christian Nation Are Bad Ideas*. Nashville: Abingdon, 1991.

Hauerwas, Stanley, and Allen Verhey. "From Conduct to Character: A Guide to Sexual Adventure." In *Christian Perspectives on Sexuality and Gender*. edited by Elizabeth Stuart and Adrian Thatcher, 175–209. Grand Rapids: Eerdmans, 1996.

Herbert, George. "The Pulley." In *The Norton Anthology of English Literature: The Major Authors*, 7th ed., edited by M. H. Abrams et al., 664. New York: Norton, 2001.

Hirst, Michael. *Elizabeth*. Directed by Shekhar Kapur. Polygram, 1998.

Hoffeditz, David M. *They Were Single Too: Eight Biblical Role Models*. Grand Rapids: Kregel, 2005.

"Home Front." *Brothers and Sisters*. Written by Monica Owusu-Breen. Directed by Ken Olin. ABC. September 30, 2007.

Hsu, Albert Y. *Singles at the Crossroads: A Fresh Perspective on Christian Singleness*. Downers Grove, IL: InterVarsity, 1997.

"I Will Remember You." *Angel*. Written by David Greenwalt and Jeannine Renshaw. Directed by David Grossman. WB. November 23, 1999.

Jameson, Anna. *Sisters of Charity, Catholic and Protestant, Abroad and at Home*. 2nd ed. London: Longman, Brown, Green and Longman, 1855.

Jerome. "Against Jovinianus." In *The Principle Works of St. Jerome*. Translated by W. H. Fremantle, with the assistance of G. Lewis and W. G. Martley. A Select Library of the Nicene and Post-Nicene Fathers of the Christian Church, edited by Philip Schaff and Henry Wace, 2nd ser., 6. Christian Classics Ethereal Library. http://www.ccel.org/ccel/schaff/npnf206.vi.vi.I.html (accessed May 23, 2008).

———. "To Eustochium." In *The Principle Works of St. Jerome*. Translated by W. H. Fremantle, with the assistance of G. Lewis and W. G. Martley. A Select Library of the Nicene and Post-Nicene Fathers of the Christian Church, edited by Philip Schaff and Henry Wace, 2nd ser., 6. Christian Classics Ethereal Library. http://www.ccel.org/ccel/schaff/npnf206.v.XXII.html (accessed May 23, 2008).

———. "To Lucinius." In *The Principle Works of St. Jerome*. Translated by W. H. Fremantle, with the assistance of G. Lewis and W. G. Martley. A Select Library of the Nicene and Post-Nicene Fathers of the Christian Church, edited by Philip Schaff and Henry Wace, 2nd ser., 6. Christian Classics Ethereal Library. http://www.ccel.org/ccel/schaff/npnf206.v.LXXI.html (accessed May 23, 2008).

———. "The Perpetual Virginity of Blessed Mary." In *The Principle Works of St. Jerome*. Translated by W. H. Fremantle, with the assistance of G. Lewis and W. G. Martley. A Select Library of the Nicene and Post-Nicene Fathers of the Christian Church, edited by Philip Schaff and Henry Wace, 2nd ser., 6. Christian Classics Ethereal Library. http://www.ccel.org/ccel/schaff/npnf206.vi.v.html (accessed May 23, 2008).

Jethani, Skye. "United Through Christ's Suffering." Sermon, Blanchard Alliance Church, Wheaton, IL, 2006.

———. "What Child Is This Who Came Not to Bring Peace?" Sermon, Blanchard Alliance Church, Wheaton, IL, December 2, 2007.

John Paul II. *Theology of the Body: Human Love in the Divine Plan*. Boston: Pauline Books and Media, 1997.

Jones, Stanton L.. and Mark A. Yarhouse. *Ex-gays? A Longitudinal Study of Religiously Mediated Change in Sexual Orientation*. Downers Grove, IL: InterVarsity, 2007.

Keller, Tim. "A New Kind of Urban Church." ChristianityToday.com. May 2006. http://www.christianitytoday.com/ct/2006/may/1.36.html (accessed May 23, 2008).

Keller, Wendy. *The Cult of the Born-Again Virgin: How Single Women Can Reclaim Their Sexual Power*. Deerfield Beach, FL: Health Communications, 1999.

Kempis, Thomas á. *The Imitation of Christ*. New York: Barnes and Noble, 2004.

Kidder, Annemarie S. *Women, Celibacy and the Church: Towards a Theology of the Single Life*. New York: The Crossroad Publishing Company, 2003.

Kinsey, Alfred C., Wardell B. Pomeroy, and Clyde E. Martin. *Sexual Behavior in the Human Male*. Philadelphia: W. B. Saunders, 1948.

Koepp, David. *Spider-Man*. Directed by Sam Raimi. Columbia, 2002.

Koons, Carolyn. "Today's Single Adult Phenomenon: The Realities, Myths, and Identity." In *Baker Handbook of Single Adult Ministry*, edited by Douglas L. Fagerstrom, 17–26. Grand Rapids: Baker, 1997.

Lawrence, Michael. "A Theology of Sex." "Sex and the Single Man" In *Sex and the Supremacy of Christ*, edited by John Piper and Justin Taylor, 135–41. Wheaton, IL: Crossways, 2005.

Letterman, David. "Top Ten Star Wars' Fans Complaints about the New Movie." *Late Night with David Letterman*. May 6, 1999. http://www.cbs.com/latenight/lateshow/top_ten/index/php/19990506.phtml (accessed May 23, 2008).

Ludy, Eric and Leslie. *When God Writes Your Love Story*. Sisters, OR: Loyal Publishing, 1999.

Luther, Martin. *The Large Catechism*. In: *Triglot Concordia: The Symbolical Books of the Ev. Lutheran Church*. Translated by F. Bente and W. H. T. Dan. Project Wittenberg. http://www.iclnet.org/pub/resources/text/wittenberg/wittenberg-luther.html#sw-lc (accessed May 23, 2008).

———. "To Several Nuns." In *Briefe aus dem Jahre 1524* [Letters of the Year 1524]. Nos. 733–756. *Weimarer Ausgabe*. Translated by Erika Bullman Flores. Project Wittenberg. http://www.iclnet.org/pub/resources/text/wittenberg/luther/nuns.txt (accessed May 23, 2008).

Maken, Debbie. *Getting Serious about Getting Married: Rethinking the Gift of Singleness*. Wheaton, IL: Crossway, 2006.

———. "Maken on Piper." Boundless Webzine. http://www.boundlessline.org/2007/05/maken_on_piper.html (accessed May 23, 2008).

"The Man, The Myth, The Viagra." *Sex and the City*. Written by Michael Patrick King. Directed by Victoria Hochberg. HBO. July 25, 1999.

Martinez, G. M. et al. "Fertility, contraception, and fatherhood: Data on men and women from Cycle 6 (2002) of the National Survey of Family Growth," National Center for Health Statistics. Vital Health Stat. 23(26). 2006.

McCulley, Carolyn. "Sex and the Single Woman." In *Sex and the Supremacy of Christ*. edited by John Piper and Justin Taylor, 183–200. Wheaton, IL: Crossway, 2005.

McLaren, Angus. *Twentieth-Century Sexuality: A History*. Malden, MA: Blackwell, 1999.

McMinn, Lisa Graham. *Growing Strong Daughters*. Rev. ed. Grand Rapids: Baker, 2007.

———. *Sexuality and Holy Longing: Embracing Intimacy in a Broken World*. San Francisco: Jossey-Bass, 2004.

———. Wheaton College Chapel Message. Wheaton, IL, October 12, 2007.

Methodius. *The Banquet of the Ten Virgins: Or, Concerning Chastity*. Translated by William R. Clark. Ante-Nicene Fathers: The Writings of the Fathers down to A.D. 325, edited by Philip Schaff and Henry Wace, 6. Christian Classics Ethereal Library. http://www.ccel.org/ccel/schaff/anf06.xi.iii.ix.viii.html (accessed May 23, 2008).

Miguelez, Laura. Wheaton College Chapel Message. Wheaton, IL, November 28, 2007.

Miles, Carrie A. *The Redemption of Love: Rescuing Marriage and Sexuality from the Economics of a Fallen World*. Grand Rapids: Brazos, 2006.

Milton, John. "Aereopagetica." In *Seventeenth Century Prose and Poetry*, 2nd ed. edited by Alexander M. Witherspoon and Frank J. Warnke, 395–417. Chicago, Harcourt Brace Jovanovich, 1982.

Mohler, R. Albert. "The Mystery of Marriage." 2004 New Attitude Conference. http://www.albertmohler.com/audio_archive.php (accessed May 23, 2008).

Moll, Rob. "The New Monasticism." ChristianityToday.com. September 2, 2005. http://www.christianitytoday.com/outreach/articles/newmonasticism.html (accessed May 23, 2008).

"The Name of the Game." *Grey's Anatomy*. Written by Blythe Robe. Directed by Seith Mann. ABC. April 2, 2006.

"Nearly 3 in 10 Young Teens 'Sexually Active': NBC News, PEOPLE Magazine Commission Landmark National Poll." January 31, 2005, 7. http://www.msnbc.msn.com/id/6839072 (accessed May 23, 2008).

"Never Kill a Boy on the First Date." *Buffy, the Vampire Slayer*. Written by Rob Des Hotel and Dean Batali. Directed by David Semel. WB. March 31, 1997.

Nicholson, William, and Michael Hirst. *Elizabeth: The Golden Age*. Directed by Shekhar Kapur. Universal, 1997.

Noelliste, Leila. "Single, Not Inferior: No Pity Please." *The Wheaton Record* December 3, 2004.

Norris, Kathleen. *The Cloister Walk*. New York: Riverhead, 1997.

"No Sure Thing." *Everwood*. Written by Joan Binder Weiss. Directed by Perry Lang. WB. February 9, 2004.

Nouwen, Henri. "Loneliness." In *Seeds of Hope: A Henri Nouwen Reader*, edited by Robert Durback. New York: Doubleday, 1997. 60–2.

———. "A Suffocating Closeness." In *Seeds of Hope: A Henri Nouwen Reader*. Edited by Robert Durback, 70. New York: Doubleday, 1997.

———. *The Wounded Healer*. New York: Doubleday, 1972.

Olsen, Ted. "Abolishing Abstinence." *Christianity Today*. 49.9 (2005): 98. Online. 8/24/2005. http://www.ctlibrary.com/ct/2005/september/12.98.html (accessed May 23, 2008).

"The One That Could Have Been (Part 1)." *Friends*. Written by Greg Malins and Adam Chase. NBC. February 17, 2000.

"The One Where Mr. Heckles Dies." *Friends*. Written by Michael Curtis and Greg Malins. NBC. October 5, 1995.

Osteen, Joel. *Your Best Life Now: 7 Steps to Living at Your Full Potential*. New York: Warner Faith, 2004.

Patterson, Randall. "Students of Virginity." *New York Times*, March 30, 2008. http://www.nytimes.com/2008/03/30/magazine/30Chastity-t.html?scp=1&sq=students+of+virginity&st=nyt (accessed May 23, 2008).

Perez, Rob. *40 Days and 40 Nights*. Directed by Michael Lehmann. Miramax, 2002.

Peterson, Eugene H. *A Long Obedience in the Same Direction: Discipleship in an Instant Society*. 2nd ed. Downers Grove, IL: InterVarsity Press, 2000.

Peterson, Paul M. "Let's Begin at Church." In *Baker Handbook of Single Adult Ministry*. edited by Douglas L. Fagerstrom, 255–63. Grand Rapids: Baker, 1997.

Pinkston, Ron. "Testimonials." http://www.embracemarriage.org (accessed May 23, 2008).

Piper, John. "Sex and the Supremacy of Christ: Part One." In *Sex and the Supremacy of Christ*, edited by John Piper and Justin Taylor, 25–35. Wheaton, IL: Crossway, 2005.

———. "Sex and the Supremacy of Christ: Part Two." In *Sex and the Supremacy of Christ*, edited by John Piper and Justin Taylor, 37–46. Wheaton, IL: Crossway, 2005.

———. "Single in Christ: A Name Better than Sons and Daughters." Sermon, Bethlehem Baptist Church, Minneapolis, MN, April 29, 2007. http://www.desiringgod.org/ResourceLibrary/Sermons/ByDate/2007/2162_Single_in_Christ_A_Name_Better_Than_Sons_and_Daughters (accessed May 23, 2008).

"Poll." ChristianSinglesToday.com. http://www.christianitytoday.com/singles. February 2008.

Prince, Derek. *God Is a Matchmaker*. Grand Rapids: Chosen Books, 1986.

Rainey, Dennis. "Fatherly Advice to Singles—Get Married." *Family Life Today*. June 22, 2004. http://www.familylife.com/fltoday/default.asp?id=7402 (accessed May 21, 2007; 2004 archives no longer available).

Rector, Robert E., Kirk A. Johnson, and Jennifer A. Marshall, "Teens Who Make Virginity Pledges Have Substantially Improved Life Outcomes." September 21, 2004. http://www.heritage.org/Research/Abstinence/cda04–07.cfm (accessed May 23, 2008).

Reed, Cheryl L. *Unveiled: The Hidden Life of Nuns*. New York: Berkley Publishing Group, 2004.

Reno, R. R. *In the Ruins of the Church: Sustaining Faith in an Age of Diminished Christianity*. Grand Rapids: Brazos, 2002.

Rolheiser, Ronald. *Forgotten among the Lilies: Learning to Love Beyond Our Fears*. New York: Doubleday, 2005.

———. *The Holy Longing: The Search for a Christian Spirituality*. New York: Doubleday, 1999.

Rooney, Andy. "Those Rotten Apples." *60 Minutes*. CBS. March 31, 2002. http://www.cbsnews.com/stories/2002/03/29/60minutes/main504971.shtml?source=search_story (accessed May 23, 2008).

Rosenau, Doug, and Michael Todd Wilson. *Soul Virgins: Redefining Single Sexuality*. Grand Rapids: Baker, 2006.

Schmucker, Matt. "Physical Intimacy and the Single Man." "Sex and the Single Man." In *Sex and the Supremacy of Christ*. Edited by John Piper and Justin Taylor. Wheaton, IL: Crossways, 2005. 141–45.

"Sexy Christian Singles." ChristianityToday.com. April 18, 2007. http://www.christianitytoday.com/singles/newsletter/2007/mind0418.html (accessed May 23, 2008).

Shalit, Wendy. *A Return to Modesty: Discovering the Lost Virtue*. New York: Touchstone, 2000.

Sharlet, Jeff. "The Young and the Sexless: A New Generation of Young Men and Women is Embracing Celibate Life." Rollingstone.com. June 23, 2005. http://www.rollingstone.com/nes/story/7418688/the_young_the_sexless/ (accessed May 23, 2008)

Sherman-Palladino, Amy. "The Morning After, Part 1." *TVGuide*. September 19–25, 2004, 50.

"Single Men and the Church: 9 guys talk about their relationship with their faith community." ChristianityToday.com. August 8, 2007. http://www.christianitytoday.com/singles/newsletter/2007/mind0808.html (accessed May 23, 2008).

Skinner, Mary. "Benedictine Life for Women in Central France, 850–1100: A Feminist Revival." In *Distant Echoes*. Vol. 1 of *Medieval Religious Women*. Kalamazoo, MI: Cistercian Publications, 1984.

Slater, Ted. "Boundless Passion." Boundless Webzine. March 18, 2008. http://www.boundlessline.org/2008/03/boundless-passi.html (accessed May 23, 2008).

Smedes, Lewis B. *Sex for Christians*. Grand Rapids: Eerdmans, 1976.

Smit, Laura. *Loves Me, Loves Me Not: The Ethics of Unrequited Love*. Grand Rapids: Baker, 2005.

Smith, Lori. *The Single Truth: Challenging the Misconceptions of Singleness with God's Consuming Truth*. Shippensberg, PA: Treasure House, 2002.

"So . . . Good Talk." *Gilmore Girls*. Written by Lisa Randolph. Directed by Jamie Bobbit. WB. February 29, 2005.

Somerset, Anne. *Elizabeth I*. New York: St. Martin's Press, 1991.

Sondheim, Stephen. "Being Alive." *Company*. Sony. 1998. Compact disc.

"Sunday." *7th Heaven*. Written by Brenda Hampton. Directed by Joel J. Feigenbaum. WB. January 6, 2003.

Tauber, Edward M., and Jim Smoke. *Finding the Right One after Divorce*. Eugene, OR: Harvest House Publishers, 2007.

Tertullian. *On Exhortation to Chastity*. Translated by S. Thelwell. Ante-Nicene Fathers: The Writings of the Fathers down to A.D. 325, edited by Philip Schaff, 4. Christian Classics Ethereal Library. http://www.ccel.org/ccel/schaff/anf04.iii.vi.ix.html (accessed May 23, 2008).

———. *On the Apparel of Women*. Translated by S. Thelwell. Ante-Nicene Fathers: The Writings of the Fathers down to A.D. 325, edited by Philip Schaff, 4. Christian Classics Ethereal Library. http://www.ccel.org/ccel/schaff/anf04.iii.iii.i.i.html (accessed May 23, 2008).

Thomas, Gary. *Sacred Marriage*. Grand Rapids: Zondervan, 2000.

"Twenty-Something Girls vs. Thirty-Something Women." *Sex and the City*. Written and directed by Darren Star. HBO. September 26, 1999.

Twohey, Megan. "Discovering fellowship in faith." *Chicago Tribune*. August 17, 2007, Sec. 2 Metro.

U2. "Miracle Drug." *How to Dismantle an Atomic Bomb*. Interscope Records, 2004. Compact disc.

U. S. Census Bureau. "2006 American Community Survey, Custom Table." http://factfinder.census.gov/servlet/CustomTableServlet (accessed May 23, 2008).

"Virginity Pledge Helps Teens Delay Sexual Activity." National Institutes of Health. January 5, 2001. http://www.nichd.nih.gov/news/releases/virginity.cfm#cpc (accessed May 23, 2008).

Warren, Diane. "How Do I Live?" *You Light Up My Life*. Performed by LeAnn Rimes. Curb Records, 2007. Compact disc.

Warren, Neil Clark. *Date . . . or Soul Mate? How to Know if Someone Is Worth Pursuing in Two Dates or Less*. Nashville: Thomas Nelson, 2002.

Watters, Candice. *Get Married: What Women Can Do To Help It Happen*. Chicago: Moody, 2008.

Wheat, Ed, et al. *Sex and the Single Christian: Candid Conversations*. Ventura, CA: Regal, 1985.

Whitehead, Barbara Dafoe, and David Popenoe. "Why Men Won't Commit: Exploring Young Men's Attitudes about Sex, Dating, and Marriage." *The State of Our Unions: The Social Health of Marriage in America 2002. A Publication of the National Marriage Project*. June 2002. August 13, 2006. http://marriage.rutgers.edu (accessed May 23, 2008).

"Why We Think Christians Aren't Dating." ChristianSinglesToday.com. September 4, 2002. http://www.christianitytoday.com/singles/newsletter/mind20904.html (accessed May 23, 2008).

Widder, Wendy. "Bringing in the Single Sheep." OnMission.com. March 18, 2005. http://www.onmission.com/site/c.cnKHIPNuEoG/b.830379/k.9B25/Bringing_in_the_single_sheep.htm (accessed May 23, 2008).

———. *Living Whole Without a Better Half*. Grand Rapids: Kregel, 2000.

Willard, Dallas. *The Spirit of the Disciplines: Understanding How God Changes Lives*. New York: Harper & Row, 1988.

Winner, Lauren F. *Real Sex: The Naked Truth about Chastity*. Grand Rapids: Brazos, 2005.

Zacharias, Ravi. *I, Isaac, Take Thee, Rebekah: Moving from Romance to Lasting Love*. Nashville: Thomas Nelson, 2004.

Zumbrun, Joshua. "Albania's sworn 'virgins': women give up sex to live as men." *Chicago Tribune*. August 22, 2007, Sec. 5.

Notes

Introduction

1. Abbott, *History of Celibacy,* 426.
2. U.S. Census Bureau, "2006 Current Population Survey."
3. Barna Group, "Evangelical Christians."
4. Ibid.
5. "Alone in the Pew."
6. Franck, *Reaching Single Adults*, 43.
7. Bearman and Brückner, "Relationship between Virginity Pledges in Adolescence."
8. Barna, *Single Focus*, 7.
9. "Why We Think Christians Aren't Dating."

Chapter 1 Repression & Neuroses

1. "Twenty-Something Girls vs. Thirty-Something Women," *Sex and the City*.
2. Quoted. in Olsen, "Abolishing Abstinence."
3. Rooney, "Those Rotten Apples."
4. Abbott, *History of Celibacy*, 426.
5. McLaren, *Twentieth-Century Sexuality*, 112.
6. Ibid., 62.
7. Kinsey, *Sexual Behavior in the Human Male*, 325.
8. Perez, *40 Days and 40 Nights*.
9. "No Sure Thing," *Everwood*.
10. "Best Laid Plans," *Everwood*.
11. Fielding, Davies, and Curtis, *Bridget Jones's Diary*.
12. "Nearly 3 in 10 Young Teens 'Sexually Active.' "
13. "The Big One," *Gilmore Girls*.
14. Sherman-Palladino, "The Morning After, Part I."
15. "The One That Could Have Been (Part 1)," *Friends*.
16. Davis, *I Love You, Don't Touch Me*.
17. Letterman, "Top Ten Star Wars' Fans Complaints."
18. Apatow and Carell, *The 40-Year-Old Virgin*.

19. Dickinson, "Male virgin's letter inspires·critics and defenders," 2.

20. Sondheim, "Being Alive."

21. Fielding, Davies, and Curtis, *Bridget Jones's Diary*.

22. "The One Where Mr. Heckles Dies," *Friends*.

23. "The Agony and the 'Ex'-Tasy," *Sex and the City*.

24. While the film version of *Sex and the City* revises this ending by having Samantha break up with her longtime boyfriend, it doesn't change the fact that the writers of the original series felt that pairing everyone up was an appropriate ending for these four women.

25. "No Sure Thing," *Everwood*.

Chapter 2 Power & Freedom

1. "Home Front," *Brothers and Sisters*.

2. Brown, *New Celibacy*, xi.

3. Ibid., 1.

4. Somerset, *Elizabeth I*, 353.

5. Hirst, *Elizabeth*.

6. Hampton, *Elizabeth: The Golden Age*.

7. Zumbrun, "Albania's sworn 'virgins,'" 5, 1, 9.

8. Ibid., 5, 9.

9. Ibid.

10. Brown, "The New Sexual Deviant," 71.

11. "The Drought," *Sex and the City*.

12. Perez, *40 Days and 40 Nights*.

13. Keller, *Cult of the Born-Again Virgin*, 11–15.

14. Ibid., 15–16.

15. Ibid., 113.

16. Shalit, *Return to Modesty*, 12.

17. Patterson, "Students of Virginity."

18. "The Name of the Game," *Grey's Anatomy*.

19. www.lifeathletes.org.

20. "The Drought," *Sex and the City*.

21. "The Abstinence," *Seinfeld*.

22. Ibid.

23. Koepp, *Spider-Man*.

24. Epstein, Epstein, and Koch, *Casablanca*.

25. "Arrival," *Smallville*.

26. "Never Kill a Boy on the First Date," *Buffy the Vampire Slayer*.

27. "I Will Remember You," *Angel*.

28. Ahbez, "Nature Boy."

29. U2, "Miracle Drug."

Chapter 3 Chastity & Holiness

1. "So . . . Good Talk," *Gilmore Girls*.

2. McMinn, *Growing Strong Daughters*, 143.

3. Smedes, *Sex for Christians*, 108.

4. Augustine, *Sermons on Selected Lessons of the New Testament*, 7.82.

5. "Virginity Pledge Helps Teens Delay Sexual Activity."

6. Rector, Johnson, and Marshall, "Teens Who Make Virginity Pledges."

7. "Sunday," *7th Heaven.*
8. "The Best Laid Plans," *7th Heaven.*
9. Sharlet, "The Young and the Sexless."
10. Keller, "A New Kind of Urban Church."
11. Harris, *I Kissed Dating Goodbye,* 40–41.
12. Courtney and Hertz, *Unguide to Dating,* 13.
13. Warren, *Date . . . or Soul Mate?* 170–71.
14. Ibid., xiii.
15. Ibid., xv.
16. Clark, *I Gave Dating a Chance,* 62.
17. "The Man, The Myth, The Viagra," *Sex and the City.*
18. McCully, "Sex and the Single Woman," 189–90.
19. Widder, *Living Whole,* 11.
20. Farmer, *Rich Single Life,* 119.
21. Hoffeditz, *They Were Single Too,* 134.
22. Ibid., 59.
23. Ibid., 60.
24. Dawn, *I'm Lonely Lord,* 222.
25. Dever, "Singleness," 135.
26. Ibid., 135.
27. Lawrence, "A Theology of Sex," 136.
28. Ibid., 136.
29. Ibid., 138.
30. McCully, "Sex and the Single Woman," 187, 191.
31. Ibid., 200.
32. Winner, *Real Sex,* 15.
33. Ibid., 100.
34. Ibid., 123.
35. Rosenau and Wilson, *Soul Virgins,* 31.
36. Ibid., 31.
37. Ibid., 98.
38. Ibid., 140.
39. Ibid., 141.
40. Winner, *Real Sex,* 56–57.
41. Ibid., 57.
42. Rosenau and Wilson, *Soul Virgins,* 98.
43. Ibid., 243.

Chapter 4 Sin & Selfishness

1. Maken, *Getting Serious,* 17–18.
2. Barna Group, Evangelical Christians.
3. Barna Group, Unchurched.
4. Barna Group, Evangelical Christians.
5. U.S. Census Bureau, "2006 American Community Survey."
6. "Poll," ChristianSinglesToday.com.
7. Courtney, "Single on Sunday Morning."
8. Widder, "Bringing in the Single Sheep."
9. Barna Group, "Born Again Adults."
10. "Sunday," *7th Heaven.*

11. Courtney, "Why Aren't Christians Dating?"

12. Barna Group, "Born Again Adults."

13. Martinez, "Fertility, contraception, and fatherhood," 52 (Table 21).

14. Associated Press, "No easy answers in the 'Book of Daniel.'"

15. Reno, *In the Ruins of the Church*, 116–17.

16. Wheat, *Sex and the Single Christian*, 109.

17. Ibid., 110.

18. Pinkston, "Testimonials."

19. Slater, "Boundless Passion."

20. Mohler, "The Mystery of Marriage."

21. Ibid.

22. Crittenden, *What Our Mothers Didn't Tell Us*, 64.

23. "Bay of Married Pigs," *Sex and the City*.

24. Crittenden, *What Our Mothers Didn't Tell Us*, 69.

25. Mohler, "The Mystery of Marriage."

26. Thomas, *Sacred Marriage*, 21.

27. Crittenden, *What Our Mothers Didn't Tell Us*, 67.

28. Maken, *Getting Serious*, 98.

29. Ibid., 22.

30. Rainey, "Fatherly Advice to Singles."

31. Clark, *I Gave Dating a Chance*, 56.

32. Cloud and Townsend, *Boundaries in Dating*, 73.

33. Ibid., 83.

34. Courtney, "The Problem with Platitudes."

35. Noelliste, "Single, Not Inferior," 11.

Chapter 5 Lust & Avoidance

1. Harris, *Not Even a Hint*, 19.

2. Courtney and Hertz, *Unguide to Dating*, 8.

3. Eldredge, *Captivating*, 165.

4. Jerome, "To Eustochium," 22.7.

5. Interview with John Stott, in Hsu, *Singles at the Crossroads*, 179.

6. Roseneau and Wilson, *Soul Virgins*, 37.

7. Ibid., 219.

8. Dawn, *Sexual Character*, 58.

9. John Paul II, *Theology of the Body*, 157.

10. Foster, *Challenge of the Disciplined Life*, 121.

11. Harris, *Not Even a Hint*, 122–23.

12. Milton, "Areopagitica," 401.

13. Ibid., 402.

14. Carlson, "Revolutionary Theology of Sex."

15. Ibid.

16. Luther, "To Several Nuns."

17. Watters, *Get Married*, 31.

18. Ibid., 32.

19. Mohler, "The Mystery of Marriage."

20. Harris, *Not Even a Hint*, 111.

21. Maken, *Getting Serious*, 50.

22. Hsu, *Singles at the Crossroads*, 181.

23. Whitehead and Popenoe, "Why Men Won't Commit."

24. Harris, *Not Even a Hint*, 111.

25. Maken, *Getting Serious*, 115.

26. Courtney, "Why Aren't Christians Dating?"

27. Maken, *Getting Serious*, 185.

28. Elliot, *Keep a Quiet Heart*, 165–66.

29. Courtney and Hertz, *UnGuide to Dating*, 14.

30. Harris, *I Kissed Dating Goodbye*, 128.

31. Schmucker, "Physical Intimacy and the Single Man," 141.

32. Harris, *Not Even a Hint*, 111.

33. Folger, *What's a Girl to Do?* 52.

34. Luther, *Large Catechism*, Part 7.

35. Budziszewski, "Called to Singleness."

36. 2 Corinthians 12:9.

37. "Sexy Christian Singles"

38. Rosenau and Wilson, *Soul Virgins*, 37.

39. Ibid., 138.

Chapter 6 Happiness & Maturity

1. Sharlet, "The Young and the Sexless."

2. Eden, *The Thrill of the Chaste*, xi.

3. Courtney, "Singles in the Hands of a Manipulative God?"

4. Ludy, *When God Writes Your Love Story*, 148.

5. Prince, *God Is a Matchmaker*, 77.

6. Thomas, *Sacred Marriage*, 20.

7. Ibid., 22.

8. Ibid., 207.

9. Ibid., 206.

10. Ibid., 226, 241.

11. Brown, *Da Vinci Code*, 308–9.

12. Dillow and Pintus, *Intimate Issues*, 178.

13. Winner, *Real Sex*, 99.

14. Ibid., 81–83.

15. Dobson, *Marriage under Fire*, 17.

16. Osteen, *Your Best Life Now*, 3–4.

17. McCulley, "Sex and the Single Woman," 197.

18. Clark, *I Gave Dating a Chance*, 10.

19. Folger, *What's a Girl to Do?* 39.

20. Psalm 84:11 and Psalm 145:16 are verses that are also frequently cited in discussions about God's faithfulness in providing a spouse.

21. Peterson, *Long Obedience*, 118.

22. Ibid., 138.

23. Nouwen, *The Wounded Healer*, 93.

24. Peterson, *Long Obedience*, 144.

25. Tauber and Smoke, *Finding the Right One*, 20.

26. Thomas, *Sacred Marriage*, 220.

27. Dawn, *Sexual Character*, 109.

28. Jones and Yarhouse, *Ex-gays?* 282–83.

29. Ibid., 280–81.

30. Dobson, "Marriage on the Ropes."

31. Harris, *I Kissed Dating Goodbye*, 169.

32. Harris, *Stop Dating the Church!* 15, 30.

33. Ibid., 53.

34. Stott in Hsu, *Singles at the Crossroads*, 180.

35. Dawn, *I'm Lonely, Lord*, 172.

36. Smit, *Loves Me, Loves Me Not*, 79.

37. "Single Men and the Church."

38. 1 Timothy 3:2, 12.

39. Peterson, "Let's Begin at Church," 257.

40. Hsu, *Singles at the Crossroads*, 180.

Chapter 7 Covenant & Inclusion

1. Miles, *Redemption of Love*, 168.

2. Grenz, *Sexual Ethics*, 171.

3. Ibid., 171–72.

4. Ibid., 159.

5. Maken, *Getting Serious*, 27.

6. Hsu, *Singles at the Crossroads*, 67–68.

7. Ibid., 68.

8. Maken, *Getting Serious*, 38–39.

9. Watters, *Get Married*, 24.

10. Maken, *Getting Serious*, 160.

11. Examples include *Secret Power to Faith, Family, and Getting the Guy: A Personal Bible Study on the Book of Ruth* by Susie Shellenberger, and *I, Isaac, Take Thee, Rebekah: Moving from Romance to Lasting Love* by Ravi Zacharias.

12. Thomas, *Sacred Marriage*, 80.

13. Ibid.

14. Ibid.

15. Garland, *1 Corinthians*, 246.

16. Ibid., 267.

17. Ibid., 260.

18. Maken, *Getting Serious*, 32.

19. Hsu, *Singles at the Crossroads*, 36.

20. Maken, *Getting Serious*, 111.

21. McMinn, Wheaton College Chapel Message.

22. Rosenau and Wilson, *Soul Virgins*, 39.

23. Clapp, *Families*, 96.

24. Ibid.

25. In addition to Jeremiah, several other Old Testament prophets such as Elijah, Elisha, and Daniel are traditionally thought to have remained single.

26. Maken, "Maken on Piper."

27. Maken, *Getting Serious*, 100.

28. Smit, *Loves Me, Loves Me Not*, 63–64.

29. Piper, "Single in Christ."

30. Winner, *Real Sex*, 143.

31. Smit, *Loves Me, Loves Me Not*, 64.

32. Hauerwas, *After Christendom?* 128.

33. Maken, *Getting Serious*, 30.